Rescue from Death
The Good News of John 3:16

ROBERT TAYLOR

© 2021 Robert Taylor
All Rights Reserved.

Unless otherwise noted, scripture taken from the New King James Version®. Copyright © 1982 by Thomas Nelson. Used by permission. All rights reserved.

Scripture quotations marked (NASB) are from the New American Standard Bible®, Copyright © 1960, 1962, 1963, 1968, 1971, 1972, 1973, 1975, 1977, 1995 by The Lockman Foundation. Used by permission. www.Lockman.org

Scripture quotations marked (NIV) are from the Holy Bible, New International Version®, NIV®. Copyright © 1973, 1978, 1984, 2011 by Biblica, Inc.™ Used by permission of Zondervan. All rights reserved worldwide. www.zondervan.com

Scripture quotations marked (NET) are from the NET Bible® copyright ©1996-2006 by Biblical Studies Press, L.L.C. All rights reserved. Scripture quoted by permission. http://netbible.com

Italics in scripture quotations have not been retained from the original. Italics are the author's own emphasis.

Unless otherwise noted, italics in quotations from reference works, commentaries, and other writers are from the original source cited.

Rescue from Death was first published in 2012 by Outskirts Press, with the subtitle: *John 3:16 Salvation*. A much more thorough presentation was published in 2016 by Dog Ear Publishing, with revisions published in 2017. The Dog Ear editions did not have a subtitle.

Published by Sherwood Heritage Press
SherwoodHeritagePress@outlook.com

ISBN: 978-0-578-83091-9

Printed in the United States of America

To my grandchildren,
Taylor, Caleb, Ella,
Oliver, and Clark.

CONTENTS

Preface 7

Introduction 9

1 In The Beginning: The Genesis Passages 13

2 Warnings Of Hell: The Gehenna Passages 44

3 Unquenchable Fire And Undying Worm: Isaiah 66:23-24 86

4 Matthew: The Foundational Book On Hell 119

5 The Price Of Redemption: The Precious Blood Of Christ 167

6 The Revelation Passages 190

7 What Must I Do To Be Saved? 256

8 Reflections And Practical Issues 264

Small Group Discussion Questions 293

Endnotes 309

PREFACE

For God so loved the world that He gave His only begotten Son, that whoever believes in Him should not perish but have everlasting life.

Read John 3:16 with the heart of a child and the truth of God's amazing grace shines forth. For whom did Christ die? In giving His Son as a sacrifice for sin, God loved the world. Does this mean everyone will be saved? Notice that John 3:16 contains a condition, *whoever believes in Him*. It is possible for everyone to be saved, but only if everyone believes.

Though an advocate of taking John 3:16 at face value, I was blind to my own failure to do so when it came to the words *should not perish*. I read *perish* but thought *eternally suffer torment*. For about thirty years, this was such an automatic practice that it never occurred to me that I might be reading theology into the text rather than coming to it as a learner. But something unexpected happened that led me to be a more diligent student of God's Word.

A brother in Christ was talking about Revelation 21:4, "And God will wipe away every tear from their eyes; there shall be no more death, nor sorrow, nor crying. There shall be no more pain, for the former things have passed away." He felt this indicated that in the new earth we won't remember those who died without Christ. Then he commented, *God alone will bear that sorrow.* His words stopped me in my tracks.

Given the traditional evangelical understanding of hell, the thought of God mourning the loss of those who had rejected Him took me by surprise. The picture was consistent with God's heart as revealed in Jesus' lament over Jerusalem: "O Jerusalem, Jerusalem, the one who kills the prophets and stones those who are sent to her! How often I wanted to gather your children together, as a hen gathers her chicks under her wings, but you were not willing!" (Matt. 23:37). It also brought to mind Jesus' words at Calvary: "Father, forgive them, for they do not know what they do" (Luke 23:34). Still, the thought stunned me, and I knew that I had been confronted with something that merited investigation.

Right then and there, I purposed to take a fresh, unbiased look at what the scriptures had to say about the destiny of the unsaved. I would study the key biblical texts as if for the first time.

This book is the result of that journey.

INTRODUCTION

Will the Church Come to Its Evangelistic Senses?

Have you ever tried to visualize endless suffering? Can you imagine relentless misery lasting week after week, month after month, year after year, century after century, and millennium after millennium? Could there be anything more dreadful than mothers and fathers and sons and daughters experiencing agony forever, throughout all of eternity?

How do Christians live with the traditional eternal conscious torment (ECT) view of hell? Speaking as a long-time traditionalist, as much as possible, we avoid thinking about it. When we do, we use language that shields us from facing its horror. Our most popular Gospel tracts warn of *death* rather than endless suffering. Typically, we speak of hell as separation from God and leave it at that. We seldom go on to consider what it would mean to be separated from the goodness of God. It's that intimidating. This probably helps explain why many believers are hesitant to evangelize. It's one thing to compartmentalize hell to get through the day; it's another to potentially have to defend the eternal suffering of friends and loved ones who don't choose to trust Christ.

No one has ever given a sufficient explanation for the ECT of sinners who are loved so much by God that He gave His only

Son for them. Why a holy God would eternally sustain sinfulness is another mystery that remains unanswered. This should not surprise us. The traditional view of hell was not built on the testimony of scripture that God's unquenchable judgment fire serves to burn up, incinerate, chaff and tares. ECT came to prominence in conjunction with the ascendance of the Roman Catholic Church which held to the view of Augustine, who was enamored with Greek philosophy, including the immortality of the soul, to the point that it colored his understanding of the biblical record.

Modern-day traditionalists defend their view by practically reducing God to the status of a bystander. *The impenitent want to be free from God, and God grants their wish*, they say. Yet, no sinner asked to be born; none of us decreed the penalty for sin; and no one desires endless misery. Whatever the nature of hell, the buck must stop with God, for though we sin of our own free will, the consequence of impenitence is the Creator's prerogative to determine.

Often, we hear traditionalists say that the need for justice demands ECT, as if no other alternative existed. What perfect justice truly requires is a *fair and just penalty* for sin. Indeed, we can be sure that the Day of Judgment will be consistent with the character of the Lord Jesus. It will satisfy the holiness of God without violating any of His other attributes.

Since God is good, hell shouldn't be unreasonable in severity, nor should it make God look like a monster. Because God is all-wise, hell should make sense. For rejecting the Creator, what could be more appropriate than to be denied a place in the Creator's eternal universe? Is this not what the Bible has repeatedly said all along? Does not the scripture warn of final judgment using terms such as perish, die, death, destruction, consume, and burn up? Do not believers look forward to a new earth and new heavens in which righteousness dwells and God is all in all?

When genuine justice is usurped, trouble follows. Substitute eternal misery for death and the Gospel becomes a hybrid of *Good News* and *Horrific News*. This is tragic not only because God is misrepresented and His love obscured, but because we shoot ourselves in the foot with regard to evangelism. Given how horrific the thought of mothers and fathers and sons and daughters endlessly suffering is, should we be surprised if the world turns away? Make no mistake about it, ECT is one of the primary reasons, if not the number one reason, for the rejection of Christianity.

Two paths are before us: We can hold to a penalty for sin that the literate secular world doesn't take seriously because it's inconceivable. Or, we can read John 3:16 with the heart of a child and provide humanity with the answer to a profound concern that everyone longs for a solution to.

Through faith in Christ, there is not only forgiveness of sins and a love relationship with God, there is rescue from death. Believers will not *perish* but have eternal life. If Christians were to take John 3:16 at face value, what a powerful message we would have to share with the world!

With so much at stake, shouldn't investigating the destiny of the unsaved and learning the truth about divine justice be a top priority? To be sure, there are hindrances, not the least of which is the inclusion of ECT in doctrinal statements that many evangelical Bible teachers and pastors have to sign annually to retain employment. Martin Luther faced similar pressure, and much more, for Christ. Will evangelicals follow in the footsteps of the Jews at Berea, who welcomed challenging issues and diligently sought to know what scripture actually teaches (Acts 17:10-11)? Will our generation rise to the occasion and take on the most crucial unfinished business of the Reformation? Will the twenty-first century be "The Century of *Good* News"?

God is good! He is truly, thoroughly, and transparently good. Yes, some will still reject Him, but let it not be because we have failed to declare the true love and true justice of John 3:16.

1
IN THE BEGINNING: THE GENESIS PASSAGES

What is the Creator's penalty for sin? Since it was Adam's disobedience in the Garden of Eden that brought condemnation to humanity (Rom. 5:12-18), our investigation of heaven's justice begins with the Genesis record of Adam's creation and fall.

IN THE BEGINNING, GOD CREATED ADAM AND EVE

> Then God said, "Let us make humankind in our image, after our likeness, so they may rule over the fish of the sea and the birds of the air, over the cattle, and over all the earth, and over all the creatures that move on the earth." God created humankind in his own image, in the image of God he created them, male and female he created them. —Genesis 1:26-27 (NET)

The Lord God formed the man from the soil of the ground and breathed into his nostrils the breath of life, and the man became a living being. —Genesis 2:7 (NET)

The Lord God formed out of the ground every living animal of the field and every bird of the air. He brought them to the man to see what he would name them, and whatever the man called each living creature, that was its name. So the man named all the animals, the birds of the air, and the living creatures of the field, but for Adam no companion who corresponded to him was found. So the Lord God caused the man to fall into a deep sleep, and while he was asleep, he took part of the man's side and closed up the place with flesh. Then the Lord God made a woman from the part he had taken out of the man, and he brought her to the man. Then the man said, "This one at last is bone of my bones and flesh of my flesh; this one will be called 'woman,' for she was taken out of man." —Genesis 2:19-23 (NET)

IN THE BEGINNING, GOD WARNED OF DEATH

The Lord God planted a garden eastward in Eden, and there He put the man whom He had formed. And out of the ground the Lord God made every tree grow that is pleasant to the sight and good for food. The tree of life was also in the midst of the garden, and the tree of the knowledge of good and evil. —Genesis 2:8-9

> And the LORD God commanded the man, saying, "Of every tree of the garden you may freely eat; but of the tree of the knowledge of good and evil you shall not eat, for in the day that you eat of it you shall surely die."
> —Genesis 2:16-17

All that God created was "very good" (Gen. 1:31). God designed a paradise in which Adam would live and work and make a home for his family. Moreover, Adam enjoyed fellowship with the Creator Himself. Only one limitation was placed on Adam: God commanded Adam not to eat from a particular tree in Eden. He also warned that disobedience would cost Adam his life: "Of the tree of the knowledge of good and evil you shall not eat, for in the day that you eat of it you shall surely die." Why such a severe consequence? The text doesn't say, but the universe belongs to God, and honoring Him is clearly very important.

IN THE BEGINNING, ADAM AND EVE SINNED

> Now the serpent was more cunning than any beast of the field which the LORD God had made. And he said to the woman, "Has God indeed said, 'You shall not eat of every tree of the garden'?" And the woman said to the serpent, "We may eat the fruit of the trees of the garden; but of the fruit of the tree which is in the midst of the garden, *God has said, 'You shall not eat it, nor shall you touch it, lest you die.'*" Then the serpent said to the woman, "You will not surely die. For God knows that in the day you eat of it your eyes will be opened, and

you will be like God, knowing good and evil." So when the woman saw that the tree was good for food, that it was pleasant to the eyes, and a tree desirable to make one wise, *she took of its fruit and ate.* She also gave to her husband with her, and *he ate.* Then the eyes of both of them were opened, and they knew that they were naked; and they sewed fig leaves together and made themselves coverings. And they heard the sound of the LORD God walking in the garden in the cool of the day, and Adam and his wife hid themselves from the presence of the LORD God among the trees of the garden.
—Genesis 3:1-8

Eating the forbidden fruit may seem like a small transgression, but it wasn't. Adam and Eve chose to disregard the will of their Creator. God would not ignore this. He had personally instructed Adam on the penalty for disobedience, and Adam had apparently passed the warning to Eve. "You shall surely die," Adam and Eve had been warned, yet they ate from the tree of the knowledge of good and evil. What now? When and how would "you shall surely die" be fulfilled?

THE MEANING OF "YOU SHALL SURELY DIE"

Preliminary Considerations

Adam's fall had broad ramifications. It affected him morally, socially, spiritually, and physically. It is tempting to read results of Adam's fall back into Genesis 2:17; however, the question is, what

RESCUE FROM DEATH

did God actually say in Genesis 2:17? To properly interpret God's penalty for sin, we must consider the Hebrew phraseology behind it, especially in the writings of Moses.

The Hebrew verb *mooth*, "die," is found more than 800 times in the Old Testament.[1] In the vast majority of cases, *mooth* indicates physical death. For example:

> And the fish that are in the river shall *die*, the river shall stink, and the Egyptians will loathe to drink the water of the river (Exod. 7:18).
> Then David called one of the young men and said, "Go near, and execute him!" And he struck him so that he *died* (2 Sam. 1:15).
> For Jozachar the son of Shimeath and Jehozabad the son of Shomer, his servants, struck him [Jehoash]. So he *died*, and they buried him with his fathers in the City of David (2 Kings 12:21).
> So all the days that Adam lived were nine hundred and thirty years; and he *died* (Gen. 5:5).

Adam did not *mooth* until 930 years had passed—hardly "in the day" he ate the forbidden fruit. Many have sought to reconcile this apparent discrepancy by suggesting that Adam immediately experienced spiritual death, followed by the slow decay of his body, eventually resulting in physical death, but this misses the meaning of the Hebrew text, which does *not* indicate two aspects of death.[2]

Writing for the Christian apologetics ministry Answers in Genesis-U.S., Bodie Hodge points out that in Genesis 2:17, the Hebrew word for day (*yom*) refers to the day Adam and Eve ate the fruit. It does not refer to the day they would die.[3] It is very much like King Solomon's edict forbidding Shimei from crossing the Brook Kidron: "For it shall be, on the day you go out and cross the Brook Kidron," said Solomon to Shimei, "know for certain you shall surely die; your blood shall be on your own head" (1 Kings 2:37).

Shimei had yelled curses at Solomon's father, King David, and thrown stones at David and his servants (2 Sam. 16:5-6). Though Abishai urged that Shimei be put to death (2 Sam. 16:9), David refused to allow it. When Solomon became king, he respected his father's decision not to kill Shimei; however, he restricted Shimei's ability to travel by imposing death as a consequence of leaving Jerusalem (1 Kings 2:36-38). About three years later, two of Shimei's slaves fled to Gath, a town about thirty miles southwest of Jerusalem. Shimei traveled to Gath, regained his runaway slaves, and returned to Jerusalem (1 Kings 2:39-40). When King Solomon heard what had happened, he called for Shimei. Solomon reminded Shimei of the penalty for traveling outside of Jerusalem and ordered Shimei's execution (1 Kings 2:41-46). How long these events took is unknown but surely required more than a day.

Solomon had not guaranteed that Shimei would die on the day he crossed the Brook Kidron but had promised that crossing Kidron would guarantee Shimei's execution. Likewise in Genesis 2:17, nothing in the language indicates an immediate death. The language indicates the certainty of death.[4]

RESCUE FROM DEATH

Mooth Mooth

The single occurrence of the Hebrew *mooth* is frequent and easily understood, but God's warning to Adam was a more distinct phrase. Occasionally in biblical Hebrew, *mooth* is repeated consecutively. This is the case in Genesis 2:17: "but of the tree of the knowledge of good and evil you shall not eat, for in the day that you eat of it you shall surely die [*mooth mooth*]."[5]

What is the significance of the double verb expression *you will surely die*? In *The Expositor's Bible Commentary*, John H. Sailhamer writes,

> In the remainder of the Pentateuch, the expression... means that one has come under the verdict of the death penalty (cf. 20:7; Exod 31:14; Lev 24:16). It is a pronouncement of a judge on one who has been condemned to die.[6]

In Exodus 31:14, we read that whoever profanes the Sabbath *mooth mooth* [shall surely be put to death]. Likewise, in Leviticus 24:16, whoever blasphemes the name of the Lord *mooth mooth* [shall surely be put to death] by stoning. Sailhamer's observation is also readily demonstrated in the narrative of Abraham and Sarah's sojourn in Gerar:

> And Abraham journeyed from there to the South, and dwelt between Kadesh and Shur, and stayed in Gerar. Now Abraham said of Sarah his wife, "She is my sister." And Abimelech king of Gerar sent and took Sarah. But God came to Abimelech in a dream by night, and said to him, "Indeed you are a dead man because of the woman whom you have taken, for she is a man's wife."

But Abimelech had not come near her; and he said, "Lord, will You slay a righteous nation also? Did he not say to me, 'She is my sister'? And she, even she herself said, 'He is my brother.' In the integrity of my heart and innocence of my hands I have done this." And God said to him in a dream, "Yes, I know that you did this in the integrity of your heart. For I also withheld you from sinning against Me; therefore I did not let you touch her. Now therefore, restore the man's wife; for he is a prophet, and he will pray for you and you shall live. But if you do not restore her, know that you shall surely die [*mooth mooth*], you and all who are yours." (Gen. 20:1-7)

"You're a dead man," God said to Abimelech. It was not that Abimelech had died in any manner. Abimelech understood that God had pronounced a death sentence against him and his people, and he asked, "Lord, will You slay a righteous nation also?"

Because Abimelech had not known that Sarah was married, God extended grace, giving Abimelech the opportunity to restore Sarah to her husband, Abraham; however, if Abimelech did not return Sarah, he and his people would *mooth mooth*—surely die. According to the ancient Hebrew, a death sentence hung over Abimelech until Sarah was restored to her husband's side.

God is not only the Creator; He is also the Ruler of the universe—the King of kings and Lord of lords (1 Tim. 6:13-16). Furthermore, He is the righteous Judge of all the earth (Gen. 18:25). In Numbers 15, a man was found in violation of the Sabbath. God imposed the death sentence: "Then the LORD said to Moses, 'The man must surely be put to death [*mooth mooth*]; all the congregation shall stone him with stones outside the camp'" (Num. 15:35).

A death sentence is one event; the execution of the death penalty is another. This too is seen in Numbers 15:

> Then the LORD said to Moses, "The man must surely be put to death [*mooth mooth*]; all the congregation shall stone him with stones outside the camp." So, as the LORD commanded Moses, all the congregation brought him outside the camp and stoned him with stones, and he died [*mooth*]. (Num. 15:35-36)

In Genesis 2:17, *mooth mooth* is a judicial statement: the declaration of the death penalty, the promise of certain *mooth*.

Before the Law, before the curse, before sin and before death, God established the death penalty as the consequence for disobedience: "You shall surely die." Historically, there have been two distinct understandings of God's death penalty: the conditional immortality view and the traditional eternal conscious torment (ECT) view.

THE CONDITIONAL IMMORTALITY VIEW OF GOD'S DEATH PENALTY

The conditional immortality view takes the penalty for sin— death— at face value, namely, cessation or end of life.

I say *face value* with the support of both testaments. Not only does *mooth* primarily refer to physical death but cessation or end of life is the standard usage of *death* in the Greek language[7] and in the New Testament. *Nekros* is consistently translated *dead*. I count more than seventy instances in the New Testament where *nekros* is connected with resurrection, primarily the resurrection of Christ. For example: "Now when they had fulfilled all that was written concerning Him, they took Him down from the tree and laid Him in a tomb. But God raised Him from the *dead*" (Acts 13:29-30). *Dead* here obviously refers to the lifeless crucified body of Christ lying in the tomb. In Acts 5:10, Sapphira's sudden death is recorded: "Then immediately she fell down at his feet and breathed her last. And the young men came in and found her *dead*, and carrying her out, buried her by her husband." In Sapphira's body, life was *absent*; it had *ceased*, come to an *end*. Other Greek words for death have this same meaning.[8]

If the conditional immortality understanding of God's justice had been carried out when Adam and Eve sinned, the human race would have ended in Eden, yet Adam and Eve lived for hundreds of years and the human race multiplied in the earth. Why? God had a solution for Adam's fall. Rather than terminating Adam and Eve's lives, God acted in grace.

God's grace grants opportunity for reconciliation (2 Cor. 5:18-21). Paul tells us that on the basis of Jesus' propitiating blood, God "passed over" Adam's transgression (Rom. 3:25). Peter tells us why: "The Lord is not slack concerning His promise, as some count slackness, but is longsuffering toward us, not willing that any should perish but that all should come to repentance" (2 Pet. 3:9).

When God extended grace, the sinner's separation from God became an unavoidable reality until reconciliation could take place. Those that receive God's gift of salvation become members of His family (John 1:12) and have everlasting life (Rom. 6:23). Those who spurn God's grace, however, will perish (John 3:16).

Every unbeliever will face final judgment. Sinners without a Savior will be cast into the lake of fire (Matt. 25:31-46; Rev. 20:11-15), where both soul and body will be killed, put to death (Matt. 10:28). Explicitly, the unrepentant will burn up in God's judgment fire (Matt. 3:12; 13:30, 40). To paraphrase Peter: When God turned the cities of Sodom and Gomorrah into ashes, He set forth an example of what the ungodly can expect to experience (2 Pet. 2:6). As Ignatius (AD 50-116) succinctly states, "For were He to reward us according to our works, we should cease to be."[9]

Important Notes

Christ's crucifixion was an extremely painful death. The amount of pain involved in the second death will be in accordance with the hardness and impenitence of the unbeliever's heart toward God (Rom. 1:32-2:12).

Conditional immortality (aka, conditionalism, CI), evangelical annihilationism, and terminal punishment are labels for the belief that the unsaved will face a final judgment before God prior to the irreversible cessation of life. Throughout this book, I use the terms *annihilationism*, *conditionalism*, and *terminal punishment* interchangeably, always carrying the evangelical understanding.

The Rationale for Terminal Punishment

The rationale for terminal punishment is straightforward: To reject the Creator is to forfeit the privilege of life in the Creator's universe. This penalty is just and understandable, even by the unsaved.

In Romans, his treatise on sin and death and grace and life, Paul affirms that death is God's righteous penalty for sin and assures us that the ancient idol worshippers were not ignorant of heaven's justice:

> For since the creation of the world His invisible attributes are clearly seen, being understood by the things that are made, even His eternal power and Godhead, so that they are without excuse, because, although they knew God, they did not glorify Him as God, nor were thankful, but became futile in their thoughts, and their foolish hearts were darkened. Professing to be wise, they became fools, and changed the glory of the incorruptible God into an image made like corruptible man—and birds and four-footed animals and creeping things.... and worshiped and served the creature rather than the Creator... they are whisperers, backbiters, haters of God, violent, proud, boasters, inventors of evil things, disobedient to parents, undiscerning, untrustworthy, unloving, unforgiving, unmerciful; who, knowing the *righteous judgment of God*, that those who practice such things are *deserving of death*, not only do the same but also approve of those who practice them. (Rom. 1:20-23, 25b, 29b-32)

Many of Adam and Eve's descendants chose not to worship the Creator who gave them life. While these did not desire to honor God, they did retain the testimony of Adam and Eve that death is the penalty for sin. The ancient idol worshippers knew the righteous judgment of God. They knew they deserved to *die* because of the things they were doing.

THE TRADITIONAL UNDERSTANDING OF GOD'S DEATH PENALTY

The traditional view of hell also holds that death is the penalty for sin. Henry C. Thiessen, in his classic *Lectures in Systematic Theology*, writes, "It takes only one word to state the penalty of sin, and thus it is given in the Scriptures, death."[10] The traditionalist definition of death, however, is rather complex. Thiessen continues, "It is a threefold death: physical, spiritual, and eternal."[11] Robert P. Lightner explains,

> The moment Adam and Eve broke God's command and acted independently of His will, three forms of death became operative. This was in fulfillment of the Creator's clear statement, "For in the day that you eat of it you shall surely die" (Gen. 2:17). *Spiritual death* was immediate: they were separated from God. They hid themselves from the presence of the Lord God. Adam and Eve revealed their newly sinful hearts as they accused each other for their own sin. The fact that man was expelled from the garden "lest he put out his hand and take also of the tree of life, and eat, and live forever" (Gen. 3:22) substantiates the reality of *physical death* for him. The repetition of the phrase "and he died" in chapter 5 affirms the presence of physical death. In addition to these two forms of death, man became subject to *eternal death*. Eternal death is the final result of spiritual death. It was the potential fate of Adam and Eve and is the potential fate of all their posterity, apart from the acceptance of redemption provided by God in Christ. Without salvation in Christ all would be eternally separated from God.[12]

Eternal death, as defined by the traditionalist, equals eternal separation from God and involves continual conscious suffering in the lake of fire. Traditionalist scholar Robert A. Peterson states, "Jesus paints a picture of inextinguishable hellfire to depict unbearable and enduring pain. We have all had the experience of being burned. Jesus and his apostles use this common experience to warn their hearers of a far worse fate."[13]

The Rationale behind Eternal Torment

The rationale behind eternal torment stems from the fact that Adam sinned against an infinite God. Noted theologian Millard Erickson, whom Peterson cites as one of the leading lights in church history,[14] writes,

> The fact that hell, as often understood, seems to be incompatible with God's love, as revealed in Scripture, may be an indication that we have misunderstood hell.
> We should note, first, that whenever we sin, an infinite factor is invariably involved. All sin is an offense against God, the raising of a finite will against the will of an infinite being. It is failure to carry out one's obligation to him to whom everything is due. Consequently, one cannot consider sin to be merely a finite act deserving finite punishment.[15]

In *Hell under Fire*, Christopher W. Morgan writes, "Sin is inherently *against God*, who is infinite in all his perfections. Thus, sin is an infinite evil and merits endless punishment."[16]

Building on the premise that sin against an infinite God merits an infinite penalty, the traditionalist reasons that finite sinners must be endlessly sustained by God in order to endlessly make payment on an infinite debt. This rationale is not a teaching of the Bible supported by chapter and verse; it is a philosophical argument that arose in the medieval Catholic Church. Peterson acknowledges this in the chapter "The Road to Traditionalism" in *Two Views of Hell*:

> [Thomas] Aquinas began the *Summa Theologiae*, his most outstanding work, in 1265 and was still not finished writing at the time of his death in 1273. In a section dealing with guilt he again argues for eternal punishment. To those who claim that it is unjust for God to render everlasting punishment for sins committed during the limited time span of a person's life, he replies, "The duration of a punishment does not match the duration of the act of sin but of its stain; as long as this lasts a debt of punishment remains. The severity of the punishment matches the seriousness of the sin."
>
> This prompts another question from Aquinas's imaginary partners in debate: What makes sins committed in this life so serious that they deserve a never-ending penalty? Once more (this time borrowing from the eleventh-century theologian Anselm) Thomas has a ready response:
>
> "Further, the magnitude of the punishment matches the magnitude of the sin.... Now a sin that is against God is infinite; the higher the person against whom it is committed, the graver the sin—it is more criminal to strike a head of state than a private citizen—and God is of infinite greatness. Therefore an infinite punishment is deserved for a sin committed against him."[17]

IS THERE A JUST RATIONALE FOR ETERNAL TORMENT?

Edward William Fudge, a lawyer as well as a theologian, shares this informative evaluation of the infinite suffering theory advanced by Anselm and Aquinas:

> For six or seven centuries after Augustine, most Western theologians neither developed traditional teaching nor called

it into question, but contented themselves with passing it on. Then came Anselm (d. 1117) and Thomas Aquinas (d. 1274) in the high Middle Ages.... The primary contribution of Anselm and Aquinas to traditionalism is the notion, based on feudalistic systems of justice, that finite man can pay for his sins against an infinite God only by suffering torment for an infinite period of time.

Anselm sets out his case for the traditionalist hell in his works *Cur Deus Homo* (bk. 1) and *Proslogion* (chaps. 8-11). Rather than examining scriptural language in light of scriptural usage, Anselm reasons within the framework of his feudal society. In Anselm's world the same crime could carry any one of a number of punishments depending on the rank of the criminal and especially of the victim. A serf might be executed for committing a particular crime, while a person of nobility who committed the same crime might only be assessed a fine. The king, of course, could commit the same deed with impunity. A serf who insulted a fellow serf might go unpunished. Upon insulting a lord, a serf might be jailed. Any serf who insulted the king would likely be beheaded. Taking his cue from such "justice," Anselm reasons that God is worthy of infinite honor and that sin against God therefore deserves infinite punishment. Because humans are finite, Anselm argues, they cannot suffer infinite punishment in a finite period of time. Therefore they must suffer conscious torment forever (infinitely) in hell.

Not only do all civilized nations today reject such feudalistic concepts of justice, Anselm's model actually contradicts a fundamental principle of jurisprudence presented by God in the law of Moses. God demanded that the Jews provide the same justice for every person, regardless of the person's rank or standing in society (Ex 23:3; Lev 19:15; Deut 1:17). This principle of a single standard applicable to all classes of people found clear expression in the law known as the *lex talionis*—an eye for an eye and a tooth for a tooth (Lev 24:19-22). It did not matter whose eye was at stake or whose tooth had been knocked out; the punishment was the same for all. Furthermore, Israel's laws were intended to elicit praise for the justice of God himself (Deut 4:5-8). In this light it should be clear that the arbitrary and discriminatory practices of feudal society provide no reliable starting place for developing Christian theology.[18]

In this evaluation, Fudge deals traditionalism a severe blow. Having a legitimate reason for the penalty for sin is vital. God seeks to make His righteousness evident to all. For example, in spite of His declared opposition to sin, throughout history God welcomed and blessed sinners. Such "passing over" of sin gave opportunity for God's righteousness to be called into question. God laid this issue to rest by the public crucifixion of His Son

> whom God *displayed publicly* as a *propitiation in His blood* through faith. This was to *demonstrate His righteousness*, because in the forbearance of God He passed over the sins previously committed; *for the demonstration*, I say, *of His righteousness* at the present time, *so that He would be just* and the justifier of the one who has faith in Jesus. (Rom. 3:25-26, NASB)

In Romans, Paul explains how God can declare a sinner righteous and still be just. God is righteous in justifying the one who believes in His Son because Jesus died for the sins of the world at Calvary. In the same way, there should be a straightforward rationale for the judgment of the unrepentant sinner. Terminal punishment makes good sense. It is unreasonable to expect God to sustain those who spurn Him. The sinner who turns his back on the Creator simply has no right to live in the Creator's universe. But what purpose would man's eternal torment serve? How is eternal torment a matter of justice? Anselm's feudalistic argument, at odds with the justice system of the Old Testament, is hardly persuasive.

INITIAL EVALUATION OF TRADITIONALISM IN LIGHT OF GENESIS 2:16-17

Close observation of the biblical record reveals that the traditionalist explanation of "shall surely die" exceeds the native meaning of *mooth mooth*. The traditionalist view combines the consequences of Adam's sin with ECT derived from the traditionalist interpretation of the New Testament. Are endless separation from God and eternal torment consistent with the first pages of the Bible, or does the traditionalist understanding of God's death penalty seem completely out of place?

Were Adam and Eve Traditionalists?

Would Adam and Eve be familiar with the traditional view of hell or would the thought of their unsaved grandchildren suffering endlessly come as a shock?

The essence of traditionalism is that every human being exists eternally either in God's presence or separated from Him.

Did Adam hear God say, "If you eat of the tree of the knowledge of good and evil, you will live forever, but you will do so without the benefit of My fellowship"? Did Eve understand God to have said, "If you eat the forbidden fruit, you will exist endlessly on this planet, but never again will I meet with you"?

The traditional view of hell explicitly holds that the penalty for sin is to eternally suffer torment in the lake of fire.

Did God say to Adam in the Garden of Eden, "Adam, if you eat from the tree of the knowledge of good and evil, you will experience pain and suffering that will never end"? An unbiased reading of Genesis chapter 2 could never lead to this conclusion. Nothing in Genesis 2 even hints of eternal torment. "And the LORD God commanded the man, saying, 'Of every tree of the garden you may freely eat; but of the tree of the knowledge of good and evil you shall not eat, for in the day that you eat of it you *shall surely die*'" (Gen. 2:16-17).

Traditionalism's Fair-Warning Problem

The difference between "shall surely *die*" and "shall suffer *endless torment*" is immense, yet under traditionalism, the two phrases are synonymous. The traditionalist attempt to reconcile this glaring contradiction appeals to the progressive nature of God's revelation and argues that the full implication of death in Genesis 2:17 is revealed in the New Testament. In Adam's case, however, the penalty for sin was essential information. It defined the peril that Adam faced. If the horror of unending torment was a possibility for Adam, should he not have been made aware of this?

Eat from a certain tree in the Garden and you will suffer without relief, eternally. *Under traditionalism, was Eden a paradise or an immensely fearful danger zone?* ECT is not just another doctrine. If true, it represents a danger a million times worse than the most painful death imaginable. Is it conceivable that God would fail to warn Adam of such danger, if it existed?

The traditionalist seeks refuge in progressive revelation because his view cannot be established from the pages of the Old Testament, but progressive revelation provides no satisfactory shelter from the need for fair warning. The earliest scripture cited by traditionalists in support of their position is Isaiah; therefore, for more than half of human history, according to traditionalism, God kept silent about the horrendous peril that loomed over one generation after the next. This is a huge moral problem for traditionalists because providing warning of impending judgment is a biblical principle that God takes very seriously (see Ezek. 33:1-9).

There Is a Better Answer

Revelation is progressive, but it is not contradictory. As one reads from Genesis to Revelation, he should expect to gain greater insight into the penalty for sin, such as the place and method of its execution, not to find it altered beyond recognition. God's integrity assures us that the penalty promised and the penalty executed will be one and the same.

What penalty for sin is found throughout the Bible? Paul affirms that the wages of sin is death and assures us that this has always been God's righteous judgment. In Romans 1, Paul takes us back to the creation of the world and the days of Adam, who lived for nearly a millennium. From the beginning, people knew God through the things that He made, but many did not glorify Him as God. Many of Adam's descendants became idol worshippers who knew that they *deserved to die* because of their sinful ways.

IN THE BEGINNING, MAN WAS NOT IMMORTAL

> Then the LORD God said, "Behold, the man has become like one of Us, to know good and evil. And now, *lest he put out his hand* and *take also of the tree of life*, and *eat, and live forever*"— therefore the LORD God sent him out of the garden of Eden to till the ground from which he was taken. — Genesis 3:22-23

Eat and Live Forever

In light of the widespread assumption that man was created as an eternal being, it's easy to breeze over Genesis 3:22-23, but a closer look reveals that living forever depended upon eating of the tree of life. Erickson explains,

> I would suggest the concept of *conditional immortality* as the state of Adam before the fall. He was not inherently able to live forever, but he need not have died. Given the right conditions, he could have lived on forever. This may be the meaning of God's words when he decided to expel Adam and Eve from Eden and from the presence of the tree of life: "and now, lest he put forth his hand and take also of the tree of life, and eat, and live for ever" (3:22). The impression is given that Adam, even after the fall, could have lived forever if he had eaten the fruit of the tree of life. What happened at the time of his expulsion from Eden was that man, who formerly could have either lived forever or died, was now separated from those conditions which made eternal life possible, and thus it became inevitable that he die.[19]

John W. Wenham writes,

> Immortality is something that well-doers seek (Rom. 2:7); immortality for the believer has been brought to light by the gospel (2 Tim 1:10)—he gains immortality (it would appear) when he gains eternal life and becomes partaker of the divine nature; immortality is finally put on at the last trump (1 Cor 15:53).[20]

Zondervan's *Pictorial Encyclopedia of the Bible* states,

> By the preaching of the Gospel, Christ's own are regenerated and through faith are united to their Savior. From Him they receive eternal life. Immortality is, in the Biblical pattern of thought, not a universal natural possession but the gift of redemptive grace.
>
> Because the Savior gives life at every point where death has intervened, the body also participates in immortality (1 Cor 15:54, *athanasia*).[21]

Living *forever* is a blessing God bestows on the basis of faith. This is true both before and after Adam's fall. In Eden, if Adam and Eve had believed God instead of the serpent's lie, they would have avoided the tree of the knowledge of good and evil and eaten of the tree of life. In the New Testament (John 3:16, 6:27-29, 51; Rom. 6:23), everlasting life is explicitly a gift of God received through faith.

TERTULLIAN, AUGUSTINE, AND THE IMMORTALITY OF THE SOUL

In summarizing the traditionalist position, I set forth their best contemporary case without any reference to the notion that the soul is immortal. I did so out of respect for traditionalists such as Peterson, who states,

> I do not accept traditionalism because I believe in the immortality of the soul. Rather, I believe in the immortality of human beings (united in body and soul after the resurrection of the dead) because the Bible teaches that there will be "eternal punishment" for the lost and "eternal life" for the saved (Mt 25:46).[22]

The traditionalist view that has dominated much of church history, however, was supported by the immortality of the soul. In *Two Views of Hell*, Peterson's historical review of traditionalist leaders begins with Tertullian and his *On the Resurrection of the Flesh* in which Tertullian "instructs his readers to understand the word *destroy* in Matthew 10:28 as indicating a 'never-ending "killing"'—rather than an extinction of being."[23] Peterson says it would be unwise to claim that Tertullian's understanding was influenced by Greek philosophy,[24] yet in explaining Matthew 10:28, Tertullian's very first words were "Here, then, we have a recognition of the natural immortality of the soul."[25]

At times, Tertullian differed from Plato. For example, Tertullian held that the soul had a beginning, the breath of God,[26] but he was firmly in agreement with the historic Greek view that the soul is immortal.[27] Tertullian's commitment to the immortality of the soul was strong, and it is obvious he did not set this belief aside when reading scripture. In Chapter 34 of *On the Resurrection of the Flesh*, Tertullian wrote,

> We, however, so understand the soul's immortality as to believe it "lost," not in the sense of destruction, but of punishment, that is, in hell. And if this is the case, then it

is not the soul which salvation will affect, since it is "safe" already in its own nature by reason of its immortality[28]

This prompted Fudge to aptly state, "Tertullian thus denies that the soul can be destroyed, the very fate of which Jesus sternly warns. In this way the stones of pagan Greek philosophy began to pave the road to today's traditionalism."[29]

Augustine of Hippo (AD 354-430) set forth the traditionalist case for hell in *The City of God*. The connection between eternal misery and the immortality of the soul, in Augustine's view, is not veiled: "As the soul has been created immortal, and therefore, although by sin it may be said to die… yet it does not cease living a kind of life, though a miserable [one], because it is immortal by creation."[30]

In Book 13, Chapter 2 of *The City of God*—"Of That Death Which Can Affect an Immortal Soul, and of That to Which the Body Is Subject"—we find the historic traditionalist definition of death:

> But I see I must speak a little more carefully of the nature of death. For although the human soul is truly affirmed to be immortal, yet it also has a certain death of its own. For it is therefore called immortal, because, in a sense, it does not cease to live and to feel; while the body is called mortal, because it can be forsaken of all life, and cannot by itself live at all. The death, then, of the soul takes place when God forsakes it, as the death of the body when the soul forsakes it…. In the last damnation, though man does not cease to feel, yet because this feeling of his is neither sweet with pleasure nor wholesome with repose, but painfully penal, it is not without reason called death rather than life.[31]

Augustine taught that physical death occurs when the *immortal soul* forsakes or separates from the mortal body. The soul, *being immortal*, dies in the sense that God forsakes it or separates His presence from it. Unless rectified by grace, this condition, according to Augustine, continues as everlasting punishment.

Despite traditionalist protests that their view of hell was not historically driven by Greek philosophy, the prominence of the immortality of the soul in Augustine's understanding of death is there for all to see. It is also integral to Augustine's defense of ECT. For example, in Book 21, Chapter 3, "Whether Bodily Suffering Necessarily Terminates in the Destruction of the Flesh," Augustine writes,

> And so, although it be true that in this world there is no flesh which can suffer pain and yet cannot die, yet in the world to come there shall be flesh such as now there is not, as there will also be death such as now there is not. For death will *not* be abolished, but will be eternal, since the *soul* will neither be able to enjoy God and live, *nor to die* and escape the pains of the body....
>
> Our opponents, too, make much of this, that in this world there is no flesh which can suffer pain and cannot die; while they make nothing of the fact that there is something which is greater than the body. For the *spirit*, whose presence animates and rules the body, can both suffer pain and *cannot die. Here then is something which, though it can feel pain, is immortal.* And this capacity, which we now see in the spirit of all, shall be hereafter in the bodies of the damned.... *But, seeing that that which suffers most* [the soul] *cannot die*, what ground is there for supposing that those bodies, because destined to suffer, are therefore, destined to die?[32]

Philip E. Hughes comments,

> There is no more radical antithesis than that between life and death, for life is the absence of death and death is the absence of life. Confronted with this antithesis, the position of Augustine cannot avoid involvement in the use of contradictory concepts, for the notion of death that is everlastingly endured requires the postulation that the damned be kept endlessly alive to endure it.... It would be hard to imagine a concept more confusing than that of death, which means existing endlessly without the power of dying. This, however, is the corner into which Augustine (in company with many others) argued himself.[33]

THE IMMORTALITY CARD STILL IN PLAY

Tertullian and Augustine's conflation of Plato's belief in the soul's innate immortality with the creation of man by God ultimately led to a modified version of Greek philosophy becoming entrenched in the Christian community. Augustine's view was adopted by the Roman Catholic Church and resides in the 1646 *Westminster Confession of Faith*, which states that God "created man, male and female, with reasonable and immortal souls."[34] To this day, the immortality of the soul remains a popular misconception. It also continues to bolster the traditional view of hell.

The practical reality is that phrases such as "everyone must exist somewhere forever" and "man's immortal soul" are commonplace in the evangelical world. What has been the cumulative effect of such expressions? If a survey were taken of evangelicals, asking why they believed that everyone lives eternally in heaven or hell, I wouldn't be surprised if most answered, "Because God created man as an eternal being." Perhaps this expresses the common thinking when it comes to the traditional doctrine of hell: The idea of eternal conscious suffering in hell is disturbing, but if man's soul was created immortal, what other end could there be for those who choose to reject God's salvation? Clark Pinnock writes,

> Belief in the natural immortality of the soul so widely held by Christians, although stemming more from Plato than the Bible, really drives the traditional doctrine of hell more than exegesis does. Consider the logic: if souls must live forever because they are naturally immortal, the lake of fire must be their home forever and cannot be their destruction.... I am convinced that the Hellenistic belief in the immortality of the soul has done more than anything else (specifically more than the Bible) to give credibility to the doctrine of the everlasting conscious punishment of the wicked. This belief, not Holy Scripture, is what gives this doctrine the credibility it does not deserve....
>
> The Greek doctrine of immortality... is one of several examples where there has been an undue Hellenization of Christian doctrine. The idea of souls being naturally immortal is not a biblical one, and the effect of believing it stretches the experience of death and destruction in Gehenna into endless torment. If souls are immortal, then either all souls will be saved (which is unscriptural universalism) or else hell must be everlasting torment. There is no other possibility since annihilation is ruled out from the start. This is how the traditional view of hell got constructed: add a belief in divine judgment after death (scriptural) to a belief in the immortality of the soul (unscriptural), and you have Augustine's terrible doctrine.[35]

Recognizing that immortality is a gift to be received rather than an inherent aspect of humanity allows for a more objective study of final judgment. It should also be noted that while belief in the immortality of the soul typically leads to the conclusion that everyone must live somewhere forever, this overlooks the fact that all of creation is ever dependent on God for existence. Even if "the immortality of the soul" originated in scripture rather than Greek philosophy, the soul would not be beyond God's power to annihilate. Nothing created by God is.

THE SURVIVAL OF THE SOUL WHEN THE BODY DIES

Some traditionalists point to the post physical death existence of both believers and unbelievers as evidence of the immortality of the soul. Let's investigate this claim, beginning with the believer's departure to be with Christ.

In his letter to the Philippians, Paul plainly teaches that at death he will depart from his body to be with Christ: "If I am to go on living in the body, this will mean fruitful labor for me. Yet... I desire to depart and be with Christ, which is better by far; but it is more necessary for you that I remain in the body" (1:22-24, NIV). This comforting truth provides no evidence that Adam was created with an immortal soul, however. Through faith in Christ, Paul had become a new creation (2 Cor. 5:17). Paul was in Christ, and Christ was in Paul (John 14:20). The believer's union with Christ (Col. 2:13; 1 John 5:11-12) far exceeds Adam's pre-fall reality. It is not by membership in Adam's race, but by the Spirit that the believer becomes an eternal being (John 3:5-16) blessed with assurance that absence from the body is to be present with the Lord (2 Cor. 4:16-5:8).

As for the unbeliever, it is true that physical death is not the end. There is a very specific reason for this: God has determined that the unsaved sinner will face a final judgment to demonstrate that he merits the lake of fire second death. In the words of the author of Hebrews, "It is appointed for men to die once, but after this the judgment" (Heb. 9:27).[36]

Prophecy foretells that the departed impenitent will be resurrected to stand before their Maker at the judgment at the Great White Throne (John 5:28-29; Rev. 20:11-13). It is the *time gap* between physical death and final judgment that accounts for the unbeliever continuing beyond biological death. The unbeliever must appear in God's courtroom; therefore, his existence is maintained by God for the Day of Judgment. The fact that God preserves the unsaved for final judgment does not tell us what happens to the impenitent in the lake of fire. This we must learn from the scriptures that declare the destiny of the unsaved.

IN THE BEGINNING, GOD GUARDED THE TREE OF LIFE

> So He drove out the man; and He placed cherubim at the east of the garden of Eden, and a flaming sword which turned every way, to guard the way to the tree of life. —Genesis 3:24

Integral to the eternal-torment view is the principle that unbelievers continue endlessly in a sinful state. Genesis 3:24 tells a different story.

Endless Existence in a Sinful State—Prevented by God

The tree of life was planted in the Garden of Eden (Gen. 2:9) for Adam and Eve to eat freely thereof (Gen. 2:16) and live forever (Gen. 3:22), but after they sinned, God acted decisively to keep humanity from the tree of life. Why? What did God guarantee by placing mighty cherubim and a flaming sword in Eden? The cherubim and flaming sword ensured that fallen people could not gain access to the fruit that produces immortality. This dramatic move on God's part appears to be in direct conflict with the eternal-torment view.

The traditional view maintains that to reject Christ is to exist throughout eternity as a sinner. Genesis 3:22-24 reveals that God has taken extraordinary measures to prevent the horrible possibility of human beings continuing forever in a sinful state.

Cherubim and a flaming sword guarding the tree of life make a striking picture. This scene in Eden brings to mind other Old Testament texts that indicate that the ungodly will not exist forever. Contrasting the righteous and the wicked, the psalmist declares,

> For yet a little while and the wicked shall be no more;
> Indeed, you will look carefully for his place,
> But it shall be no more.
> But the meek shall inherit the earth,
> And shall delight themselves in the abundance of peace.
> (Ps. 37: 10-11)

> The LORD knows the days of the upright,
> And their inheritance shall be forever.
> They shall not be ashamed in the evil time,

And in the days of famine they shall be satisfied.
But the wicked shall perish;
And the enemies of the LORD,
Like the splendor of the meadows, shall vanish.
Into smoke they shall vanish away. (Ps. 37:18-20)

In the New Testament, Peter tells of a coming fire in which "the earth and the works that are in it will be burned up" (2 Pet. 3:10). Peter goes on to say that God's plan for eternity calls for "new heavens and a new earth in which righteousness dwells" (2 Pet. 3:13). Likewise, John declares, "For all that is in the world—the lust of the flesh, the lust of the eyes, and the pride of life—is not of the Father but is of the world. And the world is passing away, and the lust of it; but he who does the will of God abides forever" (1 John 2:16-17).

From the beginning, God was determined to have a universe in which righteousness dwells. Should this surprise us? God is holy.

A DOOR OPENS

When I reread the Genesis account of original sin, eternal torment was conspicuous only by its absence. That Adam and Eve were not created as eternal beings was readily apparent. It also struck me that God had decisively acted to prevent people from living forever as sinners. Suddenly the traditional view of hell that I had held for over thirty years seemed out of sync with scripture. Freed from the assumption that eternal torment was a fact, I pressed on with my investigation, full of wonder as to what I might find.

2

WARNINGS OF HELL: THE GEHENNA PASSAGES

IDENTIFYING HELL

In the Greek New Testament, *Gehenna* (translated as *hell* in English) occurs twelve times (Matt. 5:22, 29, 30, 10:28, 18:9, 23:15, 33; Mark 9:43, 45, 47; Luke 12:5; James 3:6). The word *Gehenna* is derived from the Hebrew *Ge-Hinnom* (Valley of Hinnom), a valley south of Jerusalem.[37] It was in this valley that evil King Ahaz, who ruled Judah in the eighth century BC, made horrific child sacrifices:

> He [Ahaz] burned incense in the Valley of the Son of Hinnom, and burned his children in the fire, according to the abominations of the nations whom the LORD had cast out before the children of Israel. (2 Chron. 28:3)

The crimes of the evil King Manasseh also included the burning of his sons in the Valley of the Son of Hinnom (2 Chron. 33:6). This heartbreaking sin was not limited to Jewish leaders.

The word of the Lord to Jeremiah indicates that child sacrifice was once a significant problem in Israel:

> And they built the high places of Baal which are in the Valley of the Son of Hinnom, to cause their sons and their daughters to pass through the fire to Molech, which I did not command them, nor did it come into My mind that they should do this abomination, to cause Judah to sin. (Jer. 32:35)

Infamous for death by fire, *Gehenna* represents the final judgment fire, the lake of fire (Rev. 20:11-15). Traditionalists readily agree.[38] This chapter will cover the passages in which the word *Gehenna* appears. In the chapters ahead, we will examine passages that refer to the lake of fire/hell but do not contain the word *Gehenna*. For example, *Gehenna* is not mentioned by name in Matthew 25:41 ("Depart from Me, you cursed, into the everlasting fire prepared for the devil and his angels"); still, we know that the "everlasting fire" of Matthew 25:41 refers to the lake of fire because that is where Satan is cast in Revelation 20:10. (For more about Matthew 25:31-46, see Chapter 4.)

GEHENNA VS. HADES

We must be careful to consider verses that have *Gehenna* in view, though not specifically named. We must also recognize, however, that some verses do not refer to *Gehenna*, even though the word *hell* may be in the English text. Most of the confusion is with *Hades*, which occurs 11 times in the New Testament (Matt.

11:23, 16:18; Luke 10:15, 16:23; Acts 2:27, 31; 1 Cor. 15:55; Rev. 1:18, 6:8, 20:13-14).

Hades and *Gehenna* are distinct Greek words and distinct realities. Hades is the New Testament equivalent of the Old Testament *Sheol*.[39] It is commonly thought that prior to the death and resurrection of Christ everyone went to Sheol at death. Today, as noted previously, when a believer dies, his soul goes to be with the Lord in heaven. What the unsaved experience in Sheol/Hades is unclear.

The Old Testament mentions Sheol a number of times, yet it does not provide a definitive picture. In the words of M. R. Vincent, "Vagueness is its characteristic."[40] Neither does the New Testament illuminate the reality of Hades. The story of the rich man and Lazarus in Luke 16:19-31 is widely accepted as parabolic.[41] It was crafted to address issues of this world, namely, the Pharisees' materialism, self-righteousness and unbelief.[42] Perhaps, the *International Standard Bible Encyclopaedia* summarizes the situation best: "The NT places the emphasis on the eschatological developments at the end, and leaves many things connected with the intermediate state in darkness."[43]

Theologians refer to Hades as the intermediate state because the unsaved reside there from biological death to the Day of Judgment (Rev. 20:11-13) which directly leads to the casting of the unsaved into the lake of fire (Rev. 20:15). Unfortunately, some translations of the Bible are not careful to distinguish between hell and Hades.

The King James Version reads, "And in hell he [the rich man] lift up his eyes, being in torments, and seeth Abraham afar off, and Lazarus in his bosom" (Luke 16:23). The actual setting of Jesus' parable is Hades, as the New King James Version correctly states: "And being in torments in Hades, he lifted up his eyes and saw Abraham afar off, and Lazarus in his bosom." John F. Walvoord writes,

> In the Authorized Version, *Sheol* in the Old Testament and *Hades* in the New Testament are incorrectly translated by the English word *hell*. Both *Sheol* and *Hades* refer to the intermediate state or, as some believe, in certain instances to the grave. These terms *never* refer to the eternal state of punishment; therefore they should not have been translated in any instance by the word *hell*.[44]

Given the distinction between hell and Hades, it is disappointing that some traditionalists not only claim that hell is the setting of the parable of the rich man and Lazarus but cite the passage as a confirmation of their theology. In *Hell under Fire*, Robert W. Yarbrough writes,

> Jesus also speaks of hell in Luke's Gospel in the story of the rich man and Lazarus: "In *hell*, where he was in torment..." (Luke 16:23).... Significantly, this is yet another passage that points to a conscious and unending torment endured by hell's inhabitants.[45]

The traditionalist assertion that the parable of the rich man and Lazarus refers to hell is all too common. This is yet another way that false information has influenced believers to accept ECT. Even if Luke 16:19-31 is not a parable, the passage explicitly indicates no more than anguish in Hades prior to final judgment. This book pursues what Jesus actually taught about hell.

GENERAL WARNINGS OF HELL

Jesus mentions *Gehenna* three times in the Sermon on the Mount:

Matthew 5:22
> But I say to you that whoever is angry with his brother without a cause shall be in danger of the judgment. And whoever says to his brother, "Raca!" shall be in danger of the council. But whoever says, "You fool!" shall be in danger of *hell fire*.

Matthew 5:29-30
> And if your right eye causes you to sin, pluck it out and cast it from you; for it is more profitable for you that one of your members perish, than for your whole body to be cast into *hell*. And if your right hand causes you to sin, cut it off and cast it from you; for it is more profitable for you that one of your members perish, than for your whole body to be cast into *hell*.

Contrasting a part with the whole, Jesus says that is better to lose a member of one's body, such as an eye or a hand, than to have one's whole body cast into *Gehenna*. It is certainly better for one member of a person's body to perish by amputation than to have one's entire being cast into "the *Gehenna* of fire." Does Jesus say this because the lake of fire is a place of eternal torment, or is it that the lake of fire burns up those cast into it? The text does not provide the insight we need to answer this question. In short, the Sermon on the Mount *Gehenna* passages confirm the reality of hell but do not spell out what happens there.

Matthew 23:33 and Luke 12:4-5 are two more instances in which Jesus warns of hell without defining its punishment:

> *Matthew 23:33*
>
> Serpents, brood of vipers! How can you escape the condemnation of *hell*?

> *Luke 12:4-5*
>
> And I say to you, My friends, do not be afraid of those who kill the body, and after that have no more that they can do. But I will show you whom you should fear: Fear Him who, after He has killed, has power to cast into *hell*; yes, I say to you, fear Him!

Even less helpful in determining whether hell is a place of perishing or eternal torment are Matthew 23:15 and James 3:6:

> *Matthew 23:15*
>
> Woe to you, scribes and Pharisees, hypocrites! For you travel land and sea to win one proselyte, and when he is won, you make him twice as much a son of *hell* as yourselves.

> *James 3:6*
>
> And the tongue is a fire, a world of iniquity. The tongue is so set among our members that it defiles the whole body, and sets on fire the course of nature; and it is set on fire by *hell*.[46]

DISTINCTIVE WARNINGS OF HELL

Turning to Matthew 18:8-9 and Mark 9:43, 45, 47-48, we find a couple of additional details:

Matthew 18:8-9

> If your hand or your foot causes you to stumble, cut it off and throw it from you; it is better for you to enter life crippled or lame, than to have two hands or two feet and be cast into the *eternal fire*. If your eye causes you to stumble, pluck it out and throw it from you. It is better for you to enter life with one eye, than to have two eyes and be cast into the *fiery hell* (NASB).

Mark 9:43

> If your hand causes you to stumble, cut it off; it is better for you to enter life crippled, than, having your two hands, to go into *hell*, into the *unquenchable fire* (NASB) [The NKJV calls hell "the fire that shall never be quenched." However, the Greek text simply reads: τὸ πῦρ τὸ ἄσβεστον (SBLGNT)—"the fire—the unquenchable" (YLT).]

Mark 9:45

> If your foot causes you to stumble, cut it off; it is better for you to enter life lame, than, having your two feet, to be cast into *hell* (NASB)

Mark 9:47-48
> And if your eye causes you to sin, pluck it out. It is better for you to enter the kingdom of God with one eye, rather than having two eyes, to be cast into *hell fire*—where
>> "Their worm does not die
>> And the fire is not quenched."

The fires of *Gehenna* are referred to as "eternal fire" in Matthew 18 and "unquenchable fire" in Mark 9. What do these two expressions tell us about *Gehenna*? Traditionalists claim that they indicate that the fire's fuel supply—the wicked—is never consumed. Alan W. Gomes writes,

> Now, let us grant that fire normally represents that which consumes or annihilates its fuel until nothing but ashes are left. Normal fire dies out once the fuel has been consumed. But the fire of judgment is no normal fire: it is described as an *eternal* fire (Jude 7) which is *unquenchable* (Mark 9:48).... The fire is *doing* its work through a process of endless combustion.[47]

"Eternal fire" is surely unique, but what is the nature of the uniqueness? Does the paraphrase—"the fire that shall never be quenched"—point us in the right direction? Was the "eternal fire" of Jude 7 a matter of endless combustion? Not at all! The cities of Sodom and Gomorrah were burned to the ground rather quickly by fire that came from the Lord out of the heavens. Perhaps, then, eternal fire might best be understood as *divine* fire, the fire of our eternal God. As you read the story of Sodom and Gomorrah, what picture does it leave in your mind?

The two men said to Lot, "Do you have anyone else here—sons-in-law, sons or daughters, or anyone else in the city who belongs to you? Get them out of here, because we are going to destroy this place. The outcry to the Lord against its people is so great that he has sent us to destroy it."

So Lot went out and spoke to his sons-in-law, who were pledged to marry his daughters. He said, "Hurry and get out of this place, because the Lord is about to destroy the city!" But his sons-in-law thought he was joking.

With the coming of dawn, the angels urged Lot, saying, "Hurry! Take your wife and your two daughters who are here, or you will be swept away when the city is punished."…

By the time Lot reached Zoar, the sun had risen over the land. Then the Lord rained down burning sulfur on Sodom and Gomorrah—from the Lord out of the heavens. Thus he overthrew those cities and the entire plain, destroying all those living in the cities—and also the vegetation in the land. But Lot's wife looked back, and she became a pillar of salt.

Early the next morning Abraham got up and returned to the place where he had stood before the Lord. He looked down toward Sodom and Gomorrah, toward all the land of the plain, and he saw dense smoke rising from the land, like smoke from a furnace. (Gen. 19:12-15, 23-28, NIV)

The biblical record of Sodom and Gomorrah's judgment does not paint a picture of ongoing torment. Instead, it stuns us with death via catastrophic destruction. In the words of 2 Peter 2:6, God "condemned the cities of Sodom and Gomorrah by burning them to ashes, and made them an example of what is going to happen to the ungodly" (NIV). Basil F. C. Atkinson comments,

> The fire by the way of Jude 7 cannot be a fire in which the *inhabitants* of the guilty cities are burning today in another world, because they would not in such a case be "set forth for an example". It must have been the historical fire.[48]

Further, in direct contrast to the traditionalist position, scripture declares that unquenchable fire serves to *katakaio* (burn up, consume) the unsaved. The testimony of John the Baptist is explicit:

> But when he [John] saw many of the Pharisees and Sadducees coming to his baptism, he said to them, "Brood of vipers! Who warned you to flee from the wrath to come? Therefore bear fruits worthy of repentance… every tree which does not bear good fruit is cut down and thrown into the fire. I indeed baptize you with water unto repentance, but He who is coming after me is mightier than I, whose sandals I am not worthy to carry. He will baptize you with the Holy Spirit and fire. His winnowing fan is in His hand, and He will thoroughly clean out His threshing floor, and gather His wheat into the barn; but *He will burn up the chaff with unquenchable fire.*" (Matt. 3:7-12)

Walvoord identifies the time frame: "The baptism with fire seems related to the second coming of Christ, for only then will the wheat and the tares be separated and the tares, like the chaff mentioned by John the Baptist, burned with fire (cf. Mt 13:30, 38-42, 49-50)."[49]

John declared that Christ would gather His wheat (saved) into the barn and burn the chaff (unsaved). Jesus made it clear that the wheat (saved) and tares (unsaved) were to "both grow together until the harvest" (Matt. 13:30), that "the harvest is the end of the age" (Matt. 13:39), and that the reaping is done by the angels (Matt. 13:39). Thus any possibility of the fire referring to 70 AD and the fall of Jerusalem to the Romans is ruled out. Jesus' gathering of His "wheat into the barn" led H. A. Ironside to affirm that the flames of Matthew 25:41 are in view:

> The wheat are the children of the kingdom (Matt. 13:38). They are the ones who were to be baptized in the Holy Spirit. The chaff are the evil-doers who will be baptized in the fire of judgment. Nothing could emphasize our Lord's Deity more than John's declaration regarding Him and this twofold baptism. Imagine a creature baptizing in the Holy Spirit. Only One who is Himself Divine could do this. And on Pentecost Peter declares unhesitatingly that it was He who sent the Spirit (Acts 2:33). He it is who will consign the impenitent to the fire of everlasting punishment (Matt. 25:41). This is not to be confounded with the cleansing efficacy of the Holy Spirit, nor with the tongues "like as of fire" which appeared at Pentecost. "He will burn up the chaff with unquenchable fire" is placed in direct contrast with gathering the "wheat into the garner" (verse 12).[50]

What happens to the chaff in unquenchable fire? John says the chaff will burn up. Chaff is the light husk of wheat or other grains. When burned, chaff disappears into smoke. John's plain words are indeed confirmed by Jesus Himself:

> Another parable He put forth to them, saying: "The kingdom of heaven is like a man who sowed good seed in his field; but while men slept, his enemy came and sowed tares among the wheat and went his way. But when the grain had sprouted and produced a crop, then the tares also appeared. So the servants of the owner came and said to him, 'Sir, did you not sow good seed in your field? How then does it have tares?' He said to them, 'An enemy has done this.' The servants said to him, 'Do you want us then to go and gather them up?' But he said, 'No, lest while you gather up the tares you also uproot the wheat with them. *Let both grow together until the harvest*, and *at the time of harvest I will say* to the reapers, "First *gather together the tares and bind them in bundles to burn them*, but *gather the wheat into my barn.*"'" (Matt. 13:24-30)

Then Jesus sent the multitude away and went into the house. And His disciples came to Him, saying, "Explain to us the parable of the tares of the field." He answered and said to them: "He who sows the good seed is the Son of Man. The field is the world, the good seeds are the sons of the kingdom, but the tares are the sons of the wicked one. The enemy who sowed them is the devil, *the harvest is the end of the age*, and *the reapers are the angels*. Therefore *as the tares are gathered and burned in the fire, so it will be at the end of this age*. The Son of Man will send out His angels, and they will gather out of His kingdom all things that offend, and those who practice lawlessness, and will cast them into the furnace of fire. There will be wailing and gnashing of teeth. Then the righteous will shine forth as the sun in the kingdom of their Father. He who has ears to hear, let him hear!" (Matt. 13:36-43)

We must be careful in building doctrine from parables. This parable, however, comes with a commentary by the author Himself. Just as the tares of the field are gathered and burned in the fire, so shall it be with the unsaved.

Tares are weeds. If you want an illustration of what happens to the unsaved in the unquenchable flames of *Gehenna*, gather some weeds and burn them. But be sure your fire is adequate for the job. If you try to burn a pile of freshly cut weeds with a weak fire, the weeds may smother your fire. You need a fire that will not be quenched prior to completing its mission, even as God's judgment fire is unquenchable in that it cannot be prevented from completing its mission. Atkinson writes,

> The idea of unquenchable fire is taken like so much else in the New Testament from the Scriptures of the Old. In Jeremiah 17:27 we read that the Lord will kindle a fire in the gates of Jerusalem which will devour her palaces and *shall not be quenched*. The king of Babylon was the instrument through whom God fulfilled this threat, and the palaces were devoured. But is the fire burning now? Of course not. [Yet] No one in the world could quench it *till it had fulfilled the purpose for which it was kindled...* Such will be the fire that will burn up the wicked.[51]

Along with trees, grass, and the city of Babylon during the Great Tribulation (Rev. 8:7, 18:8), carcasses of sacrificial animals taken outside the camp (Heb. 13:11), and books deemed evil in a time of revival (Acts 19:19)—chaff and tares *katakaio* in fire.

As you watch the weeds burn up before your eyes, it will be a somber moment. "For I take no pleasure in the death of anyone, declares the Sovereign LORD. Repent and live!" (Ezek. 18:32, NIV).

Graphic Warnings of Eternal Torment?

Jesus' vivid teaching on the fiery destruction of the unsaved includes the statement that there will be "wailing and gnashing of teeth" (Matt. 13:42). Gomes holds that this expression indicates an endless condition of suffering. Starting with a paraphrase based notion of unquenchable fire, Gomes writes,

> A lake of fire burns but is never quenched... undying worms... chains of darkness... weeping and gnashing of teeth. Such is the powerful imagery for the horrible fate that awaits those who persist in their rejection of God and of His Christ. What else do these awesome figures force upon our imagination but a picture of unutterable suffering, fueled by the hopelessness of unceasing duration?[52]

If we look at these "awesome figures" in context, however, we find that they fall into one of three categories: irrelevant by virtue of being unrelated to humanity or hell, compatible with terminal punishment, or used to communicate hell as a place of perishing.

It is not human beings but fallen angels held in a place known as *Tartarus* to which *chains of darkness* pertain (2 Pet. 2:4).

Wailing and gnashing of teeth (found seven times in the Gospels: Matt. 8:12, 13:42, 50, 22:13, 24:51, 25:30; Luke 13:28) are never said to last eternally. The phrase does drive home, however, the reality that a terrible death awaits those whose names are not written in the Book of Life. Gnashing (grinding) of teeth reflects stress and/or may indicate anger at God on the part of the sinner (Acts 7:54). Harold E. Guillebaud comments,

> These terrible words [weeping and gnashing of teeth] do make quite clear that the destruction is not immediate, and that the purpose of the fire is not to consume only. But they do not remove the impression of the imagery that the wicked are compared to the worthless weeds which are thrown into the fire to be burned up, and to the worthless fish which are thrown away to be got rid of. Penal suffering comes into the application of the parables, for a death by fire is necessarily a very awful death, but it surely is not the main point, or it could not be so entirely lacking in the imagery of the parables themselves.[53]

Wailing, fear, anger—what else would be expected from sinners cast into an unquenchable fire that scripture declares will burn them up? Clearly, "wailing and gnashing of teeth" is compatible with the doctrine of terminal punishment.

Undying worms and fire that is not quenched are rooted in Isaiah 66:24: "And they will go out and look on the dead bodies of those who rebelled against me; the worms that eat them will not die, the fire that burns them will not be quenched, and they will be loathsome to all mankind" (NIV). Gomes takes the same interpretative stance with undying worms as he did with unquenchable fire:

> Worms are able to live as long as there is food for them to consume. Once their food supply has been consumed, the worms eventually die. But the torments of hell are likened

to *undying*, not dying worms. This is because their supply of food — the wicked — never ceases.[54]

Standing in opposition to Gomes' view is the fact that chaff is incinerated in unquenchable fire, a powerful indication that hell is a place of perishing. The undying worm and unquenchable fire of Isaiah 66:23-24 further support this conclusion. Originally, I planned for that investigation to take place now in response to Gomes' argument, but the material became so extensive that it merited its own chapter. In Chapter 3, it will become clear that the undying worm and unquenchable fire cited by Jesus have nothing to do with torment, much less eternal torment. We will discover that they are consuming agents, even as unquenchable fire is a consuming agent in Matthew 3:12.

So far, then, we have seen that several of the *Gehenna* verses strongly warn about hell without defining what happens there. The Matthew 18 and Mark 9 passages have been more helpful, though not decisive. This leaves one remaining *Gehenna* verse to examine, and it is pivotal.

THE DECISIVE GEHENNA WARNING

> And do not fear those who kill the body but cannot kill the soul. But rather fear Him who is able to destroy both soul and body in *hell*. —Matthew 10:28

In Matthew 10, Jesus sent His disciples on a challenging mission to the nation of Israel (vv. 5-6). The chapter contains both an "explicit short-term itinerary and a paradigm of the longer mission stretching into the years ahead."⁵⁵ Jesus warns of the dangers: "Behold, I send you out as sheep in the midst of wolves" (v. 16); "But beware of men, for they will deliver you up to councils and scourge you in their synagogues" (v. 17); "And you will be brought before governors and kings for My sake" (v. 18); "Now brother will deliver up brother to death" (v. 21); "And you will be hated by all for My name's sake" (v. 22).

The disciples will be denounced as evil by some (v. 25), but in the end, truth will prevail: "there is nothing covered that will not be revealed" (v. 26).

To bolster the disciples' resolve, Jesus also speaks words of encouragement. In Matthew 10:29-31, Jesus reminds the twelve of God's sovereignty and their importance to Him:

> Are not two sparrows sold for a copper coin? And not one of them falls to the ground apart from your Father's will. But the very hairs of your head are all numbered. Do not fear therefore; you are of more value than many sparrows.

In light of God's sovereignty, the disciples are to boldly proclaim Christ's words (v. 27). Wolves and haters are not to be feared, nor should the disciples be in awe of governors or kings capable only of temporal judgment. As Christ's messengers, the disciples' assignment is authorized by the ultimate Authority in the universe, the One who is able to destroy both soul and body in hell (v. 28).

In a context of God's authority over the world, we find a statement from Jesus on *Gehenna* that is invaluable. It is the only

Gehenna passage in which Jesus explicitly tells us what God can do to the soul in hell.

Man is capable of killing the body only; man cannot kill the soul. God, in contrast, is able to *destroy* both soul and body in hell. *Destroy* comes from the Greek word *apollumi*, which is also found in John 3:16 and 2 Peter 3:9. We're told in John 3:16 that God loved the world so much that He gave His only Son, that whoever trusts in Him will not perish [*apollumi*] but have eternal life. Jesus warns us to avoid *Gehenna* because He does not want "that any should perish [*apollumi*] but that all should come to repentance" (2 Pet. 3:9).

Along with *katakaio*, *apollumi* is one of the most important words in the Bible with regard to final judgment. God is able to *apollumi* both soul and body in hell, but whoever believes in the Son of God will not *apollumi*. To understand the Greek word *apollumi* in the context of Matthew 10:28 is to understand the fate of the unsaved in the lake of fire.

THE TRADITIONALIST VIEW OF MATTHEW 10:28

What is it that God is able to do to soul and body in *Gehenna*? In *Hell under Fire*, Yarbrough turns to the testimony of demons to understand the mind of Christ:

> Second, in Jesus' usage "destroy" can also mean to inflict enduring torment. That is, unclean spirits who ask whether Jesus will "destroy" them *(apollymi*; Mark 1:24; Luke 4:34) understand that destruction in terms of unending torment (*basanizo*; Matt. 8:29; Mark 5:7; Luke 8:28). In other words, the verb *apollymi* ("to destroy") in Matthew 10:28 is parallel not only with *apokteino* ("to kill") in the same verse, where

the reference is plainly to earthly death; *apollymi* can also be parallel with *basanizo* ("to torment, torture"), where the reference is to the sphere of existence beyond this earthly one.⁵⁶

Yarbrough's parallel between "destroy" and "torment" is generated by drawing upon two distinct situations involving Jesus and demonic beings, one that took place in Capernaum (where demons ask if Jesus has come to destroy them) and the other in the country of the Gerasenes (where demons beg Jesus not to torment them). If we simply took both incidents at face value, however, we would conclude that among unclean spirits there is apprehension about torment *and* destruction. Is there reason to believe that both prospects would be of legitimate concern to demons? Indeed, there is. Torment will take place in the lake of fire (Rev. 20:10), and in light of God's determination to establish new heavens in which righteousness dwells (2 Pet. 3:13), utterly unrighteous spirits have cause to anticipate utter destruction. (For more on the judgment of Satan and his angels, see Chapter 6.) Second, Yarbrough states that unclean spirits understand destruction to mean unending torment, but neither "unending" nor any such term is used by the unclean spirits. Third, Yarbrough asserts that in Jesus' usage, "destroy" can mean to inflict enduring torment, yet he does not cite Jesus' usage of *apollumi*. Yarbrough must cite the testimony of demons to make his argument because the parallel for which he reaches is not found in the words of Jesus Christ. The parallel Jesus established is between *apokteino* (kill) and *apollumi*.

Although *Hell under Fire* is lauded as one of the best defenses of traditionalism, Yarbrough's argument is rather nontraditional. Typically, traditionalists attempt to reconcile Matthew 10:28 with ECT by interpreting *apollumi* in terms of "ruin" or "loss of well-being." In his widely consulted *Expository Dictionary of New Testament Words,* under the heading DESTROY, W. E. Vine says of *apollumi*:

> a strengthened form of *ollumi*, signifies to destroy utterly; in Middle Voice, to perish. The idea is not extinction but ruin, loss, not of being, but of well-being. This is clear from its use, as, e.g., of the marring of wine skins, Luke 5:37; of lost sheep, i.e., lost to the shepherd, metaphorical of spiritual destitution, Luke 15:4, 6, etc.; the lost son, 15:24; of the perishing of food, John 6:27; of gold, I Pet. 1:7. So of persons, Matt. 2:13, "destroy;" 8:25, "perish;" 22:7; 27:20; of the loss of well-being in the case of the unsaved hereafter, Matt. 10:28, Luke 13:3, 5; John 3:16 (ver. 15 in some mss.)[57]

Understanding *apollumi* in terms of "ruin" or "loss of well-being" provides support to the traditionalist position, but is this the meaning of *apollumi* in Matthew 10:28? Has Vine correctly reviewed the biblical record?

VINE OR STOTT

Should we simply take Vine's definition as gospel? John Stott didn't. The internationally admired evangelical leader wrote of *apollumi*:

> When the verb is active and transitive, 'destroy' means 'kill', as when Herod wanted to murder the baby Jesus and the Jewish leaders later plotted to have him executed (Matthew 2:13; 12:14; 27:4). Then Jesus himself told us not to be afraid of those who kill the body and cannot kill the soul. 'Rather,' he continued, 'be afraid of the One [God] who can destroy both soul and body in hell' (Matthew 10:28; cf. James 4:12).

If to kill is to deprive the body of life, hell would seem to be the deprivation of both physical and spiritual life, that is, an extinction of being.[58]

So which scholar is right? Is it beyond us to discern the meaning of *apollumi* in Matthew 10:28? Actually, it isn't. With a little effort, everyone is able to do some firsthand biblical research.

BREAKOUT THE ENGLISHMAN'S GREEK CONCORDANCE

The meaning of a word is largely determined by its usage. This is why the *Englishman's Greek Concordance* is such a valuable tool. Its purpose is to show us every occurrence of each Greek word in the New Testament. Take the time to go through all of the pertinent passages and you can see how the biblical writers used any particular word.

Please watch out for something, however. It is common for a word to have a variety of meanings. Take the English word *pen*, for example. Most commonly, pen refers to a device that allows us to write in ink, but it might refer to an enclosure that keeps animals confined or to a female swan. We need to keep in mind that each particular meaning is valid only within a properly corresponding context. Suppose you were in a classroom and wondered out loud if anyone had a pen that they weren't using. It would be bizarre for someone to ask what type of animal you needed to house. This would be an obvious blunder, yet this type of thing is all too common when it comes to interpreting the New Testament.

In short, a Greek word might have multiple meanings, but it does not follow that you may pick whatever meaning you like when studying a passage of scripture. If we want to know what the Bible actually says, the meaning of the word and its context must match; they must rightly correspond to each other.

Like those in Berea who diligently studied the scriptures to see whether Paul's message was true (Acts 17:11), let's roll up our sleeves and investigate how *apollumi* is used in the Gospels.

APOLLUMI IN THE GOSPELS

Matthew 2:13
> Now when they had departed, behold, an angel of the Lord appeared to Joseph in a dream, saying, "Arise, take the young Child and His mother, flee to Egypt, and stay there until I bring you word; for Herod will seek the young Child to *destroy* Him."

This is the first occurrence of *apollumi* in the New Testament. It is exactly the same form of *apollumi* that appears in Matthew 10:28 (ἀπολέσαι). Does Vine's definition of *apollumi* as loss of well-being prove true? Did Herod want the young Child to grow up in some diminished capacity?

The wise men were to locate "He who has been born King of the Jews" (Matt. 2:2) and report His location to Herod (Matt. 2:8), but having been divinely warned in a dream that they should not return to Herod, the wise men departed for their own country

(Matt. 2:12). When Herod realized that the wise men weren't coming back, "he sent forth and put to death all the male children who were in Bethlehem and in all its districts, from two years old and under, according to the time which he had determined from the wise men" (Matt. 2:16). Is it not perfectly obvious that Herod sought to kill the young Child?

In Matthew 2:13, Vine's definition of "destroy" as *ruin, loss of well-being*, widely misses the mark. Ἀπολέσαι plainly equals *kill* in this context.

Matthew 5:29
> And if your right eye causes you to sin, pluck it out and cast it from you; for it is more profitable for you that one of your members *perish*, than for your whole body to be cast into hell.

Jesus emphasized the importance of avoiding hell through the drastic thought of an eye ripped out of its socket and cast away. If a person *perishes* in hell as a dislodged and discarded eye *perishes*—biological death followed by disintegration—then Jesus' warning favors terminal punishment. Nevertheless, I list Matthew 5:29 among the generic warnings. Why? I do not want to overreach. This verse does not tell us what happens in hell, and I don't want my view to be built on assumption.

Interestingly, in Matthew 5:29 and John 3:16, the form of *apollumi* is identical: ἀπόληται. Another exact match is found in John 11:50, in which Caiaphas states, "Nor do you consider that it is expedient for us that one man should die for the people, and not that the whole nation *should perish*."

RESCUE FROM DEATH

Ἀπολέσαι ("to destroy") (Matt. 2:13, 10:28) and ἀπόληται ("perish") (Matt. 5:9; John 3:16) are distinct forms of *apollumi*. The former is an active infinitive; the latter is in the middle voice and subjunctive mood. Though distinct forms of *apollumi*, with regard to people, *destroy/kill* and *perish* are essentially two sides of the same coin. To illustrate, consider these two statements: (1) Herod commanded his soldiers *to kill* the young Child, but they could not find Him; (2) The young Child would have *perished*, but Herod's soldiers could not find Him.

> *Matthew 8:23-25*
>
> Now when He got into a boat, His disciples followed Him. And suddenly a great tempest arose on the sea, so that the boat was covered with the waves. But He was asleep. Then His disciples came to Him and awoke Him, saying, "Lord, save us! We are *perishing*!"

Was the disciples' boat trip being ruined by bad weather? Or did they fear death?

> *Matthew 9:17*
>
> Nor do people put new wine into old wineskins, or else the wineskins break [burst], the wine is spilled, and the wineskins *are ruined*. But they put new wine into new wineskins, and both are preserved.
>
> And no one pours new wine into old wineskins; otherwise the skins burst and the wine is spilled out

and the skins *are destroyed*. Instead they put new wine into new wineskins and both are preserved. (NET)

A wineskin is literally a leather bottle. If you take an old wineskin with no elasticity and fill it with new wine, the new wine's ongoing fermentation will create more and more pressure, until the leather bottle bursts. The burst wineskin is far more than ruined in the sense of being *marred*. It would be correct to say that a burst wineskin is ruined in that it can no longer fulfill its purpose, yet the destruction is more profound. Just the other day, I dropped a cup, which shattered. As the porcelain scattered about my kitchen floor was no longer a cup, when an old wineskin bursts, there is one less bottle in the world.

The form of *apollumi* in the wineskin passages (Matt. 9:17; Mark 2:22; Luke 5:37) ἀπολοῦνται (Received Text; future tense) is also found in Hebrews 1:11 which contrasts the transitory nature of the present earth and heavens with the eternality of the Son. "They will perish, but You remain." With regard to human beings ἀπολοῦνται means perish in the sense of *die*: "Then Jesus said to him, 'Put your sword in its place, for all who take the sword will *perish* by the sword'" (Matt. 26:52). Most translations, however, favor the present tense ἀπόλλυνται found in the Nestle-Aland text.

Whether ἀπολοῦνται or ἀπόλλυνται, in the wineskin passages, we are dealing with material objects rather than human beings and a nonjudgment context. Hardly the best help to determine the meaning of ἀπολέσαι in Matthew 10:28.

RESCUE FROM DEATH

Matthew 21:40-41

> "When the owner of the farm comes, what will he do to those men?" They answered, "He will *kill* those bad men, and will give the farm to other men who will give him the fruit when it is time." (WE)

In Matthew 21, Jesus told a parable about a landowner who established a fenced vineyard with a winepress and lookout tower, which he leased to vinedressers before traveling to a faraway country (v. 33). When the landowner sent his servants to collect his portion of the crop, the vinedressers beat one servant, killed one, and stoned another (v. 35). Then the landowner sent his son, saying, "They will respect my son" (v. 37). Maliciously, however, the vinedressers killed the landowner's son (v. 39). What would happen now? Those listening to Jesus' story emphatically affirmed that the owner of the vineyard would *kill* the evil men and find honorable workers to take their place.

Matthew 22:7

> But when the king heard about it, he was furious. And he sent out his armies, *destroyed* those murderers, and burned up their city.

This passage is particularly significant because of its contextual similarities with Matthew 10:28. We want to know what Jesus meant when He taught that the King of the universe can *apollumi* both soul and body in hell. In Matthew 22:7, Jesus tells us about a king whose servants were mistreated and killed. This king was furious. His military, says Jesus, destroyed the murderers of his servants and burned up their city. In this context of retribution by a king, *apollumi* plainly means *killed*.

> *Matthew 27:20*
>
> But the chief priests and elders persuaded the multitudes that they should ask for Barabbas and *destroy* Jesus.

The chief priests and elders influenced the masses to have Jesus put to death. This is clear from Matthew 27:22: "Pilate said to them, 'What then shall I do with Jesus who is called Christ?' They all said to him, 'Let Him be crucified!'"

> *Mark 3:5-6*
>
> So when He had looked around at them with anger, being grieved by the hardness of their hearts, He said to the man, "Stretch out your hand." And he stretched it out, and his hand was restored as whole as the other. Then the Pharisees went out and immediately plotted with the Herodians against Him, how they might *destroy* Him.

I don't know anyone who thinks this verse teaches that the Pharisees plotted to discredit Jesus. Is it not universally accepted that the Pharisees plotted to *kill* Christ?

> *Luke 6:9*
>
> Then Jesus said to them, "I will ask you one thing: Is it lawful on the Sabbath to do good or to do evil, to save life or *to destroy it*?"

RESCUE FROM DEATH

Young's Literal Translation reads: "Is it lawful on the sabbaths to do good, or to do evil? life to save or *to kill?*" The NKJV cites "to kill" as the Majority Text reading. Charles B. Williams' *The New Testament: A Translation in the Language of the People* reads: "Is it right on the sabbath to do people good, or to do them evil, to save life or to take it?"

Luke 9:51-56

> Now it came to pass, when the time had come for Him to be received up, that He steadfastly set His face to go to Jerusalem, and sent messengers before His face. And as they went, they entered a village of the Samaritans, to prepare for Him. But they did not receive Him, because His face was set for the journey to Jerusalem. And when His disciples James and John saw this, they said, "Lord, do You want us to command fire to come down from heaven and consume them, just as Elijah did?" But He turned and rebuked them, and said, "You do not know what manner of spirit you are of. For the Son of Man did not come to *destroy* men's lives but to save them."

Here is an interesting parallel. Jesus connected literal consuming fire with *apollumi*. After encountering Samaritans who did not receive the Savior, the disciples asked Jesus if they should command fire from heaven to consume the Samaritans, even as Elijah had called down fire from heaven to consume King Ahaziah's soldiers (2 Kings 1:1-14). Jesus replied that He did not come to *apollumi*; He did not come to kill or burn up or consume by fire. His Second Coming will be with flames of fire (Isa. 66:15-16), but in His First Advent, Jesus came as a sacrificial lamb to die for the sins of the world.

This is a passage to highlight. Not only does Jesus equate *apollumi* with killing by literal consuming fire, but the form of the verb is identical to that in Matthew 10:28: ἀπολέσαι.

> *Luke 11:49-51*
>
> Therefore the wisdom of God also said, "I will send them prophets and apostles, and some of them they will kill and persecute," that the blood of all the prophets which was shed from the foundation of the world may be required of this generation, from the blood of Abel to the blood of Zechariah who *perished* between the altar and the temple.

Perished in this verse, means *died*; Zechariah was stoned to death (2 Chron. 24:20-21).

> *Luke 15:4-6*
>
> What man of you, having a hundred sheep, if he *loses* one of them, does not leave the ninety-nine in the wilderness, and go after the one which is *lost* until he finds it? And when he has found it, he lays it on his shoulders, rejoicing. And when he comes home, he calls together his friends and neighbors, saying to them, "Rejoice with me, for I have found my sheep which was *lost!*"

RESCUE FROM DEATH

In Luke 15:4-6, a man with a flock of one hundred loses (ἀπολέσας) one of his sheep. The man leaves the ninety-nine and goes after the sheep that is lost (ἀπολωλός). He finds his sheep, returns home, and calls his friends and neighbors to celebrate. This parable was spoken to the Pharisees and scribes who complained about Jesus' association with tax collectors and outcasts (Luke 15:1-3). It conveys God's faithful pursuit of sinners and the joy that restoration brings to heaven.

In the parable of the lost sheep, God is Savior, not Judge. His care and concern are on display, not His justice.

Clearly, *apollumi* has distinct meanings and is found in distinct contexts. Kittel's *Theological Dictionary of the New Testament* lists four literal meanings of *apollumi*: to destroy/kill; to perish; to lose; to be lost.[59] Vine, when defining *apollumi* under the heading LOSE, (Suffer) LOSS, LOST, also recognized that *apollumi* has distinct meanings.[60] In fact, Vine acknowledged the meaning "to destroy, destroy utterly, kill" when *apollumi* is in the active voice, *citing Matthew 10:28 as an example*.[61] Unfortunately, Vine's famous definition of *apollumi*, which many traditionalists rely upon, does not acknowledge that *apollumi* has a range of meanings.

In Vine's commonly used definition, lost sheep and lost son passages are conflated with kill/put to death passages to produce a one-size-fits-all definition of ruin/loss of well-being. This glaring inconsistency in Vine's work is unwarranted and unhelpful. Herod sought to kill. A man loses a sheep. We need to be able to appreciate what is being said in each particular context, and an artificial definition does not get us there.

Luke 15:8-9
> Or what woman, having ten silver coins, if she *loses* one coin, does not light a lamp, sweep the house, and search carefully until she finds it? And when she has found it, she calls her friends and neighbors together, saying, "Rejoice with me, for I have found the piece which I *lost!*"

Jesus describes a scene in which a woman *lost* a coin. It was *missing*. The diligent persistence of the woman illustrates God's evangelistic zeal for sinners.

"Missing" is a meaning of *apollumi* that is well suited to this parable. The most common meaning of *apollumi* in the Gospels—kill/die—would make no sense whatsoever in the story of the woman and her coins. Likewise, loses/lost/missing is foreign to the numerous contexts in which people are killed.

Luke 15:17
> But when he came to himself, he said, "How many of my father's hired servants have bread enough and to spare, and I *perish* with hunger!"

Here, *dying* from starvation is the concept in view.

Luke 15:24, 32
> "For this my son was dead and is alive again; [*and*] he was *lost* and is found." And they began to be merry. (v. 24) "It was right that we should make merry and be glad, for your brother was dead and is alive again, *and* was *lost* and is found." (v. 32)

"My son was dead and is alive again" refers to the son's spiritual state. Additionally (*and*), "he was *lost* and is found." As in Luke 15:4-6 and 8-9, *apollumi* here means *lost* or *missing*. The son, who had been missing from the fellowship of the family, returned home. In short, the father rejoiced over both his son's repentance (my son was dead and is alive again) *and* his son's return to the family (was missing and is found).

Luke 17:26-27

> As it was in the days of Noah, so it will be also in the days of the Son of Man: They ate, they drank, they married wives, they were given in marriage, until the day that Noah entered the ark, and the flood came and *destroyed* them all.

Apollumi in Luke 17:27 means *killed*. The Genesis record makes this very clear:

> The flood engulfed the earth for forty days. As the waters increased, they lifted the ark and raised it above the earth. The waters completely overwhelmed the earth, and the ark floated on the surface of the waters.... And all living things that moved on the earth died, including the birds, domestic animals, wild animals, all the creatures that swarm over the earth, and all humankind. Everything on dry land that had the breath of life in its nostrils died.... Only Noah and those who were with him in the ark survived. (Gen. 7:17-23, NET)

Imagine yourself in the ark when the waters covered the earth. Might you feel like you had just witnessed annihilation on a global scale? Yet final, complete, irreversible annihilation did not take place during Noah's flood, because the ungodly who perished will be resurrected to stand before God's Great White Throne (Rev. 20:11-13). Although Genesis 7:20-23 does not directly teach annihilationism, it is a powerful visual reminder of the primary usage of *apollumi* in the Gospels: kill, put to death, die, perish.

> *Luke 17:32-33*
> Remember Lot's wife. Whoever seeks to save his life *will lose* it, and whoever *loses* his life will preserve it.

In the days of Noah they "ate, they drank, they married wives, they were given in marriage, until the day that Noah entered the ark, and the flood came and destroyed them all" (17:27). In the days of Lot, they "ate, they drank, they bought, they sold, they planted, they built; but on the day that Lot went out of Sodom it rained fire and brimstone from heaven and destroyed them all" (17:28-29). That is, people were occupied with the things of this world to the point that they were unprepared for the judgment that came upon them. In both examples provided by Jesus, the worldly-minded experienced a violent death.

The ungodly will likewise be in danger of judgment at the Second Coming of the Lord Jesus. "Even so will it be in the day when the Son of Man is revealed" (17:30). "In that day," warns Jesus, "he who is on the housetop, and his goods are in the house, let him not come down to take them away. And likewise the one who is in the field, let him not turn back" (17:31). "Remember Lot's wife" (17:32), who looked back, revealing that her heart was still in Sodom, and became a pillar of salt (Gen. 19:26). Don't make the same mistake.

At Christ's return, whoever seeks to save his life will lose it; i.e., whoever continues to treasure this world will be *killed* in judgment. And whoever loses his life will preserve it; i.e., whoever *lets go* of his life, to turn to the Son of Man, will live.

John 3:14-15
> And as Moses lifted up the serpent in the wilderness, even so must the Son of Man be lifted up, that whoever believes in Him *should not perish* but have eternal life.

Those who believe in Christ shall not perish but have life eternal. Is this not conditional immortality?

John 6:39
> This is the will of the Father who sent Me, that of all He has given Me I should *lose* nothing, but should raise it up at the last day.

All that the Father has given to the Son will be raised, not one will be missing on that glorious day.

John 10:10
> The thief does not come except to steal, and to kill, and to *destroy*.

Edwin Blum succinctly states, "The thief, that is, a false shepherd, cares only about feeding himself, not building up the flock. He steals sheep in order to kill them, thus destroying part of the flock."[62]

John 18:14

> Now it was Caiaphas who gave counsel to the Jews that it was expedient that one man should *die* for the people.

Yet again, *apollumi* means to be put to death.

VINE'S TRADITIONALIST BIAS

Our overview of *apollumi* in the Gospels revealed serious deficiencies in Vine's definition of *destroy*. We saw that in many instances, *apollumi* means *kill/put to death*, yet Vine did not acknowledge this. Instead, he ascribed either ruin or loss of well-being to every passage he cited, even verses dealing with food and gold. As in the case of characterizing the wineskins as *marred*, this falls short of Jesus' usage of *apollumi*.

"Do not labor for the food which *perishes*, but for the food which endures to everlasting life, which the Son of Man will give you, because God the Father has set His seal on Him" (John 6:27). Vine's definition suggests that Jesus refers to food that *spoils*; however, the backdrop, the feeding of the 5000 (John 6:1-14), points to food that is *eaten*. Designed to be *consumed*, food is essential and people crave it, yet it is only of temporal value. When those who "ate of the loaves and were filled" (John 6:26) found Jesus in Capernaum, He pointed them to the "true bread from heaven" (John 6:32). In light of the immediate context, Jesus is best understood to have said: "Do not labor for the food which *perishes* [i.e., is eaten and is gone], but for the food which *endures* to everlasting life."

Vine also lists gold in 1 Peter 1:7 as an example of ruin. Peter wrote,

> In this you greatly rejoice, though now for a little while, if need be, you have been grieved by various trials, that the genuineness of your faith, being much more precious than gold that *perishes*, though it is tested by fire, may be found to praise, honor, and glory at the revelation of Jesus Christ (1 Pet. 1:6-7)

Gold has been known to corrupt people, but Peter speaks of gold itself, which is extremely resistant to corrosion. It is not a treasure that moth or rust destroys, but one that thieves steal.

How should we understand the perishing of gold? For all of its worth and durability, gold is part of the present material universe, which will one day come to an end (Rev. 21:1). The gold of this world, which ultimately will be dissolved (2 Pet. 3:11), is valuable, but faith is much more important because it results in the salvation of the soul (1 Pet. 1:9).

Vine goes on to cite four verses in Matthew as examples of *loss of well-being*. Our investigation reveals a different meaning: Herod sought to *kill* the one born King of the Jews (Matt. 2:13); the disciples feared *dying* in the storm (Matt. 8:25); it was not *loss of well-being* but rather clearly *death*, by violent killing, that the outraged king (Matt. 22:7) and the chief priests (Matt. 27:20) sought for their enemies.

In stating that the unsaved experience loss of well-being in the hereafter, Vine groups Luke 13:3, 5 with Matthew 10:28 and John 3:16. Luke 13:3, 5 describes yet more violent end-of-life scenarios:

> There were present at that season some who told Him about the Galileans *whose blood Pilate had mingled with their sacrifices.* And Jesus answered and said to them, "Do you suppose that these Galileans were worse sinners than all other Galileans, because they suffered such things? I tell you, no; but unless you repent you will all likewise *perish*. Or those eighteen on whom *the tower in Siloam fell and killed them*, do you think that they were worse sinners than all other men who dwelt in Jerusalem? I tell you, no; but unless you repent you will all likewise *perish*." (Luke 13:1-5)

How is it that Vine's famous definition failed to understand *apollumi* as *kill/put to death*? Perhaps it was the pressure of his theology. If we believe that the inerrant Word of God teaches eternal torment, we will expect to find that theology reflected throughout the Bible. Because scripture does not contradict itself, the stronger the commitment to the traditional view of hell, the greater the pressure to understand *apollumi* in terms such as *ruin* or *loss of well-being*.

Whatever the reason, Vine's famous definition of *apollumi* fails to square with the biblical record.

THE MEANING OF APOLLUMI IN MATTHEW 10:28

In my initial review of the key texts, Matthew 10:28 immediately grabbed my attention. Here was an explicit statement that directly challenged my long-held belief in ECT: God is able to destroy both soul and body in hell.

God can destroy. Jesus was not talking about something that man does to himself. Jesus warned about what *God* can do *to* man—fear Him who is able *to destroy* both soul and body in hell.

What are the chances that the disciples shared the traditionalist view of *destroy*? Did Peter and John understand Jesus to mean that God sustains the unsaved eternally in a state of ruin like "wineskins that can no longer function because they have holes in them" or "a coin that is useless because it is lost"?[63] This is what traditionalists want us to believe about destroy in Matthew 10:28. But do traditionalists arrive at this conclusion on the basis of the usage of ἀπολέσαι in the Gospels?

I want to be instructed by Matthew 10:28. It is the only time Jesus explicitly talks about the soul and *Gehenna*. In this pivotal verse, *apollumi* is an aorist active infinitive ἀπολέσαι. Turning to passages that deal with human beings, let us consider the following instances of *apollumi*:[64]

(A) instances of ἀπολέσαι where Jesus is the one speaking
(B) instances of ἀπολέσαι in Matthew
(C) instances of ἀπολέσαι in Mark, Luke, and John
(D) instances of ἀπολέσαι from Acts to Revelation

(E) other active forms of *apollumi* in the Gospels where the context is similar; i.e., where an authority acts against those who are offensive

There are two verses in category A: Luke 6:9 (life to save or to kill) and Luke 9:56. The latter is the most helpful because it directly involves Jesus in relationship to those who did not receive Him. In Luke 9:51-56, *Jesus equates* ἀπολέσαι *with killing by literal consuming fire.*

Category B has one verse, Matthew 2:13. Without a doubt, Herod sought *to kill* the young Child.

Category C also has one passage: "And He was teaching daily in the temple. But the chief priests, the scribes, and the leaders of the people sought to destroy Him, and were unable to do anything; for all the people were very attentive to hear Him" (Luke 19:47-48). Does not virtually everyone agree that the Jewish authorities sought *to kill* Jesus?

Category D has one verse, James 4:12: "There is one Lawgiver, who is able to save and to destroy. Who are you to judge another?" In James 4:12, as with Luke 6:9, when an English translation of the Bible uses a word other than destroy, it typically reads "kill" or "put to death."

We reviewed several verses that fit in category E, including: Matthew 21:41, 22:7, 27:20, and Mark 3:6. In each instance, *apollumi* plainly means *to kill.* Matthew 22:7 is most helpful because Jesus Himself uses the word *apollumi* to explain what a king does to grievously offensive individuals: The king's armies *killed* the murderers of his servants.

Now we know, from our own firsthand examination of the biblical data, how the particular form of the verb *apollumi* in Matthew 10:28 is used in the Gospels with regard to man. Overwhelmingly, the meaning of ἀπολέσαι is *to kill/put to death*. Other forms of *apollumi*, in contexts when an authority acts against those who have been grievously offensive or are perceived to be offensive, also mean *to kill*. Moreover, *to kill* perfectly fits the Matthew 10:28 context. Indeed, the verse is structured in a manner that leads one to expect ἀπολέσαι to mean *to kill*.

Thus we can say with great confidence: "And do not fear those who kill the body but cannot kill the soul. But rather fear Him who is able *to kill* both soul and body in hell" is the face value reading of Matthew 10:28 that takes ἀπολέσαι in its plain, literal, customary sense.

THE SIGNIFICANCE OF MATTHEW 10:28

There is no reason to believe that Jesus' warning is either empty or misleading. This is why Matthew 10:28 is such a problem for proponents of ECT. If God kills body and soul in *Gehenna*, the sinner's life, both biological and conscious, would come to an end and traditionalism would be undone.

Men can kill the body; men can also torment and men can corrupt. "Do not be deceived: 'Evil company corrupts good habits'" (1 Cor. 15:33). But man cannot kill the soul. God alone, Jesus reminds us, has the power to terminate a person.

Christ's warning that God is able to destroy both soul and body in hell, unlike eternal torment, is consistent with the Genesis 2:17 penalty for sin. Previously, we discovered that the phrase "you shall surely die" is a judicial death sentence. Civilized governments conduct trials to prove guilt prior to executing the death penalty. God will also formally demonstrate the guilt of the unsaved; however, the judgment that the unbeliever must face and the method of execution were not revealed in Genesis. These truths were taught in the New Testament.

In the Gospel of Matthew, Jesus foretold the final judgment of the unsaved at the time of His return to earth (Matt. 25:31-46). In John's Gospel (5:28-29), Jesus spoke of resurrection unto condemnation for the unsaved in the grave. These will come before God's Great White Throne for final judgment (Rev. 20:11-12). The verdict is executed by the unsaved being cast into the lake of fire (Matt. 25:41; Rev. 20:15).

Jesus repeatedly affirms the reality of hell and forcefully warns us that it is most certainly a place to be avoided. To its credit, traditionalism has rightly recognized and faithfully preserved this truth. The critical issue, however, is what ultimately happens to the impenitent in the lake of fire. To get this right, traditionalists need only to take Matthew 10:28 at face value: Fear Him who is able to kill both soul and body in *Gehenna*. Divine justice takes place in the unquenchable flames of hell as the impenitent, like chaff and tares, burn up in God's furnace of fire. There is no more apt term to describe *such a death* than annihilation.

Through frightful scenes of utter destruction, scripture seeks our attention and powerfully conveys the seriousness and finality of God's righteous penalty for sin—cessation of life. Thankfully, this does not have to be anyone's end. The Father so loved the world that He gave His Son to rescue from death all who believe in Him.

3

UNQUENCHABLE FIRE AND UNDYING WORM: ISAIAH 66:23-24

"And it shall come to pass
That from one New Moon to another,
And from one Sabbath to another,
All flesh shall come to worship before Me,"
says the LORD.
"And they shall go forth and look
Upon the corpses of the men
Who have transgressed against Me.
For their worm does not die,
And their fire is not quenched.
They shall be an abhorrence to all flesh."
— Isaiah 66:23-24

Why did Jesus speak of worm that does not die and fire that is not quenched in Mark 9:48? Traditionalists believe Jesus drew upon the unquenchable fire and undying worm of Isaiah 66:24 to paint a picture of eternal torment. Morgan writes,

> Mark 9 also instructs us that... hell is a place where the fire never goes out (9:43) and where suffering never ends. The agents of suffering (the worm and the fire) are never extinguished (9:48; cf. Isa. 66:24). The implication is strong: The agents of suffering never end because those in hell experience conscious suffering forever.[65]

Peterson writes,

> Because Isaiah speaks of undying worm and unquenchable fire, he intends for readers to understand "the dead bodies" as referring to resurrected human beings who suffer the second death, that is, experience everlasting disgrace in hell. Jesus' interpretation of Isaiah 66:24 in Mark 9:43-48 confirms the traditionalist interpretation. Jesus warns his hearers of being thrown into hell where "their worm does not die, and the fire is not quenched."[66]

It is commonly agreed that Jesus quoted Isaiah 66:24, but have traditionalists rightly understood Isaiah and, consequently, Jesus? If we are to understand Isaiah's graphic description of undying worm and unquenchable fire, we must first understand the prophetic Old Testament scriptures in which the terms appear.

Prophecy can be a difficult study, and the temptation arises to pass it over because of controversy and confusion, yet much of the biblical teaching on hell is rooted in prophetic passages. In this chapter, we will introduce the two major interpretative approaches to prophetic scripture—literal and allegorical—as well as provide a brief overview of premillennialism and amillennialism. The "perspective of prophecy" principle and the importance of prophetic details will also be discussed. This information will assist us in examining Isaiah 66:24 and understanding its message. It will also prove helpful when encountering prophetic scripture in key New Testament texts.

PRINCIPLES OF INTERPRETATION

Paul Lee Tan introduces the *literal method* of interpretation:

> It is proper for a word to have various meanings and senses. However, when a word is used in a given situation, it should normally possess but *one* intended sense or meaning. This is the regular law of linguistic exchange among sensible people.
>
> Music lovers seek to understand music composers, not by out-thinking and out-sensing the composers, but by following the latter's choice and use of precise musical notes. Students of Music Appreciation courses do not go about trying to listen for something which is not there, but attempt rather to know the intended meaning and mood of a given composer through his use of the notes. Otherwise what the composer is trying to say is ignored and what the interpreter wants to say becomes the important factor.
>
> Literal interpreters believe that Scriptural revelation is given to be understood by man. To "understand" a speaker or writer, one must assume that the speaker or writer is using words normally and without multiple meanings. This is what the literal method of interpretation assumes of God in Scriptural revelation. It believes the Bible to be revelation, not riddle....
>
> Like all great literatures, the Bible contains both figurative and nonfigurative languages. For instance, Christ describes Himself as "the light of the world" (John 8:12). Figurative language helps make God's Word linguistically more interesting.

The presence of figures in Scripture, however, does not militate against literal interpretation. Since literal interpretation properly accepts that which is normal and customary in language—and figurative language is certainly normal and customary—literal interpreters are not hindered by that which is figurative. There is no necessity to change to a different method of interpretation....

The literal sense conveyed by the figure, and not what the figurative words literally convey, is the original sense intended by the Biblical writer....

Fortunately for the literal interpreter, the meaning intended behind the use of figures in Scripture is often given in the text or context. Careful study of the text, context, and parallel passages will almost always bring out the figures' meaning. The identification and interpretation of Bible figures by the Bible itself is a rule and not an exception.

In the exclamation of John the Baptist, "Behold, the lamb of God" (John 1:29), the meaning intended by John's use of the figure *lamb* is to be found in the nature of Christ's life and death. Happily for the interpreter, the immediate context (v.29 "that taketh away the sins of the world") clearly explains John's use of that figure.[67]

Charles Ryrie explains the rationale behind the literal method (aka, the grammatical-historical method):

If God be the originator of language and if the chief purpose of originating it was to convey His message to man, then it must follow that He, being all-wise and all-loving, originated sufficient language to convey all that was in His heart to tell man. Furthermore, it must also follow that He would use language and expect man to use it in its literal, normal, and plain sense. The Scriptures, then, cannot be regarded as an illustration of some special use of language so that in the interpretation of these Scriptures some deeper meaning of the words must be sought. If language is the creation of God for the purpose of conveying His message, then a theist must view that language as sufficient in scope and normative in use in accomplishing that purpose for which God originated it.

A second reason why dispensationalists believe in the literal principle is a Biblical one. It is simply this: the prophecies in the Old Testament concerning the first coming of Christ—His birth, His rearing, His ministry, His death, His resurrection—were all fulfilled literally. There is no nonliteral fulfillment of these prophecies in the New Testament. This argues strongly for the literal method.

A third reason is a logical one. If one does not use the plain, normal, or literal method of interpretation, all objectivity is lost. What check would there be on the variety of interpretations which man's imagination could produce if there were not an objective standard which the literal principle provides? To try to see meaning other than the normal one would result in as many interpretations as there are people interpreting. Literalism is a logical rationale.[68]

The *allegorical method* infiltrated the early church through Greek influence. J. K. Grider states,

> The poetry of Homer, which was the oldest lit. the Greeks possessed, became quasi-sacred for the Greeks, and many of them, esp. the Stoics, tried to salvage such lit. by supposing that it did not mean what it said, and that it contained instead hidden meanings which were deeply moral and ennobling. It was popular to be known as teaching what Homer taught, so the Stoics interpreted Homer allegorically to make him not only morally palatable, but also to bring him into harmony with their own philosophy.
>
> A Jew by the name of Aristobulus, who lived during the early half of the 2nd cent. B.C., was prob. the earliest allegorist of the OT. He was confident that Moses had taught what Plato and other Gr. philosophers later advocated....
>
> Well-known is the fact that Philo of Alexandria (49 B.C.-A.D. 20) also allegorized the OT to harmonize it with Plato and other Gr. Philosophers....

While Justin Martyr, as a Christian, uses the allegorical method of interpretation... it remained for Clement of Alexandria and his successor Origen (185-254) to capitalize upon this method for commenting on the Scriptures... to baptize some of their Platonic views into Christianity (e.g., Origen's view of the soul's preexistence)...

Jerome seemed to be aware of the divorcement from Scripture which such interpretation could produce, and he said many unkind things about the allegorical method used by Origen and others. Yet, he resorted to this method frequently, even when he had no important reasons for doing so....

Augustine (354-430) likewise had sound things to say about rules for interpreting Scripture, and yet he seemed oblivious to his own rules in his actual comments on Scripture. He was even more fanciful than Jerome in his allegorizing.[69]

In his classic *Protestant Biblical Interpretation*, Bernard Ramm writes,

> The allegorical system that arose among the pagan Greeks, copied by the Alexandrian Jews, was next adopted by the Christian church and largely dominated exegesis until the Reformation, with such notable exceptions as the Syrian school of Antioch and the Victorines of the Middle Ages....
>
> Allegorical interpretation believes that beneath the letter (*rhētē*) or the obvious (*phanera*) is the real meaning (*hyponoia*) of the passage. Allegory is defined by some as an extended metaphor. There is the literary allegory which is intentionally constructed by the author to tell a message under historical form. Bunyan's *Pilgrim's Progress* is such a one and such allegories occur in Scripture too. If the writer states that he is writing an allegory and gives us the cue, or if the cue is very obvious (as in an allegorical political satire), the problem of interpretation is not too difficult. But if we presume that the document has a secret meaning

(*hyponoia*) and there are no cues concerning the hidden meaning interpretation is difficult. In fact, the basic problem is to determine if the passage has such a meaning at all. The further problem arises whether the secret meaning was in the mind of the original writer or something found there by the interpreter. If there are no cues, hints, connections, or other associations which indicate that the record is an allegory, and what the allegory intends to teach, we are on very uncertain grounds.[70]

During the Protestant Reformation, the literal method was rekindled and affirmed as the true method of biblical interpretation. Ramm writes,

> Luther maintained strongly the primacy of the literal interpretation of Scripture. In the *Table Talk* he affirms that "I have grounded my preaching upon the literal word" (*On God's Word*, XI). Farrar cites him as writing: "The literal sense of Scripture alone is the whole essence of faith and of Christian theology."…
> Calvin, with Luther, rejected allegorical interpretation. Calvin called it Satanic because it led men away from the truth of Scripture. He further stated that the inexhaustibility of Scripture *was not in its so-called fertility of meanings.*[71]

Though the literal method was reaffirmed during the Reformation, consistency has been elusive—both historically and in the present. The primary issue is the abandonment of the literal method when interpreting prophetic portions of scripture. One example of this is covenant theology. Renald Showers explains,

> Covenant Theology recognizes that the historical-grammatical method of interpreting the Bible is normal. In this method, attention is focused upon historical background and grammar to determine the correct meaning of a passage.

Words are given the common, ordinary meaning which they had in the culture and time in which the passage was written. Covenant Theology also recognizes that the employment of another method of interpretation could lead to disaster when seeking the meaning of a passage.

In spite of these recognitions, Covenant Theology uses a second method of interpretation when dealing with certain areas of biblical teaching. This is especially true in its treatment of prophetic teachings concerning the future, particularly the future of the nation of Israel and the future Kingdom of God. In these areas, Covenant Theology frequently employs the allegorical or spiritualizing method. In this method words are not given the common, ordinary meaning which they had in the culture and time in which the passage was written. Instead, they are assigned different meanings. For example, according to this method, the word *Israel* does not have to mean the nation of Israel. It could mean the Church. Thus, according to this method, the prophetic promises of future blessing for Israel do not have to be fulfilled with the nation of Israel. Rather, they are to be fulfilled with the Church.

One major problem with the allegorical method of interpreting unfulfilled prophetic Scriptures is that thus far the prophetic Scriptures which have been fulfilled have been fulfilled in accordance with the historical-grammatical method of interpretation, not in accordance with the allegorical method. This would seem to indicate the manner in which God intends prophetic passages to be interpreted. In light of this and the fact that Covenant Theology recognizes the danger of employing the allegorical method when interpreting other areas of biblical teaching, one could ask by what authority Covenant Theology uses the allegorical method when interpreting the prophetic Scriptures.[72]

ROBERT TAYLOR

PREMILLENNIALISM AND AMILLENNIALISM

Premillennialism

Consistent application of the literal method of Bible interpretation naturally leads to affirming that God's covenants with the nation of Israel will be fulfilled. As long as the sun comes up every morning and the moon can be found in the night sky, Israel remains the object of God's love and the beneficiary of His promises and covenants:

> Thus says the LORD,
> Who gives the sun for a light by day,
> The ordinances of the moon and the stars for a light by night,
> Who disturbs the sea, And its waves roar
> (The LORD of hosts is His name):
> "If those ordinances depart
> From before Me, says the LORD,
> Then the seed of Israel shall also cease
> From being a nation before Me forever."
> Thus says the LORD:
> "If heaven above can be measured,
> And the foundations of the earth searched out beneath,
> I will also cast off all the seed of Israel
> For all that they have done, says the LORD." (Jer. 31:35-37)

God's covenants with the nation of Israel involve land (Gen. 13:14-17, 15:7-21), a new heart (Deut. 30:6; Jer. 31:33, 32:40; Ezek. 36:17-27; Rom. 11:26-27), and establishment of the throne of David (2 Sam. 7:8-16, 23:5) from which the Messiah will rule the world (Isa. 9:6-7/Acts 2:30; Dan. 7:13-14/Matt. 24:30; Zech. 14:1-9).

The Old Testament prophets spoke much about life on earth when the Messiah returns to Jerusalem. Especially rich in this regard is the Book of Isaiah, which predicts Jerusalem as the capital of the world (Isa. 2), the end of war (Isa. 2), nonviolence among animals and between animals and humans (Isa. 11 & 65), the transformation of desert and wasteland into a fruitful land (Isa. 35), healing (Isa. 35), the beautification of Jerusalem (Isa. 54), true social justice (Isa. 65), and worship of the Lord (Isa. 66). The last nine chapters in Ezekiel are devoted to the temple, memorial sacrifices, life and worship, and property divisions that will exist after the Messiah's return to earth. The Old Testament does not designate the length of these conditions. The Book of Revelation unveils the thousand years (Rev. 20:4-6) between the Second Coming of Christ as conquering King (Rev. 19:11-16) and the Great White Throne judgment that precedes the creation of the new heaven and new earth (Rev. 20:11-21:1). Thus, it is common for Bible students to speak of the "millennial temple" and the "millennial Messianic reign of Christ." Many prophetic scriptures only fit within the thousand-year window between Christ's return and the eternal state described in Revelation.

The belief that Jesus Christ's Second Advent occurs prior to the establishment of His millennial earthly reign is known as *pre*millennialism. There is little doubt that premillennialism was the original teaching of the church. Some of those who expressed a premillennial view include Papias (AD 60-130), Justin Martyr (AD 100-165), Irenaeus (d. AD 200), and Tertullian (AD 150-220).[73] Numerous historians from a variety of backgrounds, including Edward Gibbon, J.C.I. Gieseler, Henry Sheldon, Philip Schaff, Adolph Harnack, and Will Durant acknowledge that premillennialism was the original view of the church.[74]

Energized by the rebirth of the Jewish state in 1948, premillennialism is firmly established in the evangelical world. The prevalent premillennial view among theologically conservative evangelical Bible colleges and seminaries holds that the nation of Israel will yet experience the aforementioned blessings and conditions prophesied by the Old Testament prophets. In this book, "premillennialist" refers to one who shares this understanding.

Amillennialism

Premillennialism was eclipsed in the fifth century by a theological view known as amillennialism. The amillennial perspective remains strong, especially in the Catholic Church, Greek Orthodox Church, and Reformed denominations. Erickson offers this concise definition of amillennialism: "Literally, amillennialism is the idea that there will be no millennium, no earthly reign of Christ. The great final judgment will immediately follow the second coming and issue directly in the final states of the righteous and the wicked."[75] *The Moody Handbook of Theology* states,

> The *a-* in *amillennialism* negates the term; hence, *amillennialism* means there will not be a literal, future millennium. Amillennialists do not deny the literal return of Christ, but they reject a literal thousand-year reign of Christ on the earth. According to amillennialism, the kingdom of God is present in the church age, and at the consummation of the present age, the eternal state is inaugurated without any intervening millennium. For this reason some amillennialists

suggest a term such as *realized millennialism* to indicate that they do not deny a millennium but believe it is fulfilled entirely in the present age.[76]

There were a number of reasons for the development of amillennialism in church history, but it is the interpretative aspect that is most relevant to our study. Showers provides insightful historical information and notes the connection between Bible interpretation and teaching regarding the Messiah's millennial reign:

> Several factors contributed to this rejection of the premillennial view in the east....
> Fifth, a new theology, known as Alexandrian theology, developed in the Greek Church. This new theology was formed by Origen (185-253 A.D.) and other Church scholars in Alexandria, Egypt....
> Origen and his associates were intensely interested in pagan Greek philosophy. They examined it extensively. Origen studied under "the heathen Ammonius Saccas, the celebrated founder of Neo-Platonism." He and other Alexandrian Church scholars tried to integrate Greek philosophy with Christian doctrine. This attempted integration played a significant role in the development of the new Alexandrian theology.
> Much of Greek philosophy advocated that anything which is physical or material is inherently evil, and only the totally spiritual or nonphysical is good. Through this influence the Alexandrian scholars developed the idea that an earthly, political Kingdom with physical blessings would be an evil thing, and that only a totally spiritual, nonphysical Kingdom would be good. That idea prompted Alexandrian theology to reject the premillennial belief in an earthly, political Kingdom of God with physical blessings....
> Sixth, Origen developed a new method of interpreting the Bible. This method has been called the allegorical or

spiritualizing method, and it stands in contrast to the literal, historical-grammatical method. This permitted him to read almost any meaning he desired into the Bible, and it led him into heresy in certain areas of doctrine (for example, he rejected the idea of physical resurrection and believed in universal salvation for all human beings and fallen angels)....

Premillennialism is strongly based upon the literal historical-grammatical interpretation of those Old Testament passages which the prophets wrote concerning the future Kingdom of God. In his opposition to Premillennialism, Origen spiritualized the language of the prophets. Once again, because of Origen's great influence, this allegorical method of interpreting the prophets was widely accepted by the Greek Church....

The Western or Latin Church remained strongly premillennial longer than the Greek Church in the east.... The reason for the longer duration of premillennial belief in the west was twofold. First, through the fourth century many western theologians "escaped the influence of Greek speculation." Second, the western church always recognized the apostolic authorship and canonicity of the Book of Revelation....

After the fourth century the western church started to join the revolt against premillennial belief. Two major factors contributed to this change. First, Alexandrian theology was brought to the west by such influential church leaders as Jerome and Ambrose. As a result of being taught by Greek theologians in the east for several years, Jerome (345-420 A.D.) declared that he had been delivered from "Jewish opinions," and he ridiculed the early premillennial beliefs....

The second major factor which prompted the rejection of Premillennialism in the west was the teaching of Augustine (354-430 A.D.), the Bishop of Hippo, concerning the Church. Augustine himself had been a premillennialist in the early days of his Christian faith; however, through time he rejected that view in favor of a new one which he developed. That new view became known as Amillennialism.

Several things prompted this change in Augustine. First, the political situation of the Church had changed radically around the period of his life. By Augustine's time the persecution of the Church by Rome had stopped, and the state had made itself the servant of the Church. As the Roman Empire crumbled, the Church stood fast, ready to rule in place of the empire. It looked as if Gentile world dominion was being crushed and that the Church was becoming victorious over it.

Under these circumstances Augustine concluded that Premillennialism was obsolete, that it did not fit the changed situation. In place of it he developed the idea that the Church is the Kingdom of Messiah foretold in such Scriptures as Daniel 2 and 7 and Revelation 20. In his book, *The City of God*, he became the first person to teach the idea that the organized Catholic (universal) Church is the Messianic Kingdom and that the Millennium began with the first coming of Christ....

The third factor in his change of view was the influence of Greek philosophy upon his thinking. Before his conversion Augustine was deeply immersed in the study of this philosophy, much of which asserted the inherent evil of the physical or material and the inherent goodness of the totally spiritual. This philosophy continued to leave its mark upon him even after his conversion. It also prompted him to reject as carnal the premillennial idea of an earthly, political Kingdom of God with great material blessings....

"Augustine's allegorical millennialism became the official doctrine of the church," and Premillennialism went underground.... The Roman Catholic Church strongly advocated and maintained Augustine's amillennial view throughout the Middle Ages.... The Lutheran, Reformed, and Anglican reformers rejected Premillennialism as being "Jewish opinions." They maintained the amillennial view which the Roman Catholic Church had adopted from Augustine.[77]

THE PERSPECTIVE-OF-PROPHECY PRINCIPLE

The prophets appear to have lacked the perspective of time (1 Pet. 1:10-12). For example, in the fourth chapter of Luke, Jesus stood up to read scripture in the synagogue. He was handed the Isaiah scroll and found the following passage:

> The Spirit of the LORD is upon Me,
> Because He has anointed Me
> To preach the gospel to the poor;
> He has sent Me to heal the brokenhearted,
> To proclaim liberty to the captives
> And recovery of sight to the blind,
> To set at liberty those who are oppressed;
> To proclaim the acceptable year of the LORD. (Luke 4:18-19)

After reading Isaiah 61:1-2a, Jesus returned the scroll to the attendant, "And He began to say to them, 'Today this Scripture is fulfilled in your hearing'" (Luke 4:21). It was no accident that Jesus stopped reading when He did. Isaiah 61:2b reads, "And the day of vengeance of our God." At His Second Coming, Jesus will bring the wrath of God to the world just as surely as He did the grace of God in His First Advent. Inasmuch as it has been approximately two thousand years since Jesus' First Advent—in a single verse, Isaiah 61:2—there is a time gap of at least two thousand years. This is known as "the perspective of prophecy." Alva McClain, founder of Grace Theological Seminary, explains,

> Although certain areas of the future are definitely clocked as to time sequence and extent, we shall find in Old Testament prophecy *no absolutely continuous and unbroken chronology*

of the future. The prophets often saw together on the screen of revelation certain events which in their fulfillment would be greatly separated by centuries of time.... The unyielding determination of numerous commentators to pour the events of Old Testament prophecy into a rigid mould of unbroken time, has led to disastrous results.... Take, for example, the anti-millennial approach to such a passage as Isaiah 9:6-7 which in part reads: "For unto us a child is born, unto us a son is given: and the government shall be upon his shoulder.... Of the increase of his government and peace there shall be no end, upon the throne of David." Now the normal and natural sense here should be perfectly obvious: A Child will be born, and He will reign universally upon the throne of David. And so we begin our interpretation with a literal child and a literal birth. But now consider what happens if an unbroken mould of continuous time is clamped on the prophecy. Because the regal Child did not *immediately* take the literal throne of David to rule the world, it is argued that such a thing will *never* come to pass. And then, to preserve the assumption of unbroken time-sequence which cannot allow room for any literal fulfillment of the second part of the prophecy at some future time, the throne of David on earth is changed into the throne of God in heaven, and Messiah's reign is reduced to the "influence of the Gospel" or the rule of God in the "hearts of men."

The prophets sometimes saw future events not only *together*; but in expanding their description of these events, they seem occasionally to *reverse* the time sequence in their record of the vision. An example of this may be seen in Isaiah 65:17-25, which opens with a divine announcement: "For, behold, I create new heavens and a new earth." Then follows a remarkable picture of millennial bliss which clearly is *on earth*. Children are born, men plant and build, long life is restored, and the race is in large measure delivered from the ordinary hazards of human life. Yet it appears that both sin and death are still possibilities, even in this glorious age. Now over in the New Testament, the Apostle John is found using the very words of Isaiah's prophecy: "And I saw," he writes, "a new heaven and a new earth" (Rev. 21:1). The description which follows, however, is unmistakably a record of things in the eternal state where all sin and death have been abolished (21:3-8). It is apparent, therefore, that Isaiah saw *together* on the screen of prophecy both the Millennial Kingdom and the Eternal Kingdom; but he expands in detail the former because it is the "nearest-coming" event and leaves the latter for fuller description in a later New Testament revelation.[78]

THE IMPORTANCE OF PROPHETIC DETAILS

In addition to recognizing the time gaps and sequential flexibility of prophecy, a second key to navigating biblical prophecy evident in McClain's comments is the importance of prophetic details. Prophetic details enable us to discern whether the millennium or new earth is in view in any given passage because significant differences exist between the millennial Messianic kingdom and the eternal state. For example, the millennial temple is so extensively described by Ezekiel that drawings of it are common in reference books. On the other hand, the temple of the eternal state is not a physical structure but rather God Almighty and the Lamb (Rev. 21:22). In the Messianic millennial earth there will be seas (Ps. 72:8; Ezek. 47:8-20; Zech. 9:9-10, 14:8-9). There is no sea in the new earth (Rev. 21:1). There are also distinctions to be observed between millennial Jerusalem and heavenly Jerusalem. McClain writes,

> In Holy Scripture there are two Jerusalems: the one is on earth in the land of Palestine; the other is "above," in heaven (Gal. 4:25-26; Heb. 12:22). Now the Old Testament prophets speak of a city which, in the coming Kingdom, shall

be reclaimed from Gentile power, rebuilt, restored to the historic nation of Israel, and made the religious center of the world. This Jerusalem cannot be the "heavenly Jerusalem," for that city is impeccably holy, the eternal dwelling of the true God, and has never been defiled or marred by human sin and rebellion. Any such notion is to the highest degree impossible and absurd. All predictions of a restored and rebuilt Jerusalem must therefore refer to the historical city of David on earth.

In Isaiah it is written that this city which in history had "become an harlot" would in the future be called "The city of righteousness, the faithful city" (1:21, 26). The nations which once "despised" Jerusalem shall call her, "The city of the LORD, The Zion of the Holy One of Israel" (Isa. 60:14). Her walls will be called "Salvation" and her gates "Praise" (Isa. 60:18). This very city is to be "a crown of glory in the hand of the LORD, and a royal diadem in the hand of thy God" (Isa. 62:3). It shall be made "a praise in the earth," not in heaven (Isa. 62:7). Here, according to the prophets, the covenant God of Israel in the person of the Mediatorial King will be present: "Thus saith the LORD; I am returned unto Zion, and will dwell in the midst of Jerusalem" (Zech. 8:3). Along with the political reunion of the nation, centered in Jerusalem, there will come also *religious* unity: Ephraim will say, "Let us go up to Zion unto the LORD our God" (Jer. 31:6).

From this world center, enlarged and rebuilt in regal magnificence, the divine Word will go forth to all nations in a way never before seen: "Out of Zion shall go forth the law, and the word of the LORD from Jerusalem" (Isa. 2:3). And to this city the nations will go "from year to year to worship the King, the LORD of hosts" (Zech. 14:16). With both religious and political activities centered in one city and under one King, the world will at last see a successful and beneficial union of religion and government.[79]

The distinction between historic and heavenly Jerusalem is especially helpful since Jerusalem is involved in many prophetic scriptures.

IDENTIFYING THE TIME FRAME OF ISAIAH 66:23

The time frame of Isaiah 66:23 is crucially important because it provides the context for understanding unquenchable fire and undying worms.

In *Two Views of Hell*, Peterson notes that Isaiah speaks of the new heavens and new earth in both Isaiah 65:17 and Isaiah 66:22.[80] From this observation, Peterson maintains that the context of Isaiah 66:23 is worship in eternity: "Isaiah foretells redeemed Jews' and Gentiles' ongoing adoration of God in the new earth."[81] This conclusion is integral to Peterson's argument that Isaiah intended for his readers to understand "dead bodies" to equal unsaved resurrected human beings who suffer everlasting disgrace in hell.[82]

Peterson starts well. I agree with Peterson's observation of Isaiah's initial reference to the new heavens and new earth; however, Peterson does not account for Isaiah's transition from the eternal state in 65:17 and 66:22 to the millennial kingdom that takes place prior to the creation of the new heavens and new earth. With regard to Isaiah 65:17-25, Walvoord explains the transition this way,

> A glorious picture was presented of the ultimate new heavens and new earth (vv. 17-19). The prophet then returned to the theme of Jerusalem in the millennial kingdom in which

there will be longevity but also death. One who will die at 100 years will be considered still in one's youth [65:20]....

In expressing Israel's future hope, the Old Testament... mingled prophecies of the millennial kingdom with that of the New Jerusalem in eternity. The distinctions are made clear when the details are observed. Here, obviously, the millennial kingdom was being described because in the New Jerusalem there will be no death, no sin, and no judgment. In the millennial kingdom it will be a time of great joy and rejoicing and deliverance for the people of God, but death and sin will still be present.[83]

The details of Isaiah 65:17-25 inform us of a transition within the passage from the new earth to the millennial earth. The same is true in Isaiah 66:22-24.

The stability of the sun and the moon was used in the Book of Jeremiah to communicate the certainty of God's commitment to Israel. In Isaiah, the enduring nature of the new heavens and new earth is cited to communicate that Israel will endure: "'As the new heavens and the new earth that I make will endure before me,' declares the LORD, 'so will your name and descendants endure'" (66:22, NIV). From this assurance, Isaiah moves immediately back to the Messianic millennial kingdom in 66:23:

"And it shall come to pass
That from one New Moon to another,
And from one Sabbath to another,
All flesh shall come to worship before Me," says the LORD.

Note that Isaiah 66:23 speaks of worshippers coming to worship God "from one New Moon to another," yet in the Jerusalem of the new earth, there will be no need for light from the moon, for "there shall be no night there" (Rev. 21:25, 22:5). Zechariah also supports the millennial kingdom context.

Isaiah declares that the Lord comes with fire and sword to judge and slay many (66:15-16). Zechariah explains that the Lord does so in response to the nations coming against Jerusalem (14:2-3). As in Isaiah 66, Zechariah foretells that the Lord's vengeance against His enemies will bring deliverance and safety to Jerusalem, as well as the wealth of the Gentiles (Isa. 66:12-13; Zech. 14:4-14). Following the Lord's return, people will come from all over the globe to worship the Lord in Jerusalem. Isaiah and Zechariah testify that the Jewish people will play a special role in this worldwide revival. Zechariah's prophecy is rather amazing:

> Thus says the LORD of hosts: "In those days ten men from every language of the nations shall grasp the sleeve of a Jewish man, saying, 'Let us go with you, for we have heard that God is with you.'" (Zech. 8:23)

Charles L. Feinberg says of Zechariah:

> The eye of the prophet looks on to the hour of Israel's greatest joy and blessing in the Millennium, that era in which Israel will fulfill the purpose of God for her which has always been in His heart. Once Israel is restored, world conversion follows. (Read carefully Ps 67.)[84]

Isaiah 66:19-21 expands on the nations streaming to Jerusalem. In *The Bible Knowledge Commentary*, John A. Martin summarizes these verses:

> The remnant of believing Israelites will travel as missionaries to other parts of the world, to tell Gentiles about God's glory.

RESCUE FROM DEATH

Those places and peoples will include Tarshish, probably in southwestern Spain (cf. 23:1, 6, 10, 14, 60:9), Libyans in northern Africa, Lydians in western Asia Minor, Tubal in northeastern Asia Minor, Greece, and distant lands. These and other peoples will be converted and will travel to Jerusalem to worship in the temple (cf. 2:2; Zech. 8:23). Some of them will even be selected as priests and Levites, thus showing that all the nations will in fact be blessed through Israel (cf. Gen. 12:3).[85]

According to Zechariah, it is those among the nations that remain after the battle at Jerusalem who "go up from year to year to worship the King, the LORD of hosts, and to keep the Feast of Tabernacles" (14:16). Feinberg comments,

> When the smoke of the conflict has cleared... the godly among the Gentiles will go up annually to worship the King, the Lord of Hosts, in Jerusalem and to celebrate the Feast of Tabernacles. The nations will go up representatively, for even all Israel never went up to the feasts to the last man (Lev 23:33-44 and Deu 16:13-17).
>
> The Feast of Tabernacles is the feast of the millennial age. It was the feast of ingathering and rest, of joy, praise, and thanksgiving... The Feast of Tabernacles was celebrated on the return of Israel from exile. (See Neh 8:14-18.) It is preeminently the feast of joy after the ingathering of the harvest.[86]

We can be sure that Zechariah prophesied of worship in the millennial earth because his prophecy goes on to stipulate punishment for any nation that is disobedient with regard to the Feast of Tabernacles (14:17-19). Disobedience is impossible in the new earth, where everyone is fully conformed to the image of Christ.

The unity of Zechariah and Isaiah's testimony provides strong evidence that Isaiah 66:23 has the Messianic millennial kingdom in view. That Isaiah speaks of worship in the millennium is also the conclusion of Alva McClain in *The Greatness of the Kingdom*[87] and J. Dwight Pentecost in *Things To Come*.[88]

INVESTIGATING THE SETTING OF ISAIAH 66:24

Together Isaiah and Zechariah foretell the Lord's coming to judge His enemies and the worship that He subsequently receives in the historic city of Jerusalem. The combined work of Isaiah and Zechariah sketches an end-time portrait sufficient to bring our target text—*their worm does not die and their fire is not quenched*—into focus.

In Isaiah 66:23-24, those who worship the Lord in millennial Jerusalem go forth and look upon the corpses of the men killed in what is commonly referred to as the Battle of Armageddon. Understanding this scene is critical to appreciating what Isaiah means by unquenchable fire and undying worms. McClain reviews the biblical record:

> The Old Testament prophets present the nations of the earth in deliberate *rebellion* against the true God and His appointed King....
>
> The climax of this rebellion against the God of heaven will be reached when the armies of the nations, under the leadership of the great evil genius of the end-time, will march against Jerusalem and its chosen people. The prophet Zechariah, speaking of this military movement against Jerusalem, affirms that "all the nations of the earth shall be gathered together against it" (12:2-3, ASV)....

RESCUE FROM DEATH

In the hour of deepest darkness for Israel and Jerusalem, when it seems that total defeat is certain, "Then shall the Lord go forth, and fight against those nations, as when he fought in the day of battle" (Zech. 14:3). And lest these words might be misunderstood as referring to some spiritual or providential coming of the Lord, the next verse adds a note of literality: "his feet shall stand in that day upon the mount of Olives, which is before Jerusalem on the east" (vs. 4). For those who may have some reluctance in accepting the literality of these details, a parallel may be cited in the same prophetic book where the lowly first coming of the King is described as follows: "behold, thy King cometh unto thee: he is just, and having salvation; lowly, and riding upon an ass, and upon a colt the foal of an ass" (Zech. 9:9). Since this has been literally fulfilled, why should the other be rejected as unreasonable? As far as plausibility is concerned, what is the difference between the King riding in humiliation upon an ass and the King standing gloriously on a mountain?—especially since it is the same King and both events occur on the same mountain (cf. Luke 19:37)....

Against all the devices of interpreters who seek to show that God is finished with the historic people of Israel and with their beloved city of Jerusalem, the prophetic ultimatum stands firm: "He that toucheth you toucheth the apple of his eye" (Zech. 2:8; cf. vss. 4-7). In this city the Theocratic Kingdom of history was once centered, and it is reserved as the place where the Kingdom shall again be established. Therefore, those who are wise have never ceased to "Pray for the peace of Jerusalem" (Ps. 122:6). For all the hopes of a future Kingdom of God on earth are in a certain sense bound up with the future of this city.

As an evidence of God's continued and loving interest in Jerusalem, it should be observed that the final assault against the city by the armies of the world, under the leadership of the blasphemous "little horn," [Dan. 7] will bring swift destruction upon these military forces. In fact, it is precisely this presumptuous assault that will bring the divine King down from heaven, and His first action on earth will be the defense of Jerusalem: "In that day shall the LORD defend the inhabitants of Jerusalem" (Zech. 12:8).... "in that day," God warns, "will I make Jerusalem a burdensome stone for all people: all that burden themselves with it shall be cut in pieces, though all the people of the earth be gathered together against it" (Zech. 12:3). "I will seek to destroy all the nations that come against Jerusalem" (Zech. 12:9)....

The prophet Isaiah has given a vivid description of this terrible judgment of God upon a wicked and rebellious world: "For, behold, Jehovah will come with fire, and his chariots shall be like the whirlwind; to render his anger with fierceness, and his rebuke with flames of fire. For by fire will Jehovah execute judgment, and by his sword, upon all flesh; and the slain of Jehovah shall be many" (Isa. 66:15-16, ASV). So staggering will be the loss of life under the divine "indignation" that in the days of the coming Kingdom men will look back to this terrible occasion as "the day of the great slaughter" (Isa. 30:25).[89]

In short, the armies of the world that invade Israel and attack Jerusalem will be slaughtered, leaving a multitude of dead soldiers on Israeli soil. This eschatological cataclysm is also spoken of in the Book of Joel:

> Proclaim this among the nations: Prepare for war! Rouse the warriors! Let all the fighting men draw near and attack.... Come quickly, all you nations from every side, and assemble there.... "Let the nations be roused; let them advance into the Valley of Jehoshaphat, for there I will sit to judge all the nations on every side. Swing the

sickle, for the harvest is ripe. Come, trample the grapes, for the winepress is full and the vats overflow—so great is their wickedness!" *Multitudes, multitudes* in the valley of decision! For the day of the LORD is near in the valley of decision. The sun and moon will be darkened, and the stars no longer shine. The LORD will roar from Zion and thunder from Jerusalem; the earth and the heavens will tremble. But the LORD will be a refuge for his people, a stronghold for the people of Israel. (Joel 3:9-16, NIV)

When Christ slays the armies of the world at His return, it finally brings peace to Israel. It also presents a huge practical problem: How will a multitude of dead bodies be cleared from the battlefield? The role of birds in the cleanup process is clear from Revelation chapter 19:

And I saw an angel standing in the sun, who cried in a loud voice to all the birds flying in midair, "Come, gather together for the great supper of God, so that you may eat the flesh of kings, generals, and the mighty, of horses and their riders, and the flesh of all people, free and slave, great and small."

Then I saw the beast and the kings of the earth and their armies gathered together to wage war against the rider on the horse and his army. But the beast was captured, and with it the false prophet who had performed the signs on its behalf. With these signs he had deluded those who had received the mark of the beast and worshiped its image. The two of them were thrown alive into the fiery lake of burning sulfur. The rest were killed with the sword coming out of the mouth of the rider on the horse, and all the birds gorged themselves on their flesh. (Rev. 19:17-21, NIV)

In his highly acclaimed exegetical commentary on Revelation, Robert L. Thomas states,

> The anticipated feast for the birds bears the name... "the great supper of God"... This is stunning language describing the battlefield after the Lamb's victory, a great supper given by God. It will be a veritable feast for the vultures. Christ comments on the habits of vultures and how carrion attracts them (Matt. 24:28; Luke 17:37). Even one dead body has a magnetic attraction for the creatures, but multiplied dead will clutter this field of battle.[90]

William R. Newell writes,

> Now we know that when the Lamb in wrath treads the battle line at Armageddon, absolutely millions upon millions pour out their blood in slaughter—even to the bridles of the horses!
> This then, in Revelation 19, is a literal call to the birds which feed upon flesh, from all over the earth: *and they come!* It is a literal feast, awful though the scene may be....
> And when we accept it as literal we see the necessity of it. God will not allow His Son's kingdom to begin with a plague, caused by the festering carcasses of slain multitudes.[91]

The unprecedented size of the slaughter will require a massive cleansing operation. Birds have a role, but, given the magnitude of the problem, it seems that more factors must be involved. Isaiah's book ends with worshippers, who have come to Jerusalem in the millennial kingdom, going forth to look upon the *corpses* of the men slain by the Lord at His return. These *dead bodies* are beset with unquenchable fire and undying worm. If the land must be cleansed for the millennial conditions articulated by Isaiah to be realized, does it not follow that fire and worm serve to consume these corpses?

UNQUENCHABLE FIRE AND UNDYING WORM

Starting and maintaining a fire can be a rigorous undertaking. Take something as burnable as an old dry log, lay it in a fireplace in a bed of newspaper, strike a match to it, and watch the flame sputter and die out. It takes intense sustained heat to kindle the log and start it burning, and it helps immensely if air is allowed to get underneath the log. Moreover, once the fire is going, it typically requires tending to keep it going. Why? Fire by nature is quenchable. Specific conditions are necessary to start and maintain a fire.

Public cremation is a historical practice in some cultures. The body is placed on a raised platform, with firewood all around, to facilitate burning. The effort required to incinerate just *one* body via normal fire calls into question the ability of everyday quenchable fire to consume those slain by the Lord at His return. It will surely take "unquenchable fire"—fire that is impervious to the combustion difficulties presented by massive piles of human corpses. This is precisely the nature of *unquenchable fire* in the writings of the Old Testament prophets. *Unquenchable fire is not fire that burns forever; it is fire that cannot be prevented from completing its mission*. This is evident in both Jeremiah and Ezekiel, as it is certain God never intended that the palaces of Jerusalem or the forest of the south burn eternally.

> *Ezekiel 20:45-48*
>
> Furthermore the word of the Lord came to me, saying, "Son of man, set your face toward the south; preach against the south and prophesy against the forest land, the South, and say to the forest of the South, 'Hear the word of the Lord! Thus says the Lord God: "Behold, I will kindle a fire in you, and it shall devour every green tree and every dry tree in you; *the blazing flame shall not be quenched*, and all faces from the south to the north shall be scorched by it. All flesh shall see that I, the Lord, have kindled it; *it shall not be quenched*.""

In this prophecy, fire is symbolic of God's judgment against Jerusalem and Judah via the Babylonians.[92] The *unquenchableness* of this *fire* does not speak of its duration but rather the certainty of its success; it was unstoppable until the prophesied purpose was accomplished.

> *Jeremiah 17:27*
>
> But if you will not heed Me to hallow the Sabbath day, such as not carrying a burden when entering the gates of Jerusalem on the Sabbath day, then I will kindle a fire in its gates, and it *shall devour the palaces* of Jerusalem, and *it shall not be quenched*.

The NET Bible reads, "It will burn down all the fortified dwellings in Jerusalem and no one will be able to put it out" (v. 27b). In this instance, the fire is literal and the palaces of Jerusalem were literally burned by the Babylonians (2 Kings 25:9).[93]

In Isaiah 66:24, we find not only unquenchable fire but also specially prepared worms, worms that are as unstoppable as unquenchable fire—*undying* worms.

Peterson writes of the need to "interpret *as a unit* the image of corpses beset by undying worm and unquenchable fire" and to see how "dead bodies" function as part of a larger picture.[94] I agree with Peterson's assessment; however, in overlooking the millennial Messianic kingdom that the Old Testament prophets wrote so much about, Peterson missed the true setting of Isaiah 66:24.

The aftermath of the Armageddon battlefield will be gruesome, with multitudes of corpses being consumed by vultures, *undying* worms, and *unquenchable* fire. This abhorrent sight will be an arresting reality in the land of Israel at the dawn of the millennial Messianic kingdom. How long this scene continues is not stated, but the prophesied fruitful conditions of the millennium provide confidence that corpses will surely give way to crops (Amos 9:11-15).

CONSISTENT LITERAL INTERPRETATION NEEDED

Historically, most premillennialists have held to the traditionalist view of hell. I believe part of the reason for this has to do with inconsistency in applying the literal method. For example, in *The Bible Knowledge Commentary*, Isaiah 66:22-24, Martin notes the contrast between the righteous and the rebellious, then continues about the rebellious:

> They will suffer eternal torment (cf. Mark 9:48). This awesome way in which the majestic Book of Isaiah concludes points to the need for unrepentant people to turn to the Lord, the only God, the Holy One of Israel.⁹⁵

Notice that no attempt is made to connect Isaiah 66:24 to Messianic end-time events. Instead, it is simply assumed that Mark 9 teaches eternal torment and that this is how Isaiah should be understood, end of story. Why isn't it pointed out that worm and fire cleanse the Armageddon battlefield?

Martin is interpreting Isaiah 66 in light of the premillennial return of Christ. He explicitly connects Isaiah 66:14-18 with Zechariah 14 and Revelation 19.⁹⁶ He also connects, as we saw previously, Isaiah 66:19-21 with the millennial temple. So why is no connection made to the millennial kingdom age when it comes to the chapter's final verse?

I believe Martin's failure to consider the contribution of Isaiah 66:24 to the aftermath of the Messiah's victory over the armies of the world reflects the quandary that the premillennialist faces. Traditionalists hold that the worm of Mark 9:48 is undying and the fire is unquenchable because, in their view, the unsaved are never consumed, yet premillennialists do not believe that maggot-infested corpses will cover the land of Israel for a thousand years or that burning corpses continually pollute the Messianic millennium. The premillennialist who consistently utilizes the literal method of interpretation ought to conclude that unquenchable fire and undying worms *consume* the physical bodies of the slain in Isaiah

66, yet such an admission would undermine the traditionalist handling of Mark 9:43-48. Perhaps this is why, time and again, Isaiah 66:24 is either glossed over or passed over altogether by premillennialist commentators.[97]

Should we not be consistent in applying the literal method? Indeed, we should. Good hermeneutics demand it.

UNDYING WORM AND UNQUENCHABLE FIRE IN ISAIAH 66 AND MARK 9

If we first look at Isaiah 66:24 in its own context, we find the remains of slain transgressors being consumed by unquenchable fire and undying worms. This in itself does not prove annihilation, as only the bodies of the rebellious are in view. Still, the fire and worm are consuming agents, so when I come to Jesus' teaching on hell in Mark 9:43-48, I look back to Isaiah 66 and see corpses being consumed by fire and worms. Then I look at biblical statements regarding the unsaved and final judgment fire. I see that Jesus taught that the unsaved would burn up like weeds cast into a furnace of fire. I hear the testimony of John the Baptist that unquenchable fire will burn up the chaff.

The traditionalist claim, in contrast, is that the fires of *Gehenna* burn eternally without ever consuming a single sinner, but if we try to apply the traditionalist interpretation of unquenchable fire and undying worm to the millennial kingdom scene of which Isaiah wrote, we have an impossible situation, absurd if you try to envision it.

Realizing that the traditionalist view is inconsistent with both Isaiah and the explicit statements about God's judgment fire made by Jesus and his forerunner, I cannot go along with transforming dead bodies into living human beings suffering unending disgrace. Jesus did not choose a portrait of torment to illuminate the danger of *Gehenna*. Jesus chose Isaiah's gruesome picture of literal physical death. Combining Isaiah 66:24 with Mark 9:43-48 and the key passages in Matthew that we have studied so far leads to the following conclusion: Just as undying worm and unquenchable fire consume literal corpses in the aftermath of the Battle of Armageddon, sinners cast into the flames of *Gehenna* will be consumed—soul and body. This is the conclusion that honors Jesus' testimony regarding *Gehenna* and the literal interpretation of Isaiah 66:23-24.

4

MATTHEW: THE FOUNDATIONAL BOOK ON HELL

THE IMPORTANCE OF MATTHEW'S GOSPEL

Need some wisdom? Try Proverbs. Want to understand justification by faith? Study Romans and Galatians. Concerned about the fate of unbelievers? More than half of the references to *Gehenna* are found in Matthew's Gospel. Matthew 3:12 and 13:30, 40-42 are key scriptures that also refer to the lake of fire.

In Matthew 7:13-14, Jesus warns, "Enter by the narrow gate; for wide is the gate and broad is the way that leads to *destruction* [*apoleia*], and there are many who go in by it. Because narrow is the gate and difficult is the way which leads to *life*, and there are few who find it." *Destruction* in Matthew 7:13 is contrasted with *life* in Matthew 7:14. The opposite of life is *death*, a basic meaning of *apoleia* (Acts 25:16, NKJV, cf. Acts 25:11, 24-25).[98]

Matthew 8:12, 22:13 and 25:30 speak of unbelievers being cast into outer darkness. Darkness typifies divine judgment and death in the Old Testament (Joel 2:1-2; Amos 5:18; Job 3:1-7, 10:20-22; Prov. 20:20). In Matthew 13:47-50, the wicked are cast into the furnace of fire.

It is appropriate that most of Jesus' teaching on hell is found in Matthew. In Matthew, Jesus is set forth as King. John G. Mitchell writes,

> Matthew, Mark, Luke, and John are four witnesses to the life and ministry of Jesus Christ as He walked among men.
> They all witness to His Person:
> Matthew sets Him forth as the Messiah, the King. cp Zechariah 9:9.
> Mark reveals Him as the Servant of Jehovah. cp Isaiah 42:1.
> Luke reveals Him as the Son of Man. cp Zechariah 6:12, 13:7.
> John reveals Him as the Son of God. cp Isaiah 40:9.[99]
>
> Matthew must prove the right of Jesus to the throne of David, hence he writes proving our Lord's legal, moral, judicial, and prophetical right to that throne....
> It is the book of the King, and as such He claims absolute authority, "But I say unto you." He also exercises absolute authority, for He pronounces judgment upon them, their city, and their temple.[100]

Traditionalists maintain that the single most important text in the Bible concerning final destinies is found in Matthew.[101] I would go further. The most important *passages* on hell are found in Matthew, making Matthew the Bible's primary book on final judgment. Is hell a place of perishing or eternal torment? Matthew contains the answer.

There are two significant passages in Matthew that we have yet to dig into: Matthew 21:33-45 and Matthew 25:31-46. The former deserves attention because it graphically pictures the fate of unbelievers, the latter because it is traditionalism's main proof text.

MATTHEW 21:33-45

Jesus was welcomed by huge crowds when He came to Jerusalem (Matt. 21:1-11), but the chief priests and elders confronted Him, demanding to know the authority by which He was operating (Matt. 21:23). At this time, Jesus began to speak in parables. On the temple grounds, Jesus told the parable of the wicked vinedressers.

> Hear another parable: "There was a certain landowner who planted a vineyard and set a hedge around it, dug a winepress in it and built a tower. And he leased it to vinedressers and went into a far country. Now when vintage-time drew near, he sent his servants to the vinedressers, that they might receive its fruit. And the vinedressers took his servants, beat one, killed one, and stoned another. Again he sent other servants, more than the first, and they did likewise to them. Then last of all he sent his son to them, saying, 'They will respect my son.' But when the vinedressers saw the son, they said among themselves, 'This is the heir. Come, let us kill him and seize his inheritance.' And they caught him, and cast him out of the vineyard, and killed him." (Matt. 21:33-39)

Having told this story, Jesus asked a seemingly simple question, "When the owner of the vineyard comes, what will he do to those vinedressers?" (Matt. 21:40).

The reply of His listeners was not unexpected, "In vengeance he will put the scoundrels to death, and rent the vineyard to other tenants who will promptly pay him the rent" (Matt. 21:41, Williams Translation).[102]

With the stage set, Jesus painted a vivid picture of coming judgment:

> Did you never read in the Scriptures: "The stone which the builders rejected Has become the chief cornerstone. This was the LORD's doing, And it is marvelous in our eyes"? Therefore I say to you, the kingdom of God will be taken from you and given to a nation bearing the fruits of it. And whoever falls on this *stone* will be broken; but *on whomever it falls, it will grind him to powder.* (Matt. 21:42-44)

Jesus' warning of the stone that grinds to powder brings to mind King Nebuchadnezzar's dream in the Book of Daniel. Nebuchadnezzar listened as Daniel recounted what the king had dreamed:

> You, O king, were watching; and behold, a great image! This great image, whose splendor was excellent, stood before you; and its form was awesome. This image's head was of fine gold, its chest and arms of silver, its belly and thighs of bronze, its legs of iron, its feet partly of iron and partly of clay. You watched while a *stone*

was cut out without hands, which *struck the image* on its feet of iron and clay, and broke them in pieces. Then the iron, the clay, the bronze, the silver, and the gold were crushed together, and became like chaff from the summer threshing floors; the wind carried them away so that *no trace of them was found*. And the *stone* that struck the image became a great mountain and filled the whole earth. (Dan. 2:31-35)

THE ANNIHILATION OF EMPIRES IN DANIEL

Written in the sixth century BC, the Book of Daniel contains remarkably detailed prophecy.[103] The great image that Nebuchadnezzar saw in his dream pictured a succession of Gentile kingdoms, beginning with the Babylonian kingdom. The dream indicated that these kingdoms will be destroyed so completely that "no trace" of them will remain. Daniel explained the dream to King Nebuchadnezzar:

> You, O king, are a king of kings. For the God of heaven has given you a kingdom, power, strength, and glory; and wherever the children of men dwell, or the beasts of the field and the birds of the heaven, He has given them into your hand, and has made you ruler over them all—you are this head of gold. But after you shall arise another kingdom inferior to yours; then another, a third kingdom of bronze, which shall rule over all the earth. And the fourth kingdom shall be as strong as iron, inasmuch as iron breaks in pieces and shatters

everything; and like iron that crushes, that kingdom will break in pieces and crush all the others. Whereas you saw the feet and toes, partly of potter's clay and partly of iron, the kingdom shall be divided; yet the strength of the iron shall be in it, just as you saw the iron mixed with ceramic clay. And as the toes of the feet were partly of iron and partly of clay, so the kingdom shall be partly strong and partly fragile. As you saw iron mixed with ceramic clay, they will mingle with the seed of men; but they will not adhere to one another, just as iron does not mix with clay. *And in the days of these kings the God of heaven will set up a kingdom which shall never be destroyed; and the kingdom shall not be left to other people; it shall break in pieces and consume all these kingdoms, and it shall stand forever.* (Dan. 2:37-44)

In his dream, King Nebuchadnezzar saw a dazzling sight: a human-like figure made of various metals. The gold, silver, bronze, and iron each represented a major Gentile kingdom. Nebuchadnezzar's Babylonian Empire was the head of gold. Daniel lived to see Babylon conquered by the silver kingdom, Medo-Persia, in 539 BC (Daniel 5). In Daniel 8, Greece is prophetically named as the third kingdom (8:3-8, 20-21). This part of the dream was literally fulfilled when Alexander the Great defeated Persian King Darius at Issus in 333 BC and at Gaugamela in 331 BC.[104] Rome succeeded Greece and ruled Israel at the time of Jesus' birth in Bethlehem (Luke 2:1-7).

Since the metals represent specific kingdoms, the presence of iron in both the legs and feet suggests connection. Clay in the feet, on the other hand, introduces distinction. Thus, the feet of iron and clay would represent an empire that is in some way connected with the historic Roman Empire (the one that "is" in John's day, Rev. 17:10) yet also distinct from it. It is at His Second Coming to establish His throne on the earth that Jesus will utterly destroy the kingdoms represented by the image that Nebuchadnezzar saw in his dream. John C. Whitcomb writes,

> It is significant that the smiting Stone crushes not only the feet and toes of iron and clay but also the entire image.... Just as the silver kingdom absorbed Neo-Babylonian religion and culture into itself (Cyrus even claimed that the gods of Babylon invited him to liberate their kingdom from Nabonidus and Belshazzar), so also Alexander the Great adapted Greek culture to Persian culture, which resulted in a new Hellenistic amalgam. And finally, Rome did not annihilate the religious, philosophic, and cultural aspects of the various Greek and Hellenistic kingdoms but incorporated them into the multifaceted empire called Rome.
>
> At the second coming of Christ, however, there will be no absorbing, adapting, modifying, merging, or restructuring of previous kingdoms. There will be total destruction. Four hundred years before Daniel, the Holy Spirit uttered these words of the coming Messiah: "I will surely tell of the decree of the Lord: He said to Me, 'Thou art my Son.... Ask of Me, and I will surely give the nations as Thine inheritance.... Thou shalt break them with a rod of iron, Thou shalt shatter them like earthenware'" (Ps. 2:7-9).
>
> Thus, every trace of gold (Babylonian), silver (Medo-Persian), and bronze (Hellenistic), as well as iron and clay (Roman) influence will be removed from the earth by the Lord Jesus Christ. In that great day, all idolatry will be smashed (Isa. 2:5-22), for "the kingdom of the world" will "become the kingdom of our Lord, and of His Christ; and He will reign forever and ever" (Rev. 11:15).[105]

Showers states,

> Rome was to be succeeded by a fifth kingdom represented by the stone in the dream (vv. 44-45). This kingdom would be set up by the God of heaven, not by man. The characteristics of this Kingdom of God would be as follows: it would never be destroyed; no other kingdoms would ever succeed it; it would destroy and end all the Gentile kingdoms portrayed in the image of the dream; it would endure forever....
>
> The stone struck the huge image on its feet, thereby causing the entire image to disintegrate....
>
> After the stone had crushed the entire image, the wind blew away every remnant of it. The Babylonians believed that wind was a divine activity. They called Marduk "Lord of the Wind." As a result of this belief, Nebuchadnezzar would understand that the divine activity would rid the earth of Gentile world power.
>
> Once every remnant of the image had been removed from the earth, the stone became a great mountain and filled the whole earth (v. 35).... It would be a kingdom on earth just as the four Gentile kingdoms had been....
>
> As noted earlier, the ancient Orient regarded kings and kingdoms as being synonymous. In light of this, the stone of the dream must be a representation, not only of the Kingdom of God, but also of its King. Other prophetic portions of the Bible indicated that that King would be the person who is called the Messiah (Ps. 2:2), the Son of God (Ps. 2:4-12) and the Son of Man who comes with the clouds of heaven (Dan. 7:13-14). The Bible also indicated that Jesus Christ is that person (Mt. 16:16; 26:63-64). It can be concluded, then, that the stone represented both the Kingdom of God and Jesus Christ. Significantly, more than once the Bible referred to Jesus as the Stone (Mt. 21:33-45; I Pet. 2:4-8).[106]

The annihilation of world powers is vividly taught in the Book of Daniel. This in itself does not prove that individual sinners will be annihilated. It is Jesus' application of the annihilation pictured in Daniel to Israel's unbelieving leadership that merits our attention:

> "And whoever falls on *this stone* will be broken; but *on whomever it falls*, it will *grind him to powder.*" Now when the chief priests and Pharisees heard His parables, they perceived that He was speaking of them. (Matt. 21:44-45)

Jesus is the chief cornerstone. He is also the grinding stone that, in righteous judgment, reduces the condemned to powder. In the words of the NASB, "on whomever it falls, it will *scatter him like dust.*"

A PICTURE OF ANNIHILATION

Scriptures such as Daniel 2 were understandably precious to first-century Jews who longed for the promised Messianic kingdom and deliverance from Roman rule (Luke 1:67-75). Israel's rejection of her King, however, would result in the Son returning to heaven "till they acknowledge their offense" and earnestly seek Him (Hosea 5:15); thus, it would be a future generation of Israelites who would be delivered from a future form of the iron empire. Regardless of end-times bias, the picture of being ground to powder by the Stone should be clear to all. As the empires of this world will be utterly destroyed at Christ's return, those that reject the Savior will also be utterly destroyed.

MATTHEW 25:31-46

We now come to the foundation of the eternal-torment view. Peterson states that Matthew 25:31-46 is "the single most important passage in the history of the doctrine of hell."[107] He holds that Revelation 20:10-15 is arguably "the second most important passage on the doctrine of hell."[108] J. I. Packer cites O. C. Quick, Regius Professor of Theology at Oxford, as naming Matthew 25:46 as "one of the two most explicit New Testament texts affirming permanent penal pain for some after death. Quick's other passage is Revelation 20:10, 15."[109] Gomes writes,

> An exhaustive study on the doctrine of hell is not necessary, for this controversy revolves around only two main points: (1) Do the wicked experience *conscious torment?*; and (2) Do they suffer this torment *eternally?* Therefore, in looking at the scriptural evidence for the historic position, we will focus on those passages that address these two questions....
>
> I believe that there are two sets of texts that answer these two questions conclusively. One set of passages comes from Matthew 25 [25:41, 46]; the other verses come from the Book of Revelation [14:9-11, 20:10]. While many other texts can be used in defense of the orthodox position, these are — in my opinion—the clearest.[110]

I agree with the importance of Matthew 25:31-46 in church *history* with regard to hell. Traditionalism has dominated much of church history. With regard to the *biblical* teaching of hell, I believe other passages are much weightier.

We have already seen that eternal torment is inconsistent with the Genesis record. Isaiah 66:24 speaks of literal physical death, not torment. Thus far in the Book of Matthew, John the

Baptist and Jesus have both taught that the unsaved will burn up. Paul's teaching in Romans is that death is the penalty for sin. Will Matthew 25:31-46 together with Revelation 20:10-15 establish traditionalism? The balance of this chapter will investigate traditionalism's best proof text. We will begin by considering four common traditionalist arguments. Then we will look closely at the setting of Matthew 25:31-46 and seek to interpret the passage in light of its context.

RESPONSES TO FOUR TRADITIONALIST CONTENTIONS

> Then He will also say to those on the left hand, "Depart from Me, you cursed, into the everlasting fire prepared for the devil and his angels" —Matthew 25:41
>
> And these will go away into everlasting punishment, but the righteous into eternal life. —Matthew 25:46

Contention One: Unsaved Human Beings Share the Same Fate as Satan.

Gomes reasons from Matthew 25:41:

> We observe first of all that the wicked share the same fate as Satan and his demonic hosts. Indeed, this text tells us that hell was created specifically for Satan and his angels. As followers of Satan, impenitent men and women will meet the same fate as he. This is significant, because when we look at other passages in the Book of Revelation that speak of the

Devil's fate, we are fully justified in ascribing this *same* fate to unredeemed men and women.[111]

RESPONSE: First, it is certainly true that unrepentant sinners and Satan share the same fate in the sense that both are cast into the lake of fire. It does not clearly follow that human beings and Satan have the same experience there, however. With regard to sin, God has dealt distinctly with men and angels. For example, Jesus died for Adam's fallen race, but He did not die for fallen angels (Heb. 2:9, 14-16).

Second, Satan and the fallen angels (Rev. 12:3-4, 7-9) are significantly more powerful beings than are men (2 Pet. 2:11). Interestingly, fire is not foreign territory to angelic beings. Consider the following verses from the Book of Ezekiel:

> In my thirtieth year, in the fourth month on the fifth day, while I was among the exiles by the Kebar River, the heavens were opened and I saw visions of God.
>
> On the fifth of the month—it was the fifth year of the exile of King Jehoiachin— the word of the LORD came to Ezekiel the priest, the son of Buzi, by the Kebar River in the land of the Babylonians. There the hand of the LORD was on him.
>
> I looked, and I saw a windstorm coming out of the north—an immense cloud with flashing lightning and surrounded by brilliant light. The center of the fire looked like glowing metal, and in the fire was what looked like four living creatures. In appearance their form was human, but each of them had four faces and four wings. (1:1-6, NIV)

The appearance of the living creatures was like burning coals of fire or like torches. Fire moved back and forth among the creatures; it was bright, and lightning flashed out of it. The creatures sped back and forth like flashes of lightning. (1:13-14, NIV)

These were the living creatures I had seen beneath the God of Israel by the Kebar River, and I realized that they were cherubim. (10:20, NIV)

Angelic beings are obviously quite different from human beings. It is noteworthy that Satan was a cherub who "walked back and forth in the midst of fiery stones" (Ezek. 28:14). Because the lake of fire was designed for celestial beings, it should not be assumed that man will have the same experience as Satan in the lake of fire. Destruction is often the result when something is put into an environment for which it was not designed.

Contention Two: Annihilation Is Not Punishment.

Gomes writes,

> In the Matthean texts before us, the final state of the wicked is described as one of everlasting *punishment (kolasin aionion)*. From this it follows that the wicked are not annihilated. William Shedd cogently argues that "the extinction of consciousness is not of the nature of punishment." If suffering is lacking, so is punishment; punishment entails suffering. But suffering entails consciousness....
>
> Punishment demands the existence of the one being punished. As Gerstner points out, "One can exist and not be punished; but no one can be punished and not exist. Annihilation means the obliteration of existence and

anything that pertains to existence, such as punishment. Annihilation avoids punishment, rather than encountering it."[112]

RESPONSE: At the heart of Gomes' argument is the premise that suffering is the only form of punishment. Books such as Exodus and Leviticus, however, teach that there is an appropriate penalty for every transgression. In many cases, death is named as the punishment for sin. In fact, death is listed as the penalty for sin multiple times even in a single chapter of scripture (Exod. 21:12, 14, 15, 16, 17, 23, 29).

Government has the power to administer capital punishment, but man can kill only the body. God alone has the power to put to death both body and soul (Matt. 10:28). Rejecting the grace of God will ultimately result in the execution of the Genesis 2:17 punishment for sin. Inasmuch as death is God's ordained penalty for sin (Gen. 2:15-17; Ezek. 18:4, 20; Rom. 1:32, 6:23), would not God's termination of body and soul constitute punishment?

When a government carries out the death penalty, we certainly do not conclude that the lawbreaker escaped punishment. Through the death penalty, the government denies the lawbreaker all that might have been in his flesh and blood life on this present earth. As government can deny egregious lawbreakers the right to belong to society, God's justice will deny unbelievers the privilege of having a place in His eternal universe and the blessings thereof.

Appreciation for annihilation as God's penalty for sin and appreciation of God's intentions for humanity go hand-in-hand. More on this shortly.

RESCUE FROM DEATH

Contention Three: Annihilation Is Incompatible with Degrees of Punishment.

Gomes writes,

There are no degrees of annihilation. One is either annihilated or one is not. In contrast, the Scripture teaches that there will be degrees of punishment on the day of judgment (Matt. 10:15; 11:21-24; 16:27; Luke 12:47-48; John 15:22; Heb. 10:29; Rev. 20:11-15; 22:12, etc.).[113]

RESPONSE: Evangelical annihilationists affirm that there will be degrees of suffering on the Day of Judgment. The key question is, does the Bible teach *eternal* degrees of suffering? Let us take a look at each of the verses cited by Gomes.

In *Matthew 10:5-15,* Jesus compared first-century Jewish cities with notoriously wicked ancient Gentile cities. Jesus said it will be more tolerable in the Day of Judgment for the Gentile cities than for Jewish cities that reject His apostles; however, Jesus did not explain *how* judgment would be more tolerable for the Gentile cities. Distinction in privilege seems to be the key to understanding Jesus' warning. Sodom had the witness of Lot (Gen. 19:9). The apostles' preaching to the cities of Israel was accompanied by healing the sick, cleansing lepers, raising the dead, and casting out demons (Matt. 10:8). Surely, the Day of Judgment will be more tolerable for Sodom and Gomorrah in the sense that they did not squander a privilege as great as having witnessed the miracles of Christ's apostles.

In *Matthew 11:21-24,* the miracles of Jesus render the unbelievers in Chorazin, Bethsaida, and Capernaum with less excuse for their unbelief than those of Tyre, Sidon, and Sodom:

"Woe to you, Chorazin! Woe to you, Bethsaida! For if the mighty works which were done in you had been done in Tyre and Sidon, they would have repented long ago in sackcloth and ashes. But I say to you, it will be more tolerable for Tyre and Sidon in the day of judgment than for you. And you, Capernaum, who are exalted to heaven, will be brought down to Hades; for if the mighty works which were done in you had been done in Sodom, it would have remained until this day. But I say to you that it shall be more tolerable for the land of Sodom in the day of judgment than for you." (Matt. 11:21-24)

It is one thing to be born into a Gentile culture and fail to believe in God. It's another to be born into the nation of Israel, regularly hear the Word of God publicly declared, have the Messiah Himself come to your town and perform miracles before your eyes, and still not believe. Jesus did not specify what He meant by "more tolerable," so dogmatic conclusions should be avoided. The basic principle in the passages just reviewed seems to be this: The greater the opportunity to succeed, the greater the failure if success is not achieved. Moreover, the misery of unsaved Israel's judgment is significantly compounded by a lifetime of working for a place in Messiah's kingdom:

> What shall we say then? That Gentiles, who did not pursue righteousness, have attained to righteousness, even the righteousness of faith; *but Israel, pursuing the law of righteousness*, has not attained to the law of

righteousness. Why? Because they did not seek it by faith, but as it were, by the works of the law. For they stumbled at that stumbling stone. As it is written: "Behold, I lay in Zion a stumbling stone and rock of offense, And whoever believes on Him will not be put to shame." (Rom. 9:30-33)

Failure to reach a lifetime goal due to misguided choices is a very bitter pill to swallow. Herein is another sense in which the Day of Judgment will be less tolerable for the Jews of Jesus' day than for Gentiles.

In *Matthew 16:24-28*, the "reward" for spurning Christ is to lose one's life (v. 25). The nature of the "reward" for the unsaved in *Revelation 22:12* is not identified.

Luke 12:47-48 speaks of "many stripes" and "few stripes." This reference in Gomes' list is actually a significant problem for the ECT view. Jesus states,

> And that servant who knew his master's will, and did not prepare himself or do according to his will, shall be beaten with many stripes. But he who did not know, yet committed things deserving of stripes, *shall be beaten with few*. For everyone to whom much is given, from him much will be required; and to whom much has been committed, of him they will ask the more.

Can anyone explain how a person could exist endlessly in the lake of fire and suffer *few stripes*? If a person received but one stripe in an entire year, a trillion years later, he would have suffered a trillion stripes. In light of eternity, that would be a drop in the bucket of the suffering yet to be experienced.

When confronted with the reality of unbelievers who are hardworking community-minded individuals, some traditionalists attempt to soften the blow of hell by pointing out that there will be sinners who are beaten with "few stripes." This is not coherent. ECT is *fundamentally* a nightmare beyond comprehension.

Conditionalism, in contrast, is able to account for *few* and *many* stripes. Physical death commonly involves pain to one degree or another. The perishing of soul and body in hell surely will. Jesus taught that when unbelievers are cast into the furnace of fire, "there will be wailing and gnashing of teeth" (Matt. 13:42). Whatever amount of suffering occurs in the process of being consumed in the lake of fire will be in accordance with what God deems appropriate for each individual.

John 15:22 teaches that experiencing the ministry of Christ leaves people with no excuse for their sin: "If I had not come and spoken to them, they would have no sin, but now they have no excuse for their sin."

Hebrews 10:29 is part of a larger context that Gomes does not reference. Hebrews 10:26-29 reads,

> For if we sin willfully after we have received the knowledge of the truth, there no longer remains a sacrifice for sins, but a *certain* fearful expectation of *judgment*, and *fiery indignation which will devour the adversaries.* Anyone who has rejected Moses' law dies without mercy on the testimony of two or three witnesses. Of how much worse punishment, do you suppose, will he be thought worthy

who has trampled the Son of God underfoot, counted the blood of the covenant by which he was sanctified a common thing, and insulted the Spirit of grace?

This passage stresses the certainty of judgment. Mitchell writes, "If judged under Moses' law, how much more sure judgment to those who despise the Son."[114] Notice that God's ultimate punishment is not undefined. Contempt for Christ and His sacrifice guarantees facing a "fury of fire that will consume God's enemies" (v. 27, NET).

In *Revelation 20:11-15*, works are judged to prove that the sinner is justly cast into the lake of fire. Pentecost writes,

> When an individual stands before God and the books are opened, there is the undeniable record of his sins, unrighteousness, and unworthiness to be received into the presence of a holy God. The record stands. And then, as though to demonstrate that no error has been made, God will take the Book of Life and look for the person's name. God won't find the name, so the sentence against the sinner will stand; the sinner did not accept God's provision of grace, so he or she must pay the sentence...
>
> Why consult the record of a person's life? Because the record will prove the person's unrighteousness and demonstrate that all have sinned and come short of the glory of God.[115]

Though the passage stresses that "the works of unbelievers will be deficient and will condemn them,"[116] it is reasonable to expect that the examination of the books will affect the painfulness of the second death. There is a world of difference, however, between degrees of pain in the termination of body and soul and degrees of endless suffering.

In summary: None of the verses Gomes cites prove that there will be eternal degrees of punishment. Some of the passages, such as Hebrews 10:26-29 and Luke 12:47-48, are actually problematic for the ECT view.

Contention Four: The Unsaved Suffer Punishment for as Long as the Saved Enjoy Life.

Regarding Matthew 25:41-46, Gomes writes,

> The Greek adjective *aionion* used in these verses means "everlasting, without end." We should note, however, that in certain contexts the adjective *aionios* is not always used of eternity. In some passages it refers to an "age" or period of time....
>
> Granting that the term may or may not refer to eternity, how can we be sure of its meaning in Matthew 25? What is particularly determinative here is the fact that the duration of punishment for the wicked forms a parallel with the duration of life for the righteous: the adjective *aionios* is used to describe both the length of punishment for the wicked and the length of eternal life for the righteous. One cannot limit the duration of punishment for the wicked without at the same time limiting the duration of eternal life for the redeemed. It would do violence to the parallel to give it an unlimited signification in the case of eternal life, but a limited one when applied to the punishment of the wicked.[117]

RESPONSE: The duration parallel in Matthew 25:46 informs us that the goats experience a punishment in the lake of fire (Matt. 25:41) that is as eternal as the life that the sheep find in Christ's kingdom (Matt. 25:34). But what is the punishment? To press the *aionios* parallel beyond the issue of duration predictably yields speculative conclusions. For example, Randy Alcorn cites the dual use of *eternal* in Matthew 25:46 and concludes, "Thus, according to our Lord, if some will consciously experience Heaven forever, then some must consciously experience Hell forever."[118] This conclusion goes beyond the words of the text. Matthew 25:46 is a verse of limited detail. It does not elaborate on the punishment.

Gomes and Alcorn assert that Matthew 25:46 teaches ECT, in part because they do not see any other viable punishment. Alcorn asks,

> In what sense does an annihilated person, who by definition experiences nothing, experience any punishment at all?[119]

Annihilation as eternal punishment is rooted in the Creator's purpose and program for humankind. The God of everlasting love and goodness created humanity with the intention that we might eternally enjoy His fellowship and immense blessing in a universe in which righteousness dwells; however, God does not force this incredible opportunity on anyone nor will His holiness allow unredeemed sinners to be part of His forever family. Thus, we find two options placed before people throughout scripture.

In the Garden of Eden were two unique trees: one that led to eternal life and one that led to death. In John 3:16, the believer in Christ shall not perish but have eternal life. The Bible closes with two ends: the second death and life in the new earth. From cover to cover, God's program is plainly declared: *"I have set before you life and death"* (Deut. 30:19).

To reject the Savior is to face a final irreversible death whereby eternal life in the new earth and heaven is irreversibly denied. Conditional immortality takes this death literally. The unsaved will burn up just as surely as do weeds cast into a furnace of fire.

This guarantees that each day believers enjoy throughout eternity is a day denied to the unsaved. Under conditionalism, then, the punishment of the unsaved is precisely as long as the life of the redeemed. Mark Galli writes,

> We have a finite beginning, but from that beginning forward, our lives are framed by eternity. The Bible says that human life is lived, then, on one of two trajectories: toward either eternal life or eternal death. Whether you understand hell as everlasting torment or as final destruction, in either case the consequence of rejecting God is eternal.[120]

The termination of the sinner in the lake of fire has ramifications that parallel the duration of the life of the redeemed, but is it biblically proper for a *one-time event* of eternal *consequence* to be designated as *eternal*? Indeed, it is. E. Earle Ellis writes,

> When Hebrews speaks of "an everlasting salvation" (σωτηρία αἰωνία, 5:9) or "an everlasting redemption" (αἰωνία λύτρωσις, 9:12) accomplished by the sacrifice of Christ "once for all" (ἐφάπαξ 9:12; cf. 7:27; 10:10), it is clear that it does not mean an everlasting process of saving or redeeming, but rather a one-time act of salvation and redemption that has an everlasting effect.[121]

What is true of salvation and redemption is also true of judgment. Ellis continues,

> The same is true of the expression "everlasting judgment" (κρίμα αἰώνιον) in Heb. 6:2.... Final judgment at Christ's second appearing... decides forever the blessedness of the righteous and the damnation of the wicked.[122]

In light of the biblical precedent for a one-time act of eternal consequence being deemed eternal, there should be no objection to the utter destruction of body and soul being deemed eternal punishment. Qualifying as eternal punishment, however, isn't determinative. The fact remains that Matthew 25:46 is too limited in content to clarify the punishment that takes place in the lake of fire. To determine the precise nature of the punishment to which Jesus refers, we need explicit biblical input on the fate of the unsaved in *Gehenna*. Identifying those scriptures is the challenge we face.

FOUR TRADITIONALIST CONTENTIONS UNSUCCESSFUL

The four arguments made by Gomes fail to establish that eternal torment is the penalty that unbelievers must pay for sin. We need unambiguous biblical declaration but receive philosophical reasoning about the nature of punishment. Additionally, more attention to the greater context is merited. If we want to know what a passage of scripture truly means, three things must be mastered: *context, context, and context*. In the pages ahead, we will attempt to develop the context of Matthew 25:31-46 so Jesus' teaching is evident.

As we continue our investigation, we should keep in mind that we are not looking for the most horrific punishment imaginable; we seek the true justice of the One who loves people so much that He gave His only Son for us.

THE SETTING OF MATTHEW 25:31-46

The setting of Matthew 25:31-46 is the dawn of the Messianic kingdom rule of Christ on earth. "When the Son of Man comes in His glory, and all the holy angels with Him, then He will sit on the throne of His glory" (Matt. 25:31). This glorious event will fulfill numerous Old Testament scriptures:

> Thus says the LORD:
> *"I will return to Zion,*
> *And dwell in the midst of Jerusalem.*
> Jerusalem shall be called the City of Truth,
> The Mountain of the LORD of hosts,
> The Holy Mountain." (Zech. 8:3)

> Many people shall come and say,
> "Come, and let us go up to the mountain of the LORD,
> To the house of the God of Jacob;
> He will teach us His ways, And we shall walk in His paths."
> *For out of Zion shall go forth the law,*
> *And the word of the LORD from Jerusalem.* (Isa. 2:3)

> "Behold, the days are coming," says the LORD,
> "That I will raise to David a Branch of righteousness;
> *A King shall reign and prosper,*
> *And execute judgment and righteousness in the earth.*
> In His days Judah will be saved, And Israel will dwell safely;
> Now this is His name by which He will be called:
> THE LORD OUR RIGHTEOUSNESS." (Jer. 23:5-6)

The Second Coming of Christ follows the seventieth week of Daniel (Dan. 9:24-27), also known as the Tribulation. Based on the historical fulfillment of the "sixty-nine weeks," which takes us from the decree to restore and rebuild Jerusalem in Nehemiah 2:1-8 to the ministry of Christ, each of the weeks is a seven-year period. The establishment of the "abomination of desolation" in the temple by Antichrist (Dan. 9:27, 12:11; Matt. 24:15) marks the midpoint of the Tribulation. The second half of the Tribulation, featuring Antichrist's rise as world dictator and archenemy of Israel (Dan. 7:23-25, 9:27), is a time of unprecedented trouble, also known as the Great Tribulation. A staggering number of people—billions, based on the population of the world today—will die during the seven-year Tribulation.[123] Jesus presents an overview of this future period in Matthew 24:4-31:

> For nation will rise against nation, and kingdom against kingdom. And there will be famines, pestilences, and earthquakes in various places. All these are the beginning of sorrows. (vv. 7-8)

> Therefore when you see the *"abomination of desolation,"* spoken of by Daniel the prophet, standing in the holy place (whoever reads, let him understand), then let those who are in Judea flee to the mountains. (vv. 15-16)

> For then there will be great tribulation, such as has not been since the beginning of the world until this time, no, nor ever shall be. (v. 21)

Immediately after the tribulation of those days the sun will be darkened, and the moon will not give its light; the stars will fall from heaven, and the powers of the heavens will be shaken. *Then the sign of the Son of Man will appear* in heaven, and then all the tribes of the earth will mourn, and *they will see the Son of Man coming on the clouds of heaven with power and great glory.* And He will send His angels with a great sound of a trumpet, and they will gather together His elect from the four winds, from one end of heaven to the other. (vv. 29-31)

The Great Tribulation concludes with the coming of the Son of Man to destroy Antichrist (Dan. 7:13-14, 26-27). After His victory in battle, the Lord Jesus will reign as King over all the earth and from His throne in Jerusalem will judge the Gentile survivors of the Tribulation. Walvoord writes,

> Although conservative expositors agree that this a judgment related to the second coming of Christ, there is extensive disagreement as to the nature of the judgment and its relation to the total prophetic plan. Amillenarians, who deny a future millennial reign of Christ, believe that this is a general judgment of all men that ushers in the eternal state....
>
> A strict exegesis of this passage [Matt. 25:31-46], however, does not support the conclusion that this is a general judgment. There is no mention of resurrection of either the righteous or the wicked, and "all nations" seems to exclude Israel.... Accordingly, if the view that there is a kingdom of Christ on earth for a thousand years after His second advent is supported by other Scriptures, this passage fits naturally in such a prophetic framework, and, as such, constitutes the judgment of the living who are on earth at the time of the second coming of Christ in respect to their entrance into

the millennial kingdom. This judgment therefore should be contrasted to the judgment of Israel (Eze 20:34-38) and the judgment of the wicked (Rev 20:11-15) which comes after the millennium has concluded. This passage, more precisely than any other, describes the judgment of the world at the beginning of Christ's millennial kingdom....

At this judgment, "all nations," better translated "all Gentiles," are gathered before Him and are described as sheep and goats intermingled.[124]

And so we come to the famous judgment of the sheep and the goats.

THE PURPOSE & BASIS OF THE MATTHEW 25:31-46 JUDGMENT

> All the nations will be gathered before Him, and He will separate them one from another, as a shepherd divides his sheep from the goats. And He will set the sheep on His right hand, but the goats on the left.
> —Matthew 25:32-33

The purpose of the judgment in Matthew 25:31-46 is to determine which Tribulation survivors are sheep (to be welcomed into the Messianic kingdom) and which are goats (to be cast into the lake of fire). The basis of the judgment centers on one's response to Christ via His brethren:

> Then the King will say to those on His *right hand*, "Come, you blessed of My Father, inherit the kingdom prepared for you from the foundation of the world: for

I was hungry and you gave Me food; I was thirsty and you gave Me drink; I was a stranger and you took Me in; I was naked and you clothed Me; I was sick and you visited Me; I was in prison and you came to Me." Then the righteous will answer Him, saying, "Lord, when did we see You hungry and feed You, or thirsty and give You drink? When did we see You a stranger and take You in, or naked and clothe You? Or when did we see You sick, or in prison, and come to You?" And the King will answer and say to them, "Assuredly, I say to you, inasmuch as you did it to one of the least of these My brethren, you did it to Me."

Then He will also say to those on the *left hand*, "Depart from Me, you cursed, into the everlasting fire prepared for the devil and his angels: for I was hungry and you gave Me no food; I was thirsty and you gave Me no drink; I was a stranger and you did not take Me in, naked and you did not clothe Me, sick and in prison and you did not visit Me." Then they also will answer Him, saying, "Lord, when did we see You hungry or thirsty or a stranger or naked or sick or in prison, and did not minister to You?" Then He will answer them, saying, "Assuredly, I say to you, inasmuch as you did not do it to one of the least of these, you did not do it to Me." (Matt. 25:34-45)

Some see these well-known words of Christ as a salvation-by-social-works gospel. The preceding chapter, Matthew 24, readily corrects this grave error. Walvoord explains,

> The answer to this problem is found in the context of this passage. Those described here are people who have lived through the great tribulation, a time of unparalleled anti-Semitism, when the majority of Jews in the land will be killed. Under these circumstances, if a Gentile befriends a Jew to the extent of feeding and clothing and visiting him, it could only mean that he is a believer in Jesus Christ and recognizes the Jews as the chosen people.[125]

Ironside comments,

> The Lord Jesus ever recognizes anything done for one of His own as done unto Himself (Matthew 10:42; Mark 9:41), and He also considers any harm done to His own as though it were done against Him (Acts 9:4). In its strictest sense, the "brethren" here will be part of a Jewish remnant in the last days, who will be witnesses for God in the dark days of the time of Jacob's trouble, the great tribulation (Daniel 12:1-3; Jeremiah 30:7).... As the King's messengers go through the world there will be some who receive them and believe their message: these are the sheep. Others will refuse them and spurn their testimony: these are the goats.[126]

J. Vernon McGee writes,

> Antichrist will have God's messengers butchered and slain, and anyone who would give them a cup of cold water will do so at the risk of his life. To hand out a cup of cold water... in the great tribulation... will have tremendous value. It will mean taking a stand for Jesus Christ. The basis on which the nations will be judged is their acceptance or rejection of Jesus Christ. He says, "Inasmuch as ye have done it unto one

of the least of these my brethren, ye have done it unto me"—because the messengers were representing Him.[127]

JESUS SENDS THE GOATS INTO EVERLASTING FIRE, THE TIME FRAME

The Lord Jesus righteously determines who, among the Tribulation survivors, is saved and who is not. It is obvious that the sheep immediately enjoy the blessings of Christ's kingdom (Matt. 25:34). When are the goats cast into the lake of fire?

Premillennialists believe that the judgment in Matthew 25:31-46 is distinct from the Great White Throne judgment. In *Things To Come*, Pentecost lists numerous differences between the Matthew 25:31-46 judgment and the Great White Throne judgment (Rev. 20:11).[128] When it comes to the *result* of the Matthew 25 judgment, however, Pentecost simply states that the goats are "excluded from the kingdom and consigned to the lake of fire."[129] This statement allows for the immediate casting of the goats into the lake of fire but does not pinpoint the time frame.

If the goats of Matthew 25 are not immediately cast into the lake of fire at Christ's command, then they must be slain, buried, and subsequently resurrected to stand before the Great White Throne judgment. This is untenable, as it would mean that the goats would go through *two* final judgments. Commenting on Matthew 25:31-46, Ironside writes,

> "Before Him shall be gathered all nations." This... judgment is to be distinguished from the judgment of the great white throne of Revelation 20, which will not take place on the earth at all, but will be the judgment of the wicked dead.

This which is before us here is a judgment of living nations prior to the Millennium. The other—that of the great white throne—is after it ends...

"Depart from Me, ye cursed, into everlasting fire, prepared for the devil and his angels." This sentence of eternal doom will be pronounced on those of the nations who have shown by their cold, indifferent behavior to His servants that they did not believe the message they carried through the world. It would seem that this is their final judgment, as the sentence coincides with that of the unrighteous dead, who stand before the great white throne after the thousand years are finished (Revelation 20:7-15)....

"These shall go away into everlasting punishment: but the righteous into life eternal.".... The wicked will be destroyed and *go into their awful destiny at once*. The righteous will enter into eternal life in the millennial kingdom and then have their portion with Christ through the unending ages that follow the destruction of the present creation.[130]

If the goats are cast into the lake of fire at Jesus' command (Matt. 25:41), then the goats enter the lake of fire shortly after the beast and the false prophet.

Revelation 19 details the triumph of Christ at His Second Advent. The beast's armies are "killed with the sword which proceeded from the mouth of Him who sat on the horse" (Rev. 19:21). The beast and false prophet, however, are captured and "cast alive into the lake of fire burning with brimstone" (Rev. 19:20). The conquering King of kings and Lord of lords establishes His throne in historic Jerusalem, and the famous judgment commences. Jesus welcomes the sheep into His kingdom and sends the goats into the lake of fire. This takes place at least a thousand years prior to the Great White Throne judgment (Rev. 20).

The beast and the false prophet are tormented in the lake of fire (Rev. 20:10). What happens to the goats in the fire prepared for the devil and his angels? Matthew 25:46 does not identify the punishment of the goats. Where shall we turn for answers?

COMPARING SCRIPTURE WITH SCRIPTURE

The principle that scripture should be interpreted in light of other scripture is basic to biblical hermeneutics. Ramm writes,

> In place of an appeal to the teaching magisterium [authority] of the Church, the Reformers proclaimed that Scripture interprets Scripture.
>
> In this expression the word "Scripture" is used in a double sense. As the first word of the formula, Scripture means the total Scripture; in the second occurrence it means a part of Scripture, either a verse or a passage. Restated the principle would read: "The entire Holy Scripture is the context and guide for understanding the particular passages of Scripture." If this is true then no appeal is necessary to the teaching magisterium of the Church.
>
> In the concrete task of writing Christian theology this principle means that the theologian must basically rest his theology on those passages that are clear and not upon those that are obscure. Or to phrase it yet another way, "Everything essential to salvation and Christian living is clearly revealed in Scripture." Essential truth is not tucked away in some incidental remark in Scripture nor in some passage that remains ambiguous in its meaning even after being subjected to very thorough research.[131]

In the practical application of this principle, we need to keep in mind that God gave the Bible to us one book at a time. Each of the Bible's sixty-six books was written for a particular purpose and has a particular flow of thought. When we study a text of scripture, the immediate context—that immediately preceding and following the scripture under consideration—demands careful attention. The interpreter should also consider the text in light of the book as a whole. Any other writings by the same author should also be considered. Other books of the same testament should be consulted, and, finally, the whole Bible should be checked for relevant insight.

The importance of reading and rereading the scripture to grasp its flow of thought was impressed upon me while I was a student at Multnomah School of the Bible.[132] Multnomah's founder, John G. Mitchell, constantly encouraged us to read the text over and over. He was someone who practiced what he preached. Known as Jack to his friends, Dr. Mitchell had a grasp of the Word that was inspirational. He also challenged us with the example of G. Campbell Morgan, which Dick Bohrer recounts in *Lion of God*:

> In 1923, Dr. G. Campbell Morgan, the great British preacher, had meetings in the Presbyterian church and his command of the Scriptures impressed Jack, who told about it later:
> *I asked him how in the world he went about his study of the Bible and he said to me, "Young man, if I were to tell you, you wouldn't do it."*
> *"Well," I said, "try me."*
> *And he said, "Well, I'll tell you. Before I start to study a book, I read it through 40 or 50 times in the English text. And I might read it through once in the Greek, but I always read it through 40 or 50 times in the English text."*
> Jack took that lesson to heart and began to do just that. He read his Bible so much that he memorized much of it. He would draw on passages from cover to cover to support and illustrate the points he was making. He would tell his students, "You've got to study the Book. Get your mind

jammed through with the text so that you can begin to think it through." He claimed that he never sat down and tried to memorize Scripture. "I've retained it in my memory by reading and reading and reading again and again," he would say.[133]

G. Campbell Morgan and John G. Mitchell set a tremendous example. If we followed in their footsteps, we would read Matthew's Gospel over and over *before* beginning to interpret Matthew 25:31-46. The value of such diligence will be evident shortly.

THE UNEQUAL YOKING OF SCRIPTURE

Traditionalists readily embrace the principle that scripture interprets scripture. In fact, interpreting Matthew 25:41-46 in light of Revelation 20:10 has long been at the heart of the traditional position. Peterson calls Revelation 20:10 "Scripture's own commentary on Matthew 25:41."[134] In a footnote on Romans 2:12, Newell wrote,

> Now, the word *perish* here is a terrible word! When used in Scripture regarding human beings it never hints of annihilation, but rather the contrary: "And be not afraid of them that kill the body, but are not able to kill the soul: but rather fear Him who is able to destroy both soul and body in Gehenna" (Matt. 10:28). What "destroy both soul and body in Gehenna" means as to time, is shown in Matthew 25:41-46: "Then shall He say unto them on the left hand, 'Depart from me, ye cursed, into the eternal fire which is prepared for the devil and his angels.' And these shall go away into eternal punishment: but the righteous into eternal life,"–compared with Revelation 20:10: "And the devil that deceived them was cast into the lake of fire and brimstone, where are also

the Beast and the False Prophet; and they shall be tormented day and night unto the ages of the ages."[135]

Newell is one of my favorite authors. His commentaries on Romans and Hebrews contain remarkable insight. But has this respected brother rightly handled Matthew 25:41-46 and Revelation 20:10? Is it appropriate to mate Revelation 20:10 with Matthew 25:41-46 to determine the eternal destiny of the unsaved?

The traditionalist premise is that Revelation 20:10 records what the Matthew 25 goats experience in the lake of fire. In Revelation 20:10, Satan is cast into the lake of fire, where the beast and the false prophet are already being tormented. *Where are the goats?* We have discovered that the goats of Matthew 25:31-46 were cast into the lake of fire shortly after the beast and false prophet—approximately 1000 years prior to Satan being cast into the lake of fire. If traditionalism is God's truth, the goats must be suffering in the lake of fire along with Satan, the beast, and the false prophet, yet Revelation 20:10 does not mention the goats.

Why are the goats of Matthew 25 not mentioned in Revelation 20:10?

It could be because the Book of Revelation neither records nor alludes to Christ's judgment of Tribulation survivors at the dawn of the millennial Messianic kingdom. This is a solid explanation; however, this explanation puts traditionalists in the awkward position of acknowledging that Revelation 20:10 does not have the famous sheep and goats judgment in view, while at the same time asserting that Revelation 20:10 is the divine explanation of the goats' punishment in Matthew 25:41-46.

The principle that scripture interprets scripture does not allow us to randomly pair scriptures. There must be a compelling basis to interpret one passage in light of another. Is humankind the subject of Revelation 20:10? Is Revelation 20:10 the opening statement on the judgment of human beings? I believe not. When we examine Revelation 20:10 in its own context, I believe we find clear evidence that it is the last verse in a section of scripture dealing with Satan.

Perhaps the beast and the false prophet may provide a reliable link between Matthew 25:41-46 and Revelation 20:10. If the beast and the false prophet are sinners like you and me, it could be argued that they are representative of humanity and foreshadow the fate of unbelievers. In reviewing the Book of Revelation, however, I saw that the beast ascends out of the abyss (Rev. 11:7, 17:8), which houses fallen angels (Luke 8:31; Rev. 20:1-3). I was reminded that the beast and the false prophet are so closely identified with Satan that even traditionalist theologians commonly refer to Satan, the beast, and the false prophet as the satanic trinity. Moreover, the crimes of Antichrist and the false prophet are absolutely unprecedented. The closer I looked, the more distinct from humankind the beast and false prophet appeared. Without rock-solid assurance that the beast and false prophet are intended to be viewed as representative of unsaved sinners in Revelation 20:10, we should not rush to interpret Matthew 25:41-46 in light of Revelation 20:10.

Where, then, should we look for an explanation? What are the appropriate scriptures that should be considered when interpreting Matthew 25:41-46?

CONTEXT, CONTEXT, CONTEXT

The Matthew 25:46 punishment is best understood in light of its *primary* context, Matthew's Gospel. God compiled the content of Matthew's Gospel and gave us this book as a basic unit of study. In Matthew's Gospel, a number of passages address the final judgment of unbelievers. *Would not God expect us to notice these texts and keep them in mind when interpreting the judgment of the goats?*

IN LIGHT OF MATTHEW'S GOSPEL

Matthew 3:12

> His [Christ's] winnowing fan is in His hand, and He will thoroughly clean out His threshing floor, and gather His wheat into the barn; but *He will burn up the chaff with unquenchable fire.*

Matthew 5:29-30

> And if your right eye causes you to sin, pluck it out and cast it from you; for it is more profitable for you that one of your members perish, than for your whole body to be cast into hell. And if your right hand causes you to sin, cut it off and cast it from you; for it is more profitable for you that one of your members perish, than for your whole body to be cast into hell.

The penalty for sin was established in the opening pages of the Old Testament: you shall surely die. The opening pages of the New Testament unambiguously affirm heaven's justice for the impenitent: the chaff will burn up in unquenchable fire. John the Baptist brings three factors together in a manner that inescapably communicates annihilation: chaff, *katakaio*, and unquenchable fire. Chaff is readily combustible. Throughout the New Testament, *katakaio* indicates that something is burned to ashes or utterly consumed (Matt. 13:30, 40; Acts 19:19; 1 Cor. 3:15; Heb. 13:11; 2 Pet. 3:10; Rev. 8:7, 17:16, 18:8). Unquenchable fire is unstoppable fire, fire that cannot be prevented from accomplishing its mission. No wonder Jesus tells us that it is better to lose an eye or a hand than to have one's whole body be cast into hell.

Early on, in powerful graphic imagery, the Book of Matthew portrays the fate of the impenitent. Grain husks have no chance of surviving indomitable fire. According to John the Baptist, unsaved sinners face utter incineration.

Matthew 7:13
> Enter by the narrow gate; for wide is the gate and broad is the way that leads to *destruction*, and there are many who go in by it.

Traditionalists make much of the fact that Jesus talked about hell more than anyone else. But what did Jesus actually say about hell? Does the broad way lead to eternal torment? According to Jesus, *destruction* is the end of the unsaved. Death, perish, die, burn up, destruction—such are the biblical terms that describe the end of the impenitent.

Matthew 10:28
> And do not fear those who kill the body but cannot kill the soul. But rather fear Him who is able to *destroy* [ἀπολέσαι] *both soul and body in hell.*

With regard to humanity, the specific form of *apollumi* in Matthew 10:28, ἀπολέσαι, plainly means *kill* in the Gospels. Jesus even equates ἀπολέσαι with killing by literal consuming fire in Luke 9:51-56. Moreover, *kill* perfectly matches the immediate context established by Jesus: "Do not fear those who kill the body but cannot kill the soul."

Man can kill the body but not the soul; God can ἀπολέσαι both soul and body. The literal, plain, customary meaning of ἀπολέσαι in Matthew 10:28 assures us that God can *kill/put to death* both soul and body in *Gehenna*.

We have no right to forget this truth when we come in our reading of Matthew's Gospel to 25:31-46. All that we read in the Book of Matthew about *Gehenna*, unquenchable fire, and coming judgment is divinely inspired context for understanding the eternal punishment of the goats.

Torment is not the penalty for sin; death is (Gen. 2:17; Rom. 1:32). In Matthew 25:31-46, we witness the execution of the Genesis 2:17 death penalty as the Lord Jesus sends the goats into the fire to perish—body and soul.

Matthew 11:24
> But I say to you [Capernaum] that it shall be *more tolerable* for the land of Sodom in the day of judgment than for you.

Luke 12:47-48
> And that servant who knew his master's will, and did not prepare himself or do according to his will, shall be beaten with many stripes. But he who did not know, yet committed things deserving of stripes, shall be *beaten with few*. For everyone to whom much is given, from him much will be required; and to whom much has been committed, of him they will ask the more.

Those in Capernaum had a far greater witness than those in Sodom. Moreover, those in Capernaum anticipated having a place in the Messiah's kingdom. Compared to the indifferent and those living only for today, unbelievers with great privilege who sought righteousness by works (Rom. 9:31-32) will find the Day of Judgment more intolerable.

Nowhere does scripture speak of eternal degrees of punishment. Moreover, "few stripes" in an eternity of suffering is mathematically impossible and functionally nonsensical. Indeed, isn't the horror of endless pain immense to the point of rendering "any relative measures of severity both arbitrary and meaningless?"[136] Varying degrees of pain in the execution of the death penalty, in contrast, reasonably flow from differences in opportunity and deeds among unbelievers.

Matthew 13:30
> Let both grow together until the harvest, and at the time of harvest I will say to the reapers, "First

> *gather together the tares and bind them in bundles to burn them,* but gather the wheat into my barn."

Matthew 13:40-42
> Therefore *as the tares are gathered and burned* [κατακαίεται] *in the fire, so it will be at the end of this age.* The Son of Man will send out His angels, and they will gather out of His kingdom all things that offend, and those who practice lawlessness, and will cast them into the furnace of fire. There will be wailing and gnashing of teeth.

Jesus warns that the defiant will be cast into a furnace of fire and burned like weeds. Here is specific input on the fate of the unsaved. Here is Jesus' explanation of hell. Here is the means by which the tares are excluded from Christ's kingdom. Here is the Bible's own commentary on eternal punishment.

What becomes of weeds cast into a furnace of fire poses no mystery. The tares *katakaio* in fire. W. E. Vine acknowledges that the Greek "signifies to burn up, burn utterly."[137] Alfred Marshall's interlinear English text translates κατακαίεται as "are consumed."[138] Only by reading Jesus' words with an everyone-must-live-somewhere-forever mindset could the plain meaning of the text be missed. The tares are destined to disappear into smoke, the very end of the ungodly prophesied by the psalmist thousands of years ago (Ps. 37:20).

To be cast into God's consuming fire is a terrible, frightening end—there will be wailing and gnashing of teeth.

Matthew 13:47-50
> Again, the kingdom of heaven is like a dragnet that was cast into the sea and gathered some of every kind, which, when it was full, they drew to shore; and they sat down and gathered the good into vessels, but *threw the bad away*. So it will be at the end of the age. The angels will come forth, separate the wicked from among the just, and *cast them into the furnace of fire*. There will be wailing and gnashing of teeth.

In this graphic warning, the good fish (the saved) are gathered into containers, but the bad (the unsaved) are cast into the furnace of fire. When corrupted things are thrown away into a furnace of blazing flames, is it not expected that the fire will consume what is discarded?

Nebuchadnezzar was astonished to see Shadrach, Meshach, and Abed-Nego unharmed in the midst of the burning fiery furnace (Dan. 3:19-25), and the bush not consumed by fire was a strange sight to Moses (Exod. 3:2-4). Is it not also astonishing and strange that traditionalists essentially turn the fires of hell into a cold-storage facility? Under traditionalism, the bad fish are preserved in the fire, yet the thought of preserving the bad fish is utterly foreign to the parable. The bad fish are *thrown away*.

Matthew 18:8-9
> And if your hand or foot causes you to sin, cut it off and cast it from you. It is better for you to enter into life lame or maimed, rather than having two

hands or two feet, to be cast into the *everlasting fire*. And if your eye causes you to sin, pluck it out and cast it from you. It is better for you to enter into life with one eye, rather than having two eyes, to be cast into hell fire.

The ashes of Sodom and Gomorrah testify to the consuming nature of God's eternal fire (Gen. 19:23-28; 2 Pet. 2:6; Jude 7).

Matthew 21:44-45
"And whoever falls on this *stone* will be broken; but *on whomever it falls, it will grind him to powder.*" Now when the chief priests and Pharisees heard His parables, they perceived that He was speaking of them.

Yet again, Jesus uses stunning annihilation imagery to describe the judgment of unbelievers.

Matthew 22:13
Then the king said to the servants, "Bind him hand and foot, take him away, and cast him into *outer darkness*; there will be weeping and gnashing of teeth."

The distinction between fire and darkness may indicate that both are figurative with regard to final judgment. If the final judgment fire is figurative, the reality it represents would still accomplish the same purpose—namely, the utter destruction of the chaff. Because final judgment fire and final judgment darkness represent the same end, final judgment darkness would also indicate cessation of life.

It may be, however, that the fire is literal, and darkness, figurative of death. Not only is fire the more dominant reference, but fire is the means by which the present universe will come to an end (2 Pet. 3:10-13).

Another possibility is that the fire and darkness are both literal. Henry M. Morris writes,

> The exact character and location of the lake of fire have not been revealed in the Scriptures, but there is no reason to question the physical reality of its fires....
>
> There are indeed, stars and galaxies that, although "burning," do not give off light in the visible part of the spectrum, so that they consist of both "fire" and "cloudy darkness."[139]

In addition to having a basis in science, the coexistence of fire and darkness is deeply rooted in Jewish history. Recall that at the giving of the Law, the Lord spoke to Israel "from the midst of the fire, the cloud, and the thick darkness, with a loud voice" (Deut. 5:22).

Ultimately, we do not know exactly how the original recipients of Matthew's Gospel understood "outer darkness." The best we can do is to treat outer darkness as functionally equal to the clearer unquenchable-fire revelation in which chaff and tares *burn up,* indicating permanent cessation of life.

PAUL'S COMMENTARY ON MATTHEW 25:31-46

Like Jesus, Paul taught that the unbeliever's end is destruction. He calls death the wages of sin (Rom. 6:23) and God's righteous judgment (Rom. 1:32). In 2 Thessalonians, Paul appears to provide a commentary on Matthew 25:31-46:

> These [who do not obey the Gospel, v. 8] shall be punished with everlasting destruction [*olethros*] from the presence of the Lord and from the glory of His power, when He comes, in that Day, to be glorified in His saints and to be admired among all those who believe, because our testimony among you was believed. (2 Thess. 1:9-10)

How do traditionalists respond to Paul's declaration that unbelievers will be punished with everlasting destruction? Peterson recognizes that *destruction* could mean annihilation but denies that it carries this sense in 2 Thessalonians 1:9. Peterson's first reason is that "everlasting destruction" would be redundant wording:

> The word *destruction*, considered by itself, could mean annihilation. In this setting, however, it signifies eternal punishment. I say this for two reasons.
> First, the expression *"everlasting* destruction" denotes the never-ending devastation of the unsaved in hell. Contrary to annihilationist claims, *"everlasting* destruction" is a cumbersome way to denote the obliteration of the wicked. If extinction were meant, why not just say "destruction?"[140]

First, Paul does just say "destruction" in Philippians: "For many walk, of whom I have told you often, and now tell you even weeping, that they are the enemies of the cross of Christ: whose end is *destruction*" (3:18-19). Second, there is precedent for the use of *everlasting* in conjunction with a one-time act of eternal consequence. We observed this previously with regard to eternal redemption and eternal judgment. Third, why should it be assumed that "everlasting" is superfluous? Is it unreasonable for Paul to make an emphatic statement in a chapter in which his mind is on the suffering of the church at the hands of unbelievers? Finally, imagine if Paul had written something like "anguishing torment" and a conditionalist argued that Paul really meant "extinction" because "anguishing torment" is cumbersome!

Peterson's second reason relies on a questionable translation:

> Second, the latter part of 2 Thessalonians 1:9 supports traditionalism rather than annihilationism. Paul writes, "They will be punished with everlasting destruction and shut out from the presence of the Lord and from the majesty of his power on the day he comes to be glorified in his holy people and to be marveled at among all those who have believed" (vv. 9-10). Here we learn what "everlasting destruction" entails—the wicked being forever excluded from the gracious presence of the Lord. This cannot be annihilation, for their separation presupposes their existence.[141]

Peterson quotes the NIV, which states that unbelievers "will be punished with everlasting destruction *and shut out from* [*apo*] the presence of the Lord" (1:9). The NIV at times is part translation, part commentary. Interpretation is integral to the work of translation, but the NIV's "dynamic equivalency" involves a greater degree of interpretation than standards such as the NKJV or NASB. In short, the words "and shut out," which could imply continued existence, are *not* in the Greek text.

The Greek word *apo* is primarily translated as *from* in the New Testament; *away from* is a common meaning. In 2 Thessalonians 1:9, the NKJV reads, "These shall be punished with everlasting destruction *from* [*apo*] the presence of the Lord and from the glory of His power." The NASB reads, "These will pay the penalty of eternal destruction, *away from* [*apo*] the presence of the Lord and from the glory of His power." Both translations are best understood in light of Matthew 25:

> When the *Son of Man comes in His glory*, and all the holy angels with Him, then *He will sit on the throne of His glory*. (v. 31)

> Then He will also say to those on the left hand, "*Depart from Me*, you cursed, *into the everlasting fire*" (v. 41a)

Destruction takes place in the lake of fire. Seated on the throne of His glory, the Lord Jesus commands the cursed into the fire. Destruction everlasting, then, comes *from* the Lord Jesus. That is, Jesus is responsible for the destruction. This is most likely Paul's meaning.

It is also true, however, that unbelievers pay the penalty of eternal destruction *away from* the presence of Christ: "*Depart from Me*, you cursed, *into the everlasting fire*" —into the fire where the chaff "will burn up" (Matt. 3:12).

HELL IN THE GOSPEL OF MATTHEW

By their own admission, Matthew 25:46 is the best support traditionalists have, yet the verse is of limited detail. Generic warning was sufficient for Augustine to embrace ECT because he was thoroughly indoctrinated in the immortality of the soul. The Gospel of Matthew gives us opportunity to do better.

Matthew's Gospel is home to the most vivid statements about hell in the Bible. In Matthew, the chaff burn up (3:12), broad is the way that leads to destruction (7:13), body and soul can be killed (10:28), tares are gathered and burned in fire (13:30, 40), the bad fish are thrown away into a furnace of fire (13:47-50), and the falling Stone grinds to powder (21:44-45).

Shouldn't our understanding of God's justice for unrepentant sinners be shaped by these explicit biblical truths?

5

THE PRICE OF REDEMPTION: THE PRECIOUS BLOOD OF CHRIST

THE PAYMENT FOR SIN MADE AT THE CROSS: THE NEED FOR CLARITY

When a sinner receives Jesus, God freely credits him with a righteousness that renders the believer blameless in God's sight (Rom. 4:5-8), providing peace with God (Rom. 5:1) and deliverance from condemnation (Rom. 8:1, 33-34). God made this incredible salvation available to the world because He loves people and desires everyone to be saved (1 Tim. 2:4). It is the one who rejects God's gift of salvation who must personally pay sin's penalty.

The payment for sin, which Jesus made at the cross, indicates the nature of the penalty that the unbeliever will have to pay. Some traditionalists teach that Christ Jesus literally experienced infinite torment in His divine nature at Calvary. Morris succinctly expresses this view:

> The Lord Jesus endured hell itself as our substitute, when He was forsaken by God for those three terrible hours on the cross....
>
> Christ, as man, suffered and died, "more than any man" (Isa. 52:14), but as God He could endure infinite and eternal punishment in a finite time and specific place, thus satisfying forever the righteousness of God and manifesting to perfection His redeeming love.[142]

There is logic to this understanding of the cross. According to traditionalism, every sinner owes God a debt of endless torment. Because Jesus paid the world's debt, if traditionalism is true, it follows that Christ experienced infinite torment at Calvary. For many Christians, the teaching that Jesus suffered infinite torment, much like the immortality of the soul, is a significant factor in the acceptance of the traditional view of hell. If someone believes that Christ suffered infinite torment in His divine nature, he is virtually forced to conclude that traditionalism must be true. Understanding what really happened at the cross, then, is critical.

THE UNITY OF GOD

The notion that Christ suffered infinite torment in His divine nature fails to take into consideration that the divine essence is not divisible but one (Deut. 6:4; James 2:19). The unity of God assures us that, with regard to the divine nature, no schism ever occurred at any time between the Father and the Son and the Holy Spirit. The claim that the Trinity was broken at the cross is heretical. God never ceased to be God. It was in the sphere of His human nature, not His divine nature, that the Son was forsaken. This reality is reflected in a comparison of the Synoptic Gospels—Matthew, Mark, and Luke—with the Gospel of John, the one Gospel explicitly written to prove Christ's divinity (John 20:30-31).

In the Garden of Gethsemane, just hours before going to the cross, the Synoptic Gospels inform us, Jesus was "sorrowful and deeply distressed" (Matt. 26:37) and "troubled and deeply distressed" (Mark 14:33), and that, "being in agony, He prayed more earnestly. And His sweat became like great drops of blood falling down to the ground" (Luke 22:44). In addition to Roman crucifixion, which He was about to suffer, the thought of separation from the Father surely brought anguish to Jesus. Taking our sins upon Himself necessitated the Son's separation, in His human experience, from the Father. It is commonly understood that the darkness that covered the land from the sixth hour to the ninth hour (12:00 p.m. to 3:00 p.m.) signaled this separation. Only Matthew, Mark, and Luke record the midday darkness that occurred while Christ was on the cross (Matt. 27:45; Mark 15:33; Luke 23:44). Jesus' cry, "My God, My God, why have You forsaken Me?" is recorded in Matthew 27:46 and Mark 15:34.

John's Gospel paints a very different picture from what we see in the Synoptic Gospels.[143] For example, John's Gospel contains no hint of distress in Gethsemane, does not include the darkness that came over the land, and states that Jesus knew "all things that would come upon Him" (18:4). John records that in the garden Jesus identified Himself with the words "*I AM*"—the result being that those who came to arrest Him drew backward and fell to the ground (18:6). Additionally, shortly before His crucifixion, Jesus told His disciples, "Indeed the hour is coming, yes, has now come, that you will be scattered, each to his own, and will leave Me alone. And yet I am not alone, because the Father is with Me" (16:32). This is found only in John, where we also hear Jesus say, "He who sent Me is with Me. The Father has not left Me alone, for I always do those things that please Him" (8:29) and "I and My Father are one" (10:30).

Writing about the Trinity, Lewis Sperry Chafer states,

> The Son, being very God, is eternally on an absolute equality with the Father. On the other hand, the First Person became the *God* of the Second Person by the incarnation. Only from His humanity could Christ address the First Person as "My God." This He did in that moment of supreme manifestation of His humanity when on the cross He said, "My God, my God, why hast thou forsaken me?"[144]

Historically, the church has tended to emphasize the deity of Christ. We must not lose sight of His humanity, however. Without the Christmas story, there would be no cross.

THE INCARNATION

Death is the penalty for sin, but God cannot die. How, then, can the eternal Son pay for the sins of the world? The solution is the incarnation. The eternal Son "became flesh and dwelt among us" (John 1:14). "For there is born to you this day in the city of David a Savior, who is Christ the Lord" (Luke 2:11). "'Behold, a virgin shall be with child, and bear a Son, and they shall call His name Immanuel,' which is translated, 'God with us'" (Matt. 1:23).

In the incarnation, the eternal Son of God added a complete human nature to His divine Person. The Lord Jesus Christ, singular in Person, the eternal Son, dual in nature: divine and human. In theology, this unfathomable truth is known as the hypostatic union. *The Moody Handbook of Theology* states,

> The hypostatic union may be defined as "the second person, the preincarnate Christ came and took to Himself a human nature and remains forever undiminished Deity and true humanity united in one person forever." When Christ came, a Person came, not just a nature; He took on an additional nature, a human nature—He did not simply dwell in a human person. The result of the union of the two natures is the theanthropic Person (the God-man)....
>
> "Though Christ sometimes operated in the sphere of His humanity and in other cases in the sphere of His deity, *in all cases what He did... could be attributed to His one Person*. Even though it is evident that there were two natures in Christ, He is never considered a dual personality." In summarizing the hypostatic union, three facts are noted: (1) Christ has two distinct natures: humanity and deity; (2) there is no mixture or intermingling of the two natures; (3) although He has two natures, Christ is one Person.[145]

Thiessen writes,

> No exact psychological analysis of the unique personality of Christ is possible; we can only say such things as are clearly evident from the Scriptures or as may be safely inferred from them....
>
> [For example] we may speak of the God-man when we wish to refer to the person; but we cannot speak of the divine-human nature, but must say the divine and the human nature in Christ. This is evident from the fact that Christ had an infinite intelligence and will and a finite intelligence and will; that He had a divine consciousness and a human consciousness. His divine intelligence was infinite; His human intelligence increased. His divine will

was omnipotent; His human will had only the power of unfallen humanity. In His divine consciousness He said, "I and the Father are one"; in His human consciousness He said, "I thirst."[146]

Much about the incarnation of the eternal Son baffles human comprehension. Still, the basics of the doctrine facilitate a more accurate understanding of what happened at the cross.

THE IMPORTANCE OF CHRIST'S HUMANITY

The eternal Son became "flesh and dwelt among us" to accomplish what was otherwise impossible for Him to do: die for the world:

> But when the fullness of the time had come, God sent forth His Son, *born of a woman*, born under the law, *to redeem* those who were under the law, that we might receive the adoption of sons. (Gal. 4:4-5)

> But we see Jesus, who was made a little lower than the angels, *for the suffering of death* crowned with glory and honor, *that He*, by the grace of God, *might taste death for everyone*. (Heb. 2:9)

Norman L. Geisler and Bill Roach state,

> But both the *Apostles' Creed* and the *Nicene Creed* (A.D. 325) made it very clear that it was Jesus alone who "suffered" for us on the Cross. And that He did this only through His human nature. To say otherwise is to engage in "confusing

the two natures" of Christ which was explicitly condemned in the *Chalcedonian Creed* (A.D. 451).[147]

Ponder it: The payment the eternal Son made for our sins, He made in His humanity— "who Himself bore our sins *in His own body* on the tree" (1 Pet. 2:24).

THE VALUE OF JESUS' SACRIFICE

The Lord Jesus paid for the sins of the world in His human nature. How could a human death have such power? It was the eternal Son incarnate who paid the price of our redemption.

There is one value to the life of animals, another value to that of angelic beings, and another to that of humanity. Then there is the value of the eternal Son of God. It is in contemplating Jesus' identity that the all-sufficient redeeming power of Calvary becomes evident. Chafer states,

> The value of the sacrifice is not to be discovered in the intensity of the Savior's anguish but rather in the dignity and infinite worth of the One who suffers. He did not give more or less; He gave *Himself*, He offered Himself, but this self was none other than the Second Person of the Godhead in whom measureless dignity and glory reside.[148]

In *Two Views of Hell*, Peterson is careful to argue his position from the standpoint that the Son "by virtue of his human nature" suffered "separation from God and the positive infliction of torments in body and soul."[149] Like Chafer, Peterson recognizes that the worth of the Savior's Person is key. He states that "because of the infinite dignity of Christ's person, his sufferings, though finite in duration, were of infinite weight on the scales of divine justice."[150] I appreciate Peterson's thoughtful presentation. What we differ on is the divine penalty for sin.

THE PAYMENT REQUIRED

The claim that Christ paid for the sins of the world by suffering infinite and eternal torment in His divine nature is inconsistent with the truth of God's indivisible essence. It also misses a supreme opportunity to contemplate the inestimable value of Christ's Person. Moreover, it fails to grasp the payment required by God's holiness. Newell writes,

> Concerning Christ's bearing in our place God's wrath against sin, let us say: To regard God as "angry," or as demanding that Christ suffer "the exact equivalent of all the agonies the elect would have suffered to all eternity," is to miss the whole meaning of propiation [that satisfaction of God's Holy Nature and law for man's sins rendered by Christ's blood[151]]....
> The conception that Christ on the cross was enduring all the agonies of the elect for all eternity grew directly out of the Romish legalism from which the Reformers did not escape... The shed blood brought in before God on the Day of Atonement simply witnessed that a life had been laid down, ended. "The sufferings of all the elect for all eternity" could never take the place of the *laid down life* of the great Sacrifice. God did not ask for *agonies*... Not the agonies of Christ could avail, but that, bearing sin, He laid His life down, poured out His soul unto *death*."[152]

God's salvation is by blood, real blood from a real body. "When I see the *blood*, I will pass over you," says the Lord (Exod. 12:13); the blood of an unblemished lamb that died as a sacrifice

(Exod. 12:1-6). The eternal Son incarnate is the holy Lamb of God who gave His flesh and His blood for our sins (John 1:1-14, 29, 6:51-54). Redemption is grounded in Christ's death and blood. There is no other price that can secure forgiveness.[153]

Paul writes, "Being justified freely by His grace through the redemption that is in Christ Jesus, whom God set forth to be a *propitiation by His blood*" (Rom. 3:24-25). "I declare to you the gospel... that Christ *died for our sins* according to the Scriptures, and that He was buried, and that He rose again the third day according to the Scriptures" (1 Cor. 15:1-4). "In Him we have *redemption through His blood*, the forgiveness of sins, according to the riches of His grace" (Eph. 1:7). "And you, who once were alienated and enemies in your mind by wicked works, yet now He has reconciled *in the body of His flesh through death*" (Col. 1:21-22).

In Hebrews we read,

> Not with the blood of goats and calves, but *with His own blood* He entered the Most Holy Place once for all, *having obtained eternal redemption*. For if the blood of bulls and goats and the ashes of a heifer, sprinkling the unclean, sanctifies for the purifying of the flesh, how much more shall the *blood of Christ*, who through the eternal Spirit offered Himself without spot to God, purge your conscience from dead works to serve the living God? And for this reason He is the Mediator of the new covenant, *by means of death*, for the redemption of the transgressions under the first covenant, that those who are called may receive the promise of the eternal inheritance. (9:12-15)

Peter writes, "You were not redeemed with perishable things like silver or gold from your futile way of life inherited from your forefathers, but with *precious blood*, as of a lamb unblemished and spotless, *the blood of Christ*" (1 Pet. 1:18-19, NASB).

WHAT HAPPENED AT THE CROSS

At the cross, Paul teaches in the Book of Colossians, Jesus "canceled out the certificate of debt consisting of decrees against us, which was hostile to us; and He has taken it out of the way, having nailed it to the cross" (2:14, NASB).

The transgressions of humanity, whether against the Mosaic Law or conscience (Rom. 2:12-16), generated the certificate of debt that demanded condemnation (Rom. 3:19). Heaven's courtroom housed the record of this debt: "And I saw the dead, small and great, standing before God, and books were opened.... And the dead were judged according to their works, by the things which were written in the books" (Rev. 20:12).

Jesus nailed my certificate of debt and your certificate of debt to His cross. In the words of Isaiah, "the Lord has laid on Him the iniquity of us all" (Isa. 53:6). In today's computer jargon, the books in God's courtroom containing the record of the world's sin were downloaded to Jesus' cross. With our sins laid upon Him, Jesus paid humanity's debt by voluntarily dying on the cross so everyone who believes in Him will not perish but have eternal life (Exod. 12:3-7, 12-13; John 1:29, 3:16; 1 Cor. 5:7b, 15:1-4).

The Lord Jesus Christ is absolutely unique and the only possible Savior. If He were not human, He could not die for our sins. If He were not the eternal Son, His shed blood would not have sufficient value to pay for the sins of the world.

JESUS' RESURRECTION: GOD'S "PAID IN FULL" GUARANTEE

Pinnock affirms the importance and authenticity of Christ's resurrection:

> The miracles of Christ provided men with a powerful incentive to trust him....
>
> But undoubtedly the greatest stress in the New Testament is placed on the bodily resurrection of Jesus Christ as *the* supreme sign of the truth of the Gospel. Jesus presented himself alive after his suffering to the disciples "with many infallible proofs" (Acts 1:3). His resurrection was an attested fact of history (Acts 2:32; 10:41; I Cor. 15:3-11). It was the supreme demonstration of the deity of Jesus Christ (Rom. 1:4). It provided mankind with an evidence of universal validity (Acts 17:31). "If Christ has not been raised, then our preaching is in vain and your faith is in vain" (I Cor. 15:14). We have a living hope *because* God raised up Jesus (I Pt. 1:3)....
>
> The appearance [of the risen Christ] to five hundred brethren at once indicates the public nature of the evidence. Many of these believers Paul knew to be alive at the time of his writing (I Cor. 15:6). The extensive series of appearances to many individuals over a period of several weeks is a phenomenon which calls for an explanation.... These appearances were either actual and substantial, or else they were hallucinatory. A hallucination is an apparent perception of an object. It appears frequently at the end of a period of anxious wishfulness for something to happen, and to isolated persons, not to groups. It is striking that all of the factors favorable to the hallucination hypothesis are absent

from the New Testament. The resurrection caught everyone off guard. The disciples were surprised and disbelieving for joy (Mk. 16:8; Mt. 28:17; Lk. 24:36-43; Jn. 20:19). They needed convincing themselves. Jesus did not come into an atmosphere of wishful thinking.... Many had the experience at the same time too, affording correlation and corroboration. Furthermore, physical aspects to the appearances such as his invitation to Thomas to touch him, and his eating with the disciples, add to the impressiveness of the appearances. The birth and growth of the early church is utterly inexplicable apart from the appearances of the risen Christ. Only the resurrection itself offers an adequate rational explanation to the facts we see.

There is a fantastic difference between the disciples who appear in the Gospel narratives and those who figure in the book of Acts. Timid, unreliable, fearful, unbelieving men emerge from the events immediately following the death of Christ bursting to tell of his resurrection whatever the cost to their own personal safety.... The entire narrative of the Acts of the Apostles is posited upon this single event. It is woven into its very fabric. The disciples were intellectually convinced that the gospel was true, because God had raised Jesus from the dead.[154]

Jesus' resurrection guarantees that humanity's debt is paid in full. The connection between Christ's successful payment for sin and His resurrection can be seen in Paul's letter to the Corinthians:

> And if Christ is not risen, your faith is futile; you are still in your sins! Then also those who have fallen asleep in Christ have *perished*. If in this life only we have hope in Christ, we are of all men the most pitiable. (1 Cor. 15:17-19)

Mitchell states,

> The cross was a tragedy apart from resurrection. The blessing of justification is secured by the resurrection of Jesus Christ from the dead. He was delivered up because of our offenses, yours and mine. He bore your sins and my sins. He bore the penalty. How do I know He put them away? God raised Him from the dead. That's why, when you come to the Book of Acts, the apostles proclaim nearly thirty times the resurrection of Jesus Christ from the dead.
>
> If there is no resurrection, there is no salvation. But if He was raised from the dead, then His work at the cross absolutely, perfectly satisfied God. The resurrection is God's personal proof to you that Jesus Christ has put away your sins. He has satisfied God. God is now free to take anyone who puts his trust in the Savior and not only forgive his sins, but also cover him with the righteousness of Christ.[155]

WHY JESUS WAS NOT ANNIHILATED BUT UNBELIEVERS WILL BE

Annihilation takes place when unbelievers burn up like weeds in a furnace of fire. Obviously, Jesus did not burn up at Calvary. Neither do we read of wailing and gnashing of teeth or unceasing hopelessness at the cross. An *exact* match between Christ's death and the fate of the unsaved in the lake of fire simply does not exist for conditionalists or traditionalists. This should not surprise us. Jesus is unique, and so is His death. A thoughtful review of God's plan of salvation reveals why the notion that Christ must replicate the second death to save sinners from it is unwarranted.

We begin with the observation that it was never God's intention for a man to be cast into the lake of fire solely on the basis of being a sinner. Before creating the universe, God determined to save sinners, by grace through faith, that He might have a redeemed family in whom He could delight. The peace made by the blood of Jesus' cross countered the world's transgressions (Col. 1:20; 2 Cor. 5:19) and made the acceptance or rejection of Christ the crucial issue. To accept Christ brings life (John 1:12, 20:30-31). To reject Christ is to face final judgment without the benefit of Jesus' shed blood. Christ paid the price of redemption—"For You were slain, And have redeemed us to God by Your blood" (Rev. 5:9)—but His sacrifice needs to be embraced by faith. This is illustrated in Exodus 12 where the blood of the sacrificed lamb had to be put on the lintel and two doorposts of one's house in order for the Lord to pass over rather than strike. It is also seen in Jesus' bread of life teaching: "I am the living bread which came down from heaven. *If* anyone *eats* of this bread, he will live forever; and the bread that I shall give is My flesh, which I shall give for the life of the world" (John 6:51). In short, the unbeliever dies a *redemptionless* death in the lake of fire.

Although Christ took the sins of the world upon Himself, to merit annihilation requires more than the issue of sin. One must also be indifferent to or spurning of God and His grace. This certainly was not true of Jesus: "But that the world may know that I love the Father, and as the Father gave Me commandment, so I do" (John 14:31). Christ died the death specified for Him by the Father—crucifixion—and did so as a sacrificial act of devotion to Him (Acts 2:23; Phil. 2:8; Heb. 10:4-10; John 8:29). Most importantly, Jesus' death at Calvary was a *redemptive* death. It may have appeared, while His disfigured lifeless body hung on the cross, as if Christ had been permanently defeated by the world, but in truth, when

Jesus laid down His holy, innocent, undefiled life for Adam's fallen race (Heb. 7:26-27), He accomplished a great redemptive victory (Matt. 26:26-28; Heb. 9:12-15). God was propitiated, His holiness satisfied (Rom. 3:25). Having completed the mission given to Him by the Father, Jesus was free to enter Paradise (Luke 23:43). On the third day, Jesus' tomb was found empty. "He is not here," said the angels, "but is risen" (Luke 24:1-7).

The distinction between redemptive and non-redemptive death is pivotal as to why Christ did not experience annihilation but unbelievers will. Annihilation takes place only in the case of *redemptionless* death, and Christ's death at Calvary was thoroughly *redemptive* in nature.

A Life Laid Down, Ended

The Father sent His Son to die for us in accordance with the biblical understanding of death—cessation or end of life. We take this up now.

In Eden, Adam was warned about eating of the tree of the knowledge of good and evil: "You shall surely die." This warning said nothing about eternal existence, much less continuing forever in torment. Rather, at face value, Genesis 2:17 cautioned Adam that to eat the forbidden fruit would result in his life coming to an *end*.

When Adam and Eve sinned, however, God responded with grace: "Also for Adam and his wife the Lord God made tunics of skin, and clothed them" (Gen. 3:21). Please do not miss this. The lives of Adam and Eve were extended rather than ended, for one reason and one reason only: God acted in grace. To miss God's grace in Eden is to overlook an essential aspect of the Fall. Allen P. Ross writes,

> All God's dealings with people as sinners can be traced back to this act of disobedience by Adam and Eve. God is a saving God, however, and the fact that He clothed… Adam and Eve testifies to that. An animal was sacrificed to provide garments of skin, and later all Israel's animal sacrifices would be part of God's provision to remedy the curse—a life for a life.[156]

We're on this planet today because God "passed over" Adam's transgression on the basis of Christ's propitiating blood (Rom. 3:25). Some traditionalists make Christ's separation from the Father the primary saving aspect of Calvary, yet we do not read that God was propitiated by forsakenness. The sins of the world were indeed imputed to Jesus, and this necessitated separation, in His human experience, from the Father. There is thus a sense in which it can be said that He was forsaken so we could be forgiven, but it was shed blood that took away our sins: "When I see the blood, I will pass over you"; Jesus is "a propitiation by His blood"; "For You were slain, And have redeemed us to God by Your blood."

Why God is satisfied by shed blood is found in the Book of Leviticus. The entire sixteenth chapter of Leviticus details the Day of Atonement. Leviticus 17 addresses the sanctity of blood. Verse 11 is key to our study:

> For *the life of the flesh is in the blood*, and I have given it to you upon the altar to make atonement for your souls; for *it is the blood that makes atonement for the soul*. (Lev. 17:11)

RESCUE FROM DEATH

God is the One who established the penalty for sin. He is also the One who determines the substitutionary payment acceptable to take away the sins of the world. It is what *He* sees at the cross and what the cross means to *Him* that matters. In Leviticus 17:11, the Lord tells us that "the life of the flesh is in the blood." Thus, the eternal Son left the glories of heaven for a manger in Bethlehem. He became incarnate to obtain a life that could be laid down, ended, for you and me, ended through death, through the shedding of His blood at Calvary (1 Cor. 11:26).

Newell, writing about the Day of Atonement set forth in Leviticus 16, states,

> When the Jewish high priest took the blood of the slain goat into the Holy of Holies on the Great Day of Atonement, with the whole congregation of Israel assembled without, he spake no word, uttered no confession, made no plea. Going to the mercy seat, the top of the ark of the covenant, he sprinkled the blood upon it, and before it, seven times, then went out. That *blood* witnessed that the goat which was "Jehovah's lot" had died; its life was poured out, ended. When the high priest went forth from the tabernacle and, laying his hands upon the head of the other goat (for the people), confessed all their sins and iniquities, it was as a result of the laying down of the life of the first goat, for the two together constituted one type of Christ's death, Christ's shedding His blood for sin, and the result. This second goat was sent away into the wilderness, not to be found.
>
> Remember, Christ did not resume the flesh and blood life that He had before dying. That life was laid down, ended. We are so accustomed to associate resurrection with sin bearing, that Christ's resurrection becomes in our mind a resuming of the life that He laid down. We forget that the blood poured out ended the life in the flesh.[157]

Newell affirms that "Christ's shedding His blood for sin" is a matter of a life ended. This conclusion is firmly rooted in the principle that the life of the flesh is in the blood and in the fact that Jesus' life blood literally poured out of His body.

Once, Jesus was arrested, bound, and brought before Caiaphas, the high priest, and the Sanhedrin, where the Savior was falsely accused and abused; now, Jesus is heaven's great High Priest who has mercy and grace for us in time of need.

The Son went to the cross in His earthly flesh and blood life and rose in His glorious (Phil. 3:21) heavenly (1 Cor. 15:45-49) flesh and bone (Luke 24:39) life. Arthur Jackson writes,

> The resurrection of Christ is unto a new creation. Christ's resurrection was not a mere reversal of the death process... His was now a "glorious body;" a body consisting of flesh and bones but—with no blood.... In the resurrected Christ we see something the world had never encountered before. Here is life on an entirely different principle [than blood]: a body, a true physical body, immortal, incorruptible, one suited for both heaven and eternity.[158]

Christ is now Head of a new race of people (Eph. 1:20-23; Rom. 5:12-21). Commenting on Romans 5:12-21, Mitchell writes,

> In the last half of Romans 5, Paul discusses what we were in Adam and what we are now in Christ. He is talking about two Adams and two races of people....
>
> When sinners accept God's precious Son as their Savior, they are born from above, they are born into a new family, they are born into a new race where death doesn't cast a shadow....
>
> That's why I read in 2 Corinthians 5:17, "If any man be in Christ [this Head of a new race], he is a new creature:

old things are passed away; behold, all things are become new."¹⁵⁹ [Brackets Mitchell's]

Christ risen as "the second Man" (1 Cor. 15:47), the Head of a new race, presupposes the laying down of His old flesh and blood life. Newell writes,

> God raised Christ from the dead in glorious triumph. And thereafter Christ walked for forty days on earth "in newness of life." He was "the First-born from the dead." He was the Last Adam... the Second Man, "a new starting point of the human race."...
>
> It was not back into the old flesh and blood earthly existence that He came. He had, indeed, His body: "Handle Me and see." "Have ye here anything to eat?" Yet He had poured out His blood. The life of the flesh was in the blood (Lev. 17:11). He had laid that life down. He is now a heavenly Man. He is in the heavenlies.¹⁶⁰

The reality that a life ended at the cross is consistent with the conditionalist view that the penalty for sin requires a life to cease or come to an end. The wonder of God's grace is that: *Jesus died a redemptive death at Calvary that we might not die a redemptionless death in the lake of fire.*

Jesus' shed blood is redemptive both because of who He is and because His blood speaks of a life sacrificially ended for sinners. As the blood of the sacrificed goat testified that its life had ended, so the pouring out of Jesus' blood witnessed that His earthly life had ended. Since the blood sustains the life of the flesh (Lev. 17:14), it could not be otherwise. That He might bring us to God, the body of the righteous One was put to death for the unrighteous (Col. 1:22; 1 Pet. 3:18). Jesus died for us because He doesn't want my life or your life to end in the flames of *Gehenna*. He loves us. He doesn't want us to perish. He wants us to believe in Him and live.

Undone by Their Own Words

Traditionalists, especially when dealing with texts and topics other than hell, recognize that Christ's death was a matter of a life laid down, ended. Furthermore, when teaching on Romans 6, outstanding Bible teachers of the twentieth century acknowledged that through union with Christ in His crucifixion, we who believe in Jesus *died* in the sight of God. What is freely admitted when teaching the riches of grace in Romans 6 should be a wake-up call to traditionalists. McClain writes,

> When He died, we died; when He was buried, we were buried (in the mind of God)....
>
> "Knowing this, that our old man was crucified with him" (v. 6).... The "old man" means the old self; what we were in Adam. That "old man" was crucified with Christ at the cross, and the task is finished in the mind of God.[161]

Ironside taught,

> I was seen by God on that cross with His blessed Son.
>
> How many people were crucified on Calvary?... Paul says in Gal. 2:20, "I am crucified with Christ.".... And each believer can say, "Our old man is crucified with Him." So untold millions were seen by God as hanging there upon that cross with Christ. And this was not merely that our sins were being dealt with, but that we ourselves as sinners, as children of Adam's fallen race, might be removed from under the eye of God and our old standing come to an end forever.[162]

RESCUE FROM DEATH

Newell writes,

> The old man was crucified with Christ, and all that belonged to "man in the flesh" was ended before God there on Christ's cross....
>
> Our old man would thus be crucified with Christ, so that all the evil of the old man, and all his responsibilities also, would be completely annulled before God for all believers. For they must righteously be released from Adam, before they are created in Christ, another Adam! And this must be by *death*.[163]

Mitchell states,

> We're dealing with a fact. God has declared that when Christ died, you and I were joined to Him. We were baptized into His death. When He was buried, we were buried. And when He came forth in resurrection, we too came forth, identified with the risen and glorified Christ. It's the end of you and me as far as our history as sinners....
>
> You and I were the ones who should have been crucified. We were the ones who had transgressed against the law of God. We were the sinners, and God says "the wages of sin is death." Either we die or somebody else dies. Christ died in our stead. We were identified with Him—we were joined with Him when He died. God saw you and me in His Son hanging on the cross and in the grave.[164]

The cross is central to the forgiveness of our sins. It is also the foundation of Paul's principles of sanctification in Romans 6–8. In discussing what was accomplished at the cross, these highly respected traditionalist teachers inadvertently affirm the conditionalist position. How? What the cross provides for the person of faith, the unbeliever lacks and must face in the final judgment.

At the heart of Romans 6 is the fact that God counts the believer as having *died* with Christ. You and I were yet future when Christ died nearly 2000 years ago at Calvary. So were all of our sins. God foresaw all, and Christ died for all. Through union with Christ, we who were under the sentence of death as members of Adam's race *died* in the sight of God. Our debt was paid in full, and our *history as sinners ended* at the cross.

What awaits those who spurn the Savior's gift of salvation?

The chance to share in Christ's crucifixion, in the sight of God, is an incredible gift of grace. The only other option is to be cast into the lake of fire and have one's history as a sinner end there. This is what Jesus Himself taught. Not only is God *able* to kill both soul and body in hell (Matt. 10:28) but the unsaved *will* burn up like weeds in a furnace of fire (Matt. 13:30, 40-42).

Conditional immortality is not only plainly taught in scripture, its understanding of the fate of the unsaved is fundamentally consistent with Calvary. At the cross, Jesus experienced intense suffering followed by literal bodily death verified by burial in Joseph of Arimathea's tomb. Conditionalism likewise affirms suffering, appropriate to one's sin, followed by death. ECT, in contrast, is a matter of suffering followed only by more suffering. Conditionalism also enjoys a parallel with Calvary in that as Christ's earthly flesh and blood life ended forever at the cross, so in the second death the impenitent come to a permanent end.

CHRIST'S DEATH AND RESURRECTION: HOPE AND WARNING

In due time, the believer in Christ will be given an imperishable flesh and bone body like the one with which Jesus came out of the grave, "For our citizenship is in heaven, from which we also eagerly wait for the Savior, the Lord Jesus Christ, who will transform our lowly body that it may be conformed to His glorious body" (Phil. 3:20-21), but there will be no happy ending for those who turn their backs on God's offer of salvation.

Jesus' resurrection also guarantees that the final judgment foretold in Revelation 20:11-15 will actually take place. When in Athens, Paul was taken to the Areopagus, where he spoke to the Greek philosophers of his day. Paul declared that God "commands all people everywhere to repent. For he has set a day when he will judge the world with justice by the man he has appointed. He has given proof of this to everyone by raising him from the dead" (Acts 17:30-31, NIV).

The second death in the lake of fire should not be sugarcoated. It is a dreadful reality. It will involve fire and unrealized hopes and dreams, and it will culminate in the permanent end of life itself. I can't think of it without tears in my eyes.

This is not a necessary end for anyone. The risen Savior welcomes all who come to Him into God's forever family. Have you put your future in Jesus' hands?

6

THE REVELATION PASSAGES

Traditionalists are confident that the Book of Revelation cements their viewpoint. In *Hell under Fire*, Gregory K. Beale states, "It still remains true that Revelation 14:11 and 20:10-15 are the Achilles' heel of the annihilationist perspective."[165]

Beale implies that Revelation 14:11 and 20:10-15 are traditionalism's clinching proof texts. Did God really wait until the last book of the Bible to confirm the high stakes of rebellion?

The penalty for sin was declared long before Revelation was written. It was revealed in the opening pages of Genesis: "You shall surely die." By the time the reader of the Bible comes to Revelation, he has already been thoroughly informed that the unsaved burn up in the fire prepared for the devil and his angels. Will we find the Genesis 2:17 penalty for sin altered beyond recognition in the Book of Revelation, or will the noncontradictory nature of God's Word prevail?

Before we examine traditionalist claims regarding Revelation 14 and 20, let's briefly get acquainted with the storyline and futuristic nature of Revelation.

OUTLINE OF REVELATION

Preliminary Note

Conditionalists are a diverse lot. We come from a variety of church backgrounds and represent a wide range of eschatological views. Many, if not most, proponents of conditional immortality, thus far have been amillennialists who remind us that in the Old Testament—burning sulfur, unquenchable fire, and smoke that ascends forever—combine to picture devastation (Isa. 34:9-10). Many have taken a preterist or partial preterist view of the Book of Revelation. Space does not allow for interaction with views held by other conditionalists, but what can be thankfully acknowledged is that conditionalists tend to be supportive of one another. We take interest in how others argue for conditionalism, believing that believers from diverse backgrounds sharing a common understanding of the fate of the unsaved reflects how thoroughly conditional immortality is imbedded in God's Word. It is in this spirit that my understanding of the Book of Revelation is presented.

The Outline

Jesus Himself gave us the broad outline of Revelation when He said to John, "Write the things which you *have seen*, and the things *which are*, and the things which *will take place after this*" (Rev. 1:19).

John had an encounter with Christ in 1:9-20. His description of Christ fulfills "the things which you have seen." The seven letters to seven churches in chapters 2 and 3 constitute "the things which are." In chapter 4, John is called up to heaven to be shown future events—"the things which will take place." A prologue in chapters 4 and 5 opens the futuristic portion of the book. Chapters 6 through 18 detail the Tribulation preceding the return of Christ in chapter 19. The restraint and torment of Satan, the millennium, and the Great White Throne judgment are found in chapter 20. The new earth and New Jerusalem are the primary focus of chapter 21 and 22:1-5, followed by an epilogue.[166]

This understanding of Revelation is known as the *futurist* view. It naturally flows from the belief that the literal method of interpretation, which gives due consideration to figures of speech and prophetic symbols, is to guide us throughout God's Word. The trustworthiness of the literal method is confirmed by the myriad of Old Testament prophecies that have been literally fulfilled.

Futurists are united with regard to the broad outline of Revelation. Understandably, given the massive amount of prophetic detail in scripture, differences exist over how all the pieces of the puzzle fit together. The study of prophecy is humbling. Not only do we not know how it all fits together, even when we think we understand something, mystery yet remains. For example, it is fairly certain that the ten kings in Daniel's chapter 7 night visions "who shall arise from" the fourth kingdom (Dan. 7:23-24) are the same ten kings seen in Revelation 17 giving their "power and authority" to Antichrist (Rev. 17:12-13). The identity of the ten kings and the nations they head, however, is an open (and much debated) question.

With regard to the chronology of Tribulation events, many believe that the seals, trumpets, and bowls follow one another sequentially. Ryrie calls chapters 6, 8-9, and 16 the "chronological framework" of the Tribulation section.¹⁶⁷ The seals appear to be associated with the first half of the Tribulation, and the trumpets and bowls with the second half. This is in keeping with Matthew 24 where beginning birth pangs precede the midpoint abomination of desolation that marks the start of unprecedented tribulation.¹⁶⁸

Outside of the seals, trumpets, and bowls, the Tribulation section is not necessarily chronological. Ryrie states,

> The chapters in this section are not unlike a conversation on the telephone between two persons. They start telling the story in order (chap. 6), but soon there is an interruption to fill in some information (chap. 7). Then the order of events is resumed (chaps. 8-9) only to return to some more fill-in (chaps. 10-15). There is a return to the progressive order of events (chap. 16)... Sometimes the "fill-in" material runs ahead of the story; at other times it backs up to add or emphasize pertinent information.¹⁶⁹

To better appreciate the gist of the conversation in Revelation, we now turn to the prologue of the Tribulation section and the scroll, which only the Lamb of God is worthy to open.

A SOVEREIGN GOD AND A SEVEN-SEAL SCROLL

In Revelation 4, the spotlight is on the throne of God and on God as Creator and Sovereign of the universe: "You are worthy, O Lord, To receive glory and honor and power; For You created all things, And by Your will they exist and were created" (4:11).

In Revelation 5, our attention is drawn to a seven-seal scroll in God's right hand: "And I saw in the right hand of Him who sat on the throne a scroll written inside and on the back, sealed with seven seals" (5:1). What is this scroll that John wept over (5:4) that no one, except the Lord Jesus, is worthy to open (5:3-9)? Many hold that the scroll is the title deed to the earth. Morris says of the scroll,

> It is nothing less than the title deed to the earth itself. This is not explained in the immediate context, but it is clearly the antitype of all the rich typological teaching associated with the divinely specified procedures for land redemption in the Old Testament.[170]

Old Testament Land Redemption

There are provisions set forth in the Old Testament that govern the land God gave to Israel. These principles are foundational to appreciation of the scroll as the title deed to the earth.

God gifted land to the people of Israel under the Abrahamic Covenant (Gen. 13:14-18, 15:7-21; Exod. 6:4), but He retained ultimate ownership: "The land shall not be sold permanently, for the land is Mine" (Lev. 25:23). Distribution of the land was made to the tribes of Israel (Josh. 13-19), and inheritance (Num. 27:8-11) and marriage (Num. 36:8) laws were established so "no inheritance shall change hands from one tribe to another" (Num. 36:9).

In cases of poverty, land could be sold (leased, really) to others; however, possession had to be returned in the Year of Jubilee (Lev. 25:28), which took place every fifty years (Lev. 25:8-10). Prior to the Year of Jubilee, an Israelite had the right to redeem his leased land by payment of the redemption price (Lev. 25:26-27). A kinsman-redeemer also had this right: "If one of your brethren becomes poor, and has sold some of his possession, and if his kinsman-redeemer comes to redeem it, then he may redeem what his brother sold" (Lev. 25:25). That is, to keep the land in the tribe, a near kinsman was allowed to pay the redemption price and take ownership of the leased land until the Year of Jubilee.

Jeremiah exercised the right of a kinsman-redeemer during the besiegement of Jerusalem by Babylon in 587 BC. In this time of national crisis brought about by Judah's disobedience (Jer. 32:23), God instructed Jeremiah to purchase a field from his cousin, Hanameel (Jer. 32:6-8). Jeremiah paid Hanameel seventeen shekels of silver for the field and gave both the sealed purchase deed and the open deed to his assistant, Baruch (Jer. 32:9-12). Knowing that Babylonian domination would continue for about five decades longer, Jeremiah charged Baruch with ensuring the preservation of the title deeds by putting them in a place where "they may last many days" (Jer. 32:14). Through this act, God affirmed that, following a period of exile, the people of Judah would return to their land (Jer. 32:42-44).

Land redemption principles not only governed the land of Israel but also reflect larger truths. Showers writes,

> In the same manner that an Israelite lost tenant possession or administration of his land inheritance to another person because of mismanagement or, as in the case of the whole nation, to foreign usurpers, because of rebellion against God (Lam. 5:2), there is a genuine sense in which mankind forfeited tenant possession or administration of their earth inheritance to Satan because they followed Satan's lead to rebel against God (Gen. 3).
>
> As a result of getting the first man, Adam, to join his revolt against God, Satan usurped tenant possession of the earth away from its original tenant and has been exercising administrative control of the world system against God ever

since.... Several things indicate that this is so. For example, Satan had the authority to offer Jesus all the power and glory of the kingdoms of the world (Lk. 4:5-6); Satan declared that it had been delivered (perfect passive verb) to him by someone else (Adam, Lk. 4:6); Jesus called Satan "the prince of this world" (Jn. 12:31; 14:30; 16:11); and Paul called him "the god of this age" (2 Cor. 4:4).[171]

Satan's rule over the world is prominently on display in Revelation, and so is this usurper's defeat. The relationship between God's land redemption program for Israel and His program to end Satan's illegitimate rule is a fascinating study.

Christ as Kinsman-Redeemer in Revelation

At the cross, Christ won a multifaceted victory. Much attention is rightly given to the great salvation truths of propitiation, justification, and redemption. Another aspect is Christ's defeat of Satan (Heb. 2:14). Satan's defeat is clearly seen in Revelation where Christ fulfills the role of humanity's Kinsman-Redeemer in accordance with the Mosaic land redemption program. Showers writes,

> Just as God intended each Israelite tenant inheritance to remain forever the possession of the tribe to which it was given originally, so He intended the tenant inheritance of the earth to remain forever the possession of mankind to whom it was given originally. Thus, parallel to the fact that an Israelite was forbidden to lose his tenant possession inheritance to a person outside his tribe is the fact that it was wrong for mankind to forfeit their tenant possession inheritance to a being outside mankind. But they did forfeit their tenant possession inheritance to Satan, a being outside mankind...

RESCUE FROM DEATH

Just as land redemption in Israel involved two significant responsibilities for the kinsman-redeemer, so the redemption of the earth involves the same two responsibilities for Christ, mankind's Kinsman-Redeemer. First, He had to pay the redemption price for the earth and thereby obtain the right of tenant possession. Second, now that Christ has obtained that right, He must take actual possession of the earth and exercise administrative control over it as the last Adam, God's representative....

Christ defeated Satan and his forces when He paid the redemption price of His shed blood. Through the payment of that price, Christ defeated Satan and his forces in the sense that He gained the right to take tenant possession of the earth away from them and rule the earth as the last Adam. This truth sheds light on the meaning of Christ's statement just before He went to the cross, "the prince of this world is judged" (Jn. 16:11). Christ's death sealed Satan's doom. At the proper time, determined sovereignly by God, Christ will exercise the right He gained at the cross to throw out the usurper....

The Scriptures indicate that Satan and his forces will challenge Christ's right to take tenant possession of the earth as the time of His return draws near. Since Christ will take actual possession of the earth in conjunction with His Second Coming immediately after the end of the 70th week and the Great Tribulation, Satan and his forces will issue their challenge during the 70th week (the last seven years before Christ takes possession). That challenge will involve strong, deceptive, violent action. For example, Satan and his forces will wage war against those who testify for Christ and the Word of God during the 70th week (Dan. 7:21-22, 25-27; Rev. 6:9-11; 11:3-10; 13:7)....

Since Christ will not crush Satan and his forces and take possession of the earth until the nation of Israel repents (Zech. 12-14; Acts 3:12, 19-21), during the 70th week Satan and his forces will exert great effort to annihilate Israel before it can repent (Dan. 9:27; Mt. 24:15-16; Rev. 12:7-17)....

By the end of the 70th week, Satan and his forces will have drawn all the rulers and armies of the world into the land of Israel for the battle of Armageddon (Rev. 16:12-16), which will take place at Christ's Second Coming and will pit Satan and his ungodly allies against Christ and His forces (Rev. 19:11-20:3). This will be Satan's ultimate challenge to Christ's right to take tenant possession of the earth and rule it. The combined military might of rebellious mankind will be gathered to the precise location to which Christ will return to take possession of the earth, because Satan will want all the help he can get to try to prevent Christ from exercising His right (Ps. 2:1-3).

Just as a challenge to an Israelite kinsman-redeemer's right of tenant possession of land in such a situation required the kinsman-redeemer to provide irrefutable evidence of his right of tenant possession before he took actual possession of the land, so Satan's challenge to Christ's Kinsman-Redeemer right of tenant possession of the earth will require Christ to provide irrefutable evidence of His right of tenant possession before He takes actual possession of the earth at His Second Coming.

The Israelite kinsman-redeemer's irrefutable evidence consisted of his taking the sealed deed of purchase from its secure place, breaking its seal or seals, opening it, and reading its contents publicly. In like manner, Christ's irrefutable evidence will consist of His taking the sealed deed of purchase of the earth from its secure place (God's right hand), breaking its seven seals, opening it, and looking at its contents (for the purpose of reading publicly)....

Just as an armed force will attack an alien occupying army with a tremendous bombardment before it launches the invasion that will evict that alien army, so Christ, through the breaking of the seals, will attack the domain of Satan and his forces (the alien forces occupying the earth since the fall of mankind) with a tremendous bombardment of divine wrath or judgment before He launches the invasion (His great and terrible Day of the Lord invasion of the earth when

He comes with His angels), which will evict Satan and his forces from the earth.

The fact that Satan and his forces will be incapable of stopping this bombardment of their domain will prove that they are not the ultimate authority over the earth. In addition, this bombardment, instigated by Christ through the breaking of the seals, will demonstrate not only that He has power and authority to fulfill the second responsibility of the Kinsman-Redeemer (the taking of tenant possession by eviction of the usurper) but also is preparing to do so.[172]

Ironside agrees with this conclusion:

> The seven-sealed book in the Revelation… is unquestionably the title-deed to this world. It remains sealed till the rightful Heir steps forth to claim it. He, the worthy One, has first to purge His heritage by judgment, before entering into possession of it. The opening of the seals is the declaration that He is about to enter into His vested rights.[173]

With Israel back in her homeland and other world developments setting the stage for Christ's prophesied Messianic return to the earth, taking a futuristic view of Revelation is now relatively common, but Ironside wrote in 1906. Like Jeremiah, he took God at His Word even though supporting circumstances were lacking.[174]

Finally, it is important to note that while Israel was given a specific land "forever" (Gen. 13:15), the context of God's promise is the present creation, not the eternal state. The entire earth is going to be utterly destroyed by fire and replaced with a new earth (2 Pet. 3:10-13). This takes place *after* God fulfills His Messianic promises during Christ's thousand-year reign with His redeemed saints (Rev. 20:4-6). In the new earth (Rev. 21:1), all things are made new (Rev. 21:5).

With this basic overview of the Book of Revelation, let us investigate the proof text that some feel is actually traditionalism's strongest.

REVELATION 14:9-11

> Then a third angel followed them, saying with a loud voice, "If anyone *worships the beast and his image*, and *receives his mark on his forehead* or *on his hand*, he himself shall also drink of the wine of the wrath of God, which is poured out full strength into the cup of His indignation. And *he* shall be tormented with fire and brimstone in the presence of the holy angels and in the presence of the Lamb. And the *smoke* of their torment *ascends* forever and ever [*eis aionas aionon*]; and they have no rest day or night, *who worship the beast and his image*, and *whoever receives the mark of his name*."

God's wrath in Revelation 14:9-11 is explicitly toward those who worship the beast and receive his mark on the forehead or hand. By beginning and ending with this fact, the passage emphasizes that the wrath in question applies to a very specific group of sinners. We are also dealing with a restricted time frame. Worshipping the beast and receiving his mark on the forehead or hand is a possibility only during the forty-two months of the Great Tribulation (Rev. 13:5, 11-18). The uniqueness of this moment is reinforced by the immediate context to which we now turn.

THE FIVE ANGELS OF REVELATION 14: THE IMMEDIATE CONTEXT

The warning against worshipping the beast is located in the midst of a series of angelic utterances. Five angels speak in Revelation 14, one after another.

First, in Revelation 14:6-7, John sees a *flying angel* preaching a message for the entire world: "Fear God and give glory to Him, for the hour of His judgment has come; and worship Him who made heaven and earth, the sea and springs of water."

To what judgment does the flying angel refer? Peterson believes the final judgment is in view:

> The angel who flies in midair announces, "Fear God and give him glory, because the hour of his judgment has come" (Rev 14:7). This refers to the Last Judgment, because the punishment of the wicked described three verses later lasts forever: "The smoke of their torment rises for ever and ever. There is no rest day or night" (v. 11).[175]

There is a key discrepancy, however, between the final judgment in the Bible and the message of the first angel. In Revelation 20:11-15, those who stand before God's Great White Throne are judged to demonstrate that they deserve to be cast into the lake of fire. In stark contrast, the angel in Revelation 14:6-7 presents an opportunity for salvation. The angel flies in midair, "having the *everlasting gospel* to preach to those who dwell *on the earth*—to every nation, tribe, tongue, and people" (14:6), calling people to "worship Him who made heaven and earth, the sea and springs of water" (14:7).[176] Ryrie states, "The message of this gospel is to all the world. It is God's last call of grace to a world that persists in rejecting Him and that openly defies Him."[177] Ironside writes,

> It is mercy indeed, to God's creatures everywhere, that in that hour of judgment, before the last blow falls, the call will still go forth to men everywhere to own the claims of the Omnipotent One whose mercies have been rejected so long.[178]

Thomas comments on Revelation 14:7:

> This is the very last chance to change allegiance to the God of heaven....
>
> The final command of the angelic gospel calls for the worship of the Creator. He who created all things has the right to expect worship as He has the right to judge what He has created (4:10; 10:6; cf. Acts 4:24; 14:15-17). This description of the Creator alludes to Neh. 9:6 and Ps. 33:6-9 (cf. Ps. 146:6) and is an appropriate appeal to natural theology with a worldwide audience... (Swete, Moffatt, Beckwith, Charles, Lenski).[179]

At present, the angel of Revelation 14:6-7 is not preaching "to every nation, tribe, tongue, and people" nor does the angel's message fit the conditions of the Messianic millennium or the new earth. Futurists have long maintained that the angelic preaching of Revelation 14:6-7 is an event exclusive to the Tribulation preceding Christ's return.

A *second angel* announces the fall of Babylon in Revelation 14:8. This angelic proclamation is also fulfilled during the Tribulation (Rev. 16:19, 17:1-19:3).

The *third angel* warns against worshipping the beast and receiving his mark on the forehead or hand. Those who follow the beast will reap the wrath of God. *When, where, and how long this wrath occurs is the focus of our present investigation.*

A *fourth angel* cries in a loud voice to One like the Son of Man (seated on a white cloud), "Thrust in Your sickle and reap, for the time has come for You to reap, for the harvest of the earth is ripe" (Rev. 14:15). In response, "He who sat on the cloud thrust in His sickle on the earth, and the earth was reaped" (Rev. 14:16).

A *fifth angel* cries out to an angel with a sharp sickle (introduced in Rev. 14:17) to "thrust in your sharp sickle and gather the clusters of the vine of the earth, for her grapes are fully ripe" (Rev. 14:18). The angel throws the harvested vine of the earth into the great winepress of the wrath of God, and blood flows for a distance of about 184 miles (Rev. 14:19-20).

The fourth and fifth angels also speak of judgment that finds its fulfillment on earth, this time at the return of Christ (Rev. 19:11-21).

In Revelation 14, then, we find a series of angels speaking about judgment. The first, second, fourth, and fifth angels tell of judgment that begins and ends on earth. Because consistency points to the third angel's judgment also being temporal, let's outline the passage and investigate whether or not there is a correlation between Revelation 14:9-11 and the events of the Great Tribulation.

OUTLINE OF THE PASSAGE

I see the passage break down in the following way:

VERSE 9 *sets the stage:* Then a third angel followed them, saying with a loud voice, "If anyone worships the beast and his image, and receives his mark on his forehead or on his hand"

VERSE 10A *is a broad picture of wrath:* "he himself shall also drink of the wine of the wrath of God, which is poured out full strength into the cup of His indignation."

VERSES 10B and 11A *spotlight a specific aspect of wrath:* "And he shall be tormented with fire and brimstone in the presence of the holy angels and in the presence of the Lamb. And the smoke of their torment ascends forever and ever;"

VERSE 11B *is a broad summary statement:* "and they have no rest day or night, who worship the beast and his image, and whoever receives the mark of his name."

REVELATION 14:9-11 AND THE EVENTS OF THE GREAT TRIBULATION

First, there is a thematic match between the third angel's message and the Great Tribulation. The third angel warns of the wrath of God, which is the implicit theme of the trumpet judgments and the explicit theme of the bowl judgments.

> Then I saw another sign in heaven, great and marvelous: *seven angels* having the *seven last plagues,* for *in them* the *wrath of God* is complete. (Rev. 15:1)

> Then I heard a loud voice from the temple saying to the *seven angels*, "Go and *pour out the bowls* of the *wrath of God* on the earth." (Rev. 16:1)

Second, fire and brimstone are key aspects of the third angel's message and God's Great Tribulation fury. The Great Tribulation begins and ends with judgment by fire. Fire plays a prominent role in the *first trumpet judgment*, burning up a third of the trees and all green grass (8:7). The *second trumpet* involves "something like a great mountain burning with fire" (8:8). The *third trumpet* sounds, and "a great star fell from heaven, burning like a torch" (8:10). Brimstone (sulfur) is not mentioned, but it is integral to events such as forest fires and volcanoes. We also know that the sun and other stars contain sulfur. Thus, it seems that fire and sulfur are present in the first three trumpet judgments. The *fourth trumpet* results in a one-third reduction of light from the sun, moon, and stars (8:12). The *fifth trumpet* brings five months of torment to those "who do not have the seal of God" via demonic locust beings (9:1-12). Fire, smoke, and brimstone are explicitly named in the *sixth trumpet* judgment (9:17). This wrath is so intense that a third of humankind will die (9:18).

In the *bowl judgments*, "a foul and loathsome sore" comes "upon the men who had the mark of the beast and those who worshiped his image" (16:2), waters are turned to blood to punish those who "have shed the blood of saints and prophets" (16:4-6), fierce heat scorches the impenitent (16:9), and painful darkness, reminiscent of the ninth Mosaic plague, afflicts the beast's kingdom (16:10; cf. Exod. 10:21). The final bowl is undoubtedly poured out just prior to Christ's return and includes the fact that "great Babylon was remembered before God, to give her the cup of the wine of the fierceness of His wrath" (Rev. 16:19). The inclusion of the fall of Babylon in the final bowl is significant because the judgment of Babylon explicitly involves not only torment and destruction by fire (Rev. 18:8-10, 15-21) but also smoke that rises "forever and ever" (Rev. 19:3).

Third, it makes sense that smoke would rise continually while judgments involving fire and sulfur bring pain and suffering to beast worshippers during the Great Tribulation. How smoke would "ascend" within a lake of fire, however, is unclear.

Fourth, the third angel states that torment by fire and brimstone takes place "in the presence of the holy angels and in the presence of the Lamb." The connection between the torment of the rebellious during the Great Tribulation and the holy angels is clear and undeniable. The trumpets are sounded by holy angels, and the bowls are poured out by holy angels. In contrast, the idea that holy angels are eternally associated with the torment of sinners lacks biblical support.

Because the holy angels who sound the trumpets and pour out the bowls serve the Lamb, Christ's participation in the wrath that falls on beast worshippers during the Great Tribulation is easy to grasp. The thought of the holy angels and Jesus eternally watching human beings suffer is difficult to envision. Even more incomprehensible is the traditionalist view that Christ will eternally reside in the lake of fire. Peterson writes,

> Furthermore, hell's torment takes place "in the presence of the holy angels and of the Lamb" (Rev 14:10). Although not many Christians conceive of Christ's being present in hell, he is there, as the word *Lamb* suggests. In fact, in twenty-seven

of the twenty-eight times that John uses the word *lamb* in Revelation, it is a symbol denoting Christ (in Rev 13:11 it occurs in a simile). However, Christ does not bring grace and peace to hell, but "the wrath of the Lamb" (6:16).[180]

Fifth, God's wrath is relentless in the third angel's message: "And they have no rest day or night, who worship the beast and his image, and whoever receives the mark of his name" (Rev. 14:11b). Similarly, the trumpet and bowl judgments ensure wave after wave of tribulation for beast worshippers. The relentlessness of God's wrath in the Great Tribulation is perhaps best captured by the Bible's birth-pangs metaphor. Showers writes,

> Christ referred to "the beginning of sorrows" (lit., "the beginning of birth pangs," Mt. 24:8). The fact that He called these "the *beginning* of birth pangs" indicates that more birth pangs would follow them....
>
> Just as a woman's beginning, less severe birth pangs precede her later, most severe pangs of hard labor, so the beginning, less severe pangs of the world's future time of trouble must precede its later, most severe pangs of hard labor....
>
> The beginning, less severe birth pangs will be in the first half of the 70th week; the later, most severe pangs will occur in the second half.[181]

Mark Robinson states,

> The judgments of the Tribulation period will come with increasing rapidity and harshness as the period progresses, in the same way that birth pains come increasingly faster and are more painful just prior to birth.
>
> Revelation chapters 6 to 19 show this reality unfolding as the seal, trumpet, and bowl judgments are unleashed, in all their fury, upon the world.[182]

Like a woman in labor prior to giving birth, those who worship the beast and take his mark will have no relief from God's wrath during the Great Tribulation.

Unfortunately, the correlation between the third angel's message and the Great Tribulation is rarely acknowledged. Though futuristic traditionalists recognize the Great Tribulation setting of Revelation 14, verses 9-11 (much like Isaiah 66:24) are typically assumed to describe eternal torment in the lake of fire. A key supporting factor for both amillennial and premillennial traditionalists is the Greek phrase *eis aionas aionon*, "forever and ever."

DOES "FOREVER AND EVER" NECESSARILY DENOTE ETERNITY?

Peterson writes, "The expression 'for ever and ever' occurs thirteen times in Revelation and each time denotes eternity."[183] Usually, "forever and ever" does involve eternity in the Book of Revelation. This is because the phrase is primarily linked to the eternal Creator. In Revelation 5:13, for example, we read, "To him who sits on the throne and to the Lamb be praise and honor and glory and power, for ever and ever!" (NIV). But must "forever and ever" always encompass eternity?

Eis aionas aionon is literally "to ages of ages." W. E. Vine states that the various "forever and ever" phrases formed in connection with *aion*, an age, such as *eis aionas aionon*, "are idiomatic expressions betokening undefined periods."[184] Gregory Beale, who wrote the chapter "The Revelation on Hell" in *Hell under*

Fire, acknowledges that *forever and ever* is a "temporal phrase" and affirms that whether or not eternity is in view depends on the "context of the passage and of the book."[185] Taken together, these traditionalist scholars inform us that *forever and ever* is an undefined period, the duration of which is contextually determined. If this is correct, then the many examples of forever and ever linked to our eternal God do not determine the meaning of forever and ever in Revelation 14:11. Every instance of the phrase must be considered in its own context.

The common characteristic of the "forever and ever" passages seems to be that something is constant. Praise and honor and glory and power continually, *always*, belong to God. Regarding the smoke that *anabaino* "ascends" forever and ever in Revelation 14:11, Greek scholar Fritz Rienecker notes, "pres. act. ind. [present active indicative] to go up, to ascend. The pres. tense connected w. the temporal designation 'forever' indicates a continual unbroken action."[186] The devil, the beast, and the false prophet will experience torment *day and night*. Moreover, quite interestingly, the origin of *aion* is thought to be a word meaning "continued *duration*."[187]

In assessing the possibility that *eis aionas aionon* in Revelation 14:11 allows for the view that smoke ascends continually from fire and brimstone judgments that torment beast worshippers during the Great Tribulation, any other examples of "forever and ever" linked to rising smoke would be of the utmost importance. We have such an instance in Revelation 19:3.

Does the smoke rising "forever and ever" from fallen Babylon rise eternally?

HER SMOKE RISES FOREVER AND EVER

The fall of Babylon is declared by an angel in Revelation 14:8. The outworking of this terrible judgment is depicted as part of the seventh bowl of wrath in Revelation 16:19. Revelation 17:1–19:3 give full coverage of the judgment of Babylon, the great harlot, declaring her final and complete destruction and the smoke that rises up "forever and ever." How the details of this prophecy will exactly play out, however, is difficult to discern. Is the destruction of Babylon in Revelation 17 and 18 the same event? This is but one question for which there is no consensus.

While the jury is still out on how all the pieces of Revelation fit together, it seems plain enough that in Revelation 18, a literal city burns until it is no more. Here is part of the revelation given to John:

> In the measure that she glorified herself and lived luxuriously, in the same measure give her torment and sorrow; for she says in her heart, "I sit as queen, and am no widow, and will not see sorrow." Therefore her plagues will come in one day—death and mourning and famine. And *she will be utterly burned with fire*, for strong is the Lord God who judges her. And the kings of the earth who committed fornication and lived luxuriously with her will weep and lament for her, when they see *the smoke of her burning*, standing at a distance for fear of her *torment*, saying, "Alas, alas, *that great city Babylon*, that *mighty city*! For in one hour your judgment has come." (18:7-10)

> And every shipmaster, all who travel by ship, sailors, and as many as trade on the sea, stood at a distance and cried out when they saw *the smoke of her burning* (18:17b-18a)

> Then a mighty angel took up a stone like a great millstone and threw it into the sea, saying, "Thus with violence *the great city* Babylon shall be thrown down, and *shall not be found anymore.*" (18:21)

This revelation is in keeping with Isaiah's prophecy that Babylon would be "as when God overthrew Sodom and Gomorrah" (Isa. 13:19). As Abraham looked toward the cities of Sodom and Gomorrah and saw "the smoke of the land which went up like the smoke of a furnace" (Gen. 19:28), eyewitnesses substantiate the literalness of Babylon's burning (Rev. 18:9, 17-18). The smoke rising from the city of Babylon at the end of the Great Tribulation, which confirmed the termination of the great harlot who shed the blood of prophets and saints, is cause for rejoicing in heaven:

> After these things I heard a loud voice of a great multitude in heaven, saying, "Alleluia! Salvation and glory and honor and power belong to the Lord our God! For true and righteous are His judgments, because He has judged the great harlot who corrupted the earth with her fornication; and He has avenged on her the blood of His servants shed by her." Again they said, "Alleluia! Her *smoke rises up forever and ever!*" (Rev. 19:1-3)

Charles H. Dyer writes,

> John summarizes heaven's response to Babylon's fall in Revelation 19:1-3. In this heavenly "Hallelujah Chorus," the multitude in heaven praise God because "He has condemned the great prostitute" (19:2). John described Babylon as a prostitute in chapter 17. The multitude continue to praise God as they shout, "Hallelujah! The smoke from her goes up for ever and ever" (19:3). The "smoke" that "goes up forever" pictures the burning of Babylon described in chapter 18.[188]

The smoke that causes the kings of the earth, shipmasters, and sailors to mourn in Revelation 18 is said, in Revelation 19:3, to rise *eis tous aionas ton aionon*—"to the ages of the ages"—yet the smoke resulting from the destruction of the city of Babylon during the Tribulation will surely not rise endlessly. Surely, it will not cloud the renewed earth during the Messianic millennial reign of Christ (Rev. 20:4-6) or pollute the new earth (Rev. 21:1). Thus, it appears that Vine and Beale are correct that "forever and ever" does not necessarily denote eternity but requires contextual verification as to the time frame involved.

The smoke of Revelation 19:3 may not rise eternally, but we can expect it to rise continually while Babylon burns. With this fresh reminder of the importance of context, let us review the setting, which holds the key to understanding the judgment of the beast's followers in Revelation 14:9-11.

THE MESSAGE OF REVELATION 14:9-11

During the Great Tribulation, the world is a giant pressure cooker under the reign of the satanic trinity. The beast with two horns (Rev. 13:11) has power to kill those who refuse to bow to the image of the beast whose death wound was healed (Rev. 13:12-15). He also denies the right to engage in commerce to any refusing to take the mark of beast (Rev. 13:17). The pressure from the beasts of Revelation 13 is immediate and intense to life and livelihood.

At such a time as this, God provides a counterbalance to Satan's tyranny: Those who take the mark of the beast to avoid the satanic trinity's wrath must instead bear the wrath of the Lord. Unleashing devastation and torment and death on the earth—one trumpet sounds after another. One by one, the bowls of the wrath of God are poured out. In the Great Tribulation, "they have no respite day and night who do homage to the beast and to its image, and if any one receive the mark of its name" (Rev. 14:11b, Darby Translation).

Traditionalists look to Revelation 14:9-11 to determine what happens to those cast into the lake of fire; however, the third angel's message best fits the Great Tribulation on earth. To overlook this is to miss the third angel's contribution to the trumpet and bowl judgments.

The choice set before the world during the Great Tribulation is hard-lined: Worship the beast or worship "Him who made heaven and earth, the sea and springs of water" (Rev. 14:7). Sadly, many will bow to the beast, but that choice will not be made in the face of intense tangible pressure from one side only. Revelation 14:9-11 promises not ECT beyond the grave but relentless wrath and suffering *on earth* for those who reject God.

REVELATION 20:10

> And the *devil*, who deceived them, was cast into the lake of fire and brimstone where the beast and the false prophet are. And they will be tormented day and night forever and ever.

Satan is a major figure in the Bible, and his casting into the lake of fire is an important event. The NIV does a good job here by correctly translating the elided Greek verb: "And the devil... was thrown into the lake... where the beast and the false prophet *had been thrown.*"

Evil must be judged, and there is no greater evil in the universe than Satan. Inasmuch as Satan, the beast, and the false prophet forcibly lead the world away from God, it is especially appropriate that this unholy trio suffer without respite in the lake of fire while unsaved men and women appear before God's Great White Throne for final judgment.

Is there more to Revelation 20:10 than this? Does this verse about the devil and his cohorts teach that human beings who fail to believe in Christ will experience unrelenting torment throughout eternity?

If we are to understand John's vision, we need an accurate assessment of the devil, the beast, and false prophet. Few question the identity of the devil, but the beast like a leopard with feet like a bear and a mouth like that of a lion, this creature with seven heads and ten horns that John saw in the lake of fire (Rev. 13:1-7, 16:13-14, 19:19-20)—who is this?

RESCUE FROM DEATH

THE IDENTITY OF THE BEAST

The Daniel—Revelation Connection

We begin our investigation in Daniel, the prophetic key to the Book of Revelation. Previously, in Chapter 4, we saw that the great image in Daniel 2 pictured four great empires: Babylon (head of gold), Medo-Persia (chest and arms of silver), Greece (belly and thighs of bronze) and the iron kingdom of Rome. The Stone struck the great image on its feet of iron and clay, completely destroying the entire image, no trace of which was to be found. This must yet be in the future because the smiting Stone (Christ) both consumes the kingdoms of this world and fills the whole earth with His righteous reign (Dan. 2:35, 44).

In Daniel 2, it is the pagan king Nebuchadnezzar who had a dream in which Gentile empires were represented by a great image of excellent splendor. In Daniel 7, a man of God, Daniel, dreams and sees these same empires as beasts.[189] The first beast was like a lion, the second like a bear, and the third like a leopard. Daniel tells us that the *dominion* of the lion (Babylon), bear (Medo-Persia), and leopard (Greece) were taken away; nevertheless, in some sense, "their lives were prolonged for a season and a time" (7:12). It seems that some aspect of each kingdom continued on in the fourth beast. Utter extinction (no trace left) of these kingdoms will not come until the final stage of the iron empire is judged (Dan. 2:41-44, 7:24-27).

Daniel 7 builds on Daniel 2 and helps set the stage for the Book of Revelation. In Daniel 7, a "little horn," with eyes like the eyes of a man, comes up among the ten horns of the fourth beast, subdues three, speaks pompous words, is greater in appearance than his fellow horns, and exercises dominion (7:8, 20, 25). When the dominion of the little horn is taken away (Dan. 7:26), the everlasting kingdom of the Most High will be given to the saints and all will serve God (Dan. 7:27). Thus, the little horn is the ruler who is defeated at Christ's Second Coming.

Like the beasts of Daniel 7, the beast of Revelation rises up out of the sea (Dan. 7:3; Rev. 13:1). The beast John saw is described in Revelation 13:2 as a composite of leopard (body), bear (feet), and lion (mouth). This can hardly be a coincidence. Nor can it be missed that Daniel's fourth beast and Revelation's beast both have ten horns (Dan. 7:7; Rev. 13:1). Moreover, in Daniel and Revelation the ten horns are ten kings (Dan. 7:24; Rev. 17:12). Clearly, Revelation is continuing the end-time message found in Daniel.

The Seven Heads of the Beast

What about the seven heads of the Revelation beast? The sevens heads are said to be seven mountains (Rev. 17:9) and are also seven kings (Rev. 17:10). This is consistent with the principle seen in Daniel 2, where the head of gold of the great image represented both an empire (Babylon) and its leader (Nebuchadnezzar). The connection between the seven mountains in Revelation 17 and the empires found in Daniel is well stated by Joseph A. Seiss:

> A *mountain*, or prominent elevation on the surface of the earth, is one of the common scriptural images, symbols, or representatives of a kingdom, regal dominion, empire, or established authority....

Of these seven regal mountains, John was told *"the five are fallen,"* dead, passed away, their day over; *"the one is,"* that is, was standing, at that moment, was then in sway and power; *"the other is not yet come, and when he shall come, he must continue a little time."* What regal mountain, then, was in power at the time John wrote? There can be no question on that point; it was the Roman empire.... Of the same class with this, and belonging to the same category, there are five others—five which had then already run their course and passed away. But what five imperial mountains like Rome had been and gone, up to that time? Is history so obscure as not to tell us with unmistakable certainty? Preceding Rome the world had but five great names or nationalities answering to imperial Rome, and those scarce a schoolboy ought to miss. They are Greece, Persia, Babylon, Assyria, and Egypt; no more, and no less. And these all were imperial powers like Rome.... Thus, then, by the clearest, most direct, and most natural signification of the words of the record, we are brought to the identification of these seven mountain kings as the seven great world-powers, which stretch from the beginning of our present world to the end of it. Daniel makes the number less; but he started with his own times, and looked only down the stream. Here the account looks backward as well as forward. That which is first in Daniel is the third here, and that which is the sixth here is the fourth in Daniel. Only in the commencing point is there any difference.[190]

If these Revelation 17 mountains overlap the empires found in Daniel as indicated by Seiss, then the *seventh kingdom* in Revelation 17, the *one yet to come*, must be the prophesied iron and clay ten nation confederation and its leader, the little horn of Daniel 7. That the little horn is one of the seven heads will prove vital to understanding the beast.

One of the Seven and Also an Eighth

The beast of Revelation is not only one of the seven kings; he is also an eighth king: "The beast that was, and is not, is himself an eighth king and yet is one of the seven" (Rev. 17:11, NET). For this understanding to be fulfilled, the beast must rule *twice*. We turn again to the Book of Daniel to discover the two distinct periods in which the beast will rule.

The Seventieth Week of Daniel

Daniel 9:24-27 is one of the most important passages in prophetic scripture. We will touch on key points historically held by futurists to identify the two periods in which the beast rules. The angel Gabriel declared to Daniel:

> Seventy weeks are determined
> For your people and for your holy city,
> To finish the transgression,
> To make an end of sins,
> To make reconciliation for iniquity,
> To bring in everlasting righteousness,
> To seal up vision and prophecy,
> And to anoint the Most Holy. (9:24)

"Seventy weeks" is literally *seventy sevens*. That is, seventy units of seven have been decreed for Israel and Jerusalem (Daniel's people and holy city). By the end of the seventy sevens, several things will have been accomplished. One significant accomplishment is the establishment of everlasting righteousness. This is in keeping with the prophetic dreams in Daniel 2 and 7 that culminate with God's righteous kingdom ruling the earth.

> Know therefore and understand,
> That from the going forth of the command
> To restore and build Jerusalem
> Until Messiah the Prince,
> There shall be seven weeks and sixty-two weeks;
> The street shall be built again, and the wall,
> Even in troublesome times. (9:25)

A starting and ending point is cited for 69 (7 + 62) of the sevens. The starting point is the command to restore and rebuild Jerusalem. Sixty-nine "sevens" later brings us to the Messiah. This is an amazing Christological prophecy. In 444 BC, King Artaxerxes issued a decree that empowered Nehemiah to rebuild Jerusalem (Neh. 2:1-8). Fast forward 483 years (sixty-nine units of seven years), and we are in the days when Jesus traveled the dusty roads of Israel. In fact, using the biblical 360-day year, it has been calculated that sixty-nine sevens takes us to the triumphal entry of Christ into Jerusalem.[191] This stunning prophetic witness to Jesus as Israel's Messiah, establishes that *each "seven" is a period of 7 years*. Thus, the seventy weeks equal a total of 490 years.

> Then after the sixty-two weeks the Messiah will be cut off and have nothing, and the people of the prince who is to come will destroy the city and the sanctuary. And its end will come with a flood; even to the end there will be war; desolations are determined. (9:26, NASB)

After the 7 + 62 sevens brings us to the Messiah, two major events will take place: (1) the Messiah will be cut off ("suffer the death penalty," NKJV explanatory note); (2) the city of Jerusalem and its temple will be destroyed (which happened in 70 AD). These two events take place in a *time gap* between the sixty-nine sevens and the seventieth seven. *Without a time break*, the 490 years would have ended no later than 40 AD, thirty years *prior* to the destruction of Jerusalem and the temple.

We also learn that it is the people of the prince to come (i.e., the people "from whom will come" a prince)[192] who destroy the city and sanctuary. This, of course, was done by the Roman Empire. The diverse ethnic composition of the historic Roman military complex, however, should temper attempts to prematurely surmise the prince's nationality.

> And he will make a firm covenant with the many for one week, but in the middle of the week he will put a stop to sacrifice and grain offering; and on the wing of abominations will come one who makes desolate, even until a complete destruction, one that is decreed, is poured out on the one who makes desolate. (9:27, NASB)

The prince who is to come (9:26) is the closest antecedent of *he* in 9:27; moreover, Jesus did not make a seven-year covenant. The *many* would be the people of Israel, as the prophecy is explicitly about Israel and Jerusalem (9:24). Thus, a prince to come, out of the people that destroyed Jerusalem and the temple, makes a covenant with Israel that initiates the final seven years prophesied by Gabriel.

In the middle of the seventieth week, the prince to come will bring an end to sacrifice and offering. In order for sacrifice and offering to be put to a stop, they must first begin. This in turn suggests a temple, which Paul and John confirm will exist in the end-times (2 Thess. 2; Rev. 11). It is likely that the treaty between the coming prince and Israel enables the rebuilding of the temple in Jerusalem and reinstitution of the Mosaic sacrificial traditions. During the first half of the seventieth week, Israel appears to be under the coming prince's protection.

Three and a half years into the treaty, the middle of the week, not only are Jewish sacrifice and offering stopped, but the prince to come "will set up an abomination that causes desolation" (9:27, NIV). Jesus warned those in Judea to flee to the mountains when they see the abomination of desolation (spoken of by Daniel the prophet) standing in the holy place because it would be the start of unprecedented tribulation (Matt. 24:15-21). This tribulation is followed by Christ's return to establish His kingdom on earth (Matt. 24:30, 25:31). During the second half of the seventieth week, the prince to come will persecute Israel.

The Two Periods of the Beast's Rule

The two forty-two month periods that comprise the seventieth week of Daniel 9 provide two distinct opportunities for the beast to rule. In the first forty-two month period, the beast, who heads a ten nation confederation, rules as the seventh king in Revelation 17, the one who "has not yet come" (v. 10). Subsequently, the beast rules as the eighth king during the forty-two months of the Great Tribulation (Rev. 17:11, 13:5). The transition from seventh king to eighth king is consistent with the beast's transition from a regional authority (during the first half of the seventieth week) to a global authority (during the second half of the seventieth week). Global authority comes to the beast from Satan, "the ruler of this world" (John 14:30). "And the dragon gave him his power, his throne, and great authority.... he was given authority to continue for forty-two months... authority was given to him over every tribe, tongue, and nation" (Rev. 13:2-7).

The Revealing of the Man of Sin

A comparison of the little horn in Daniel 7, the prince in Daniel 9, and the beast of Revelation indicates that the same individual is in view. All three have a rule of forty-two months in which God's people are persecuted (Dan. 7:25 w/ Rev. 12:6, 14; Dan. 9:27; Rev. 13:5, 7). All three are defeated, and subsequently, Christ establishes his reign of righteousness on earth (Dan. 7:26-27; Dan. 9:24, 27 w/Matt. 24:15, 30, 25:31; Rev. 19:19-21, 20:4). This evil end-time ruler is commonly referred to by the title Antichrist. Ryrie states,

> The term "antichrist" is a biblical one (1 John 2:18, 22, 4:3; 2 John 7). It is used both of false teachers in John's day (and by example it may be used of false teachers in any day) and of the coming Antichrist. In other words, the word is properly used in both the present and future and in both the singular and plural....
> The Lord predicted that there would be many false prophets and many who claim to be Christ during the tribulation days (Matt. 24:11, 23-24). The title "Antichrist," therefore, ought to be applied to the outstanding person among all these false people, and that is the first Beast [Rev. 13:1].[193]

Paul refers to Antichrist as the "man of sin." Paul assured the Thessalonians that the Day of the Lord would not begin before the man of sin was revealed (2 Thess. 2:2-3). Paul goes on to say that the man of sin "opposes and exalts himself above all that is called God or that is worshiped, so that he sits as God in the temple of God, showing himself that he is God" (2 Thess. 2:4). This passage has left some with the impression that the man of sin is revealed when Antichrist sits in the temple as if he were God. The man of sin is revealed, however, prior to this mid-Tribulation event. Showers writes,

> In the Scriptures, God has revealed other activities of the man of sin that will precede his declaration to be God and reveal who he is at least three and one-half years before that declaration. First, the man of sin will rise to power as the 11th ruler within the already formed ten-division confederation that will constitute the revived Roman Empire (Dan. 7:7-8, 20, 23-24). Second, as the man of sin rises to power, he will overthrow three of the original ten rulers of the revived Roman Empire (Dan. 7:8, 20, 24).... Fourth, as the dominant ruler of the revived Roman Empire, the man of sin will establish a seven-year covenant of peace with the nation of Israel, and the establishment of the covenant will be the historic starting point of the 70th week (Dan. 9:27)....
>
> Since these divinely foretold activities will reveal who the man of sin is, and since they will be performed by the beginning of the 70th week, we can conclude that the man of sin will be revealed by the beginning of the 70th week.[194]

Although most of Antichrist's activities in the Book of Revelation understandably occur during the second half of the Tribulation, he is seen in the first half of the tribulation as one who goes out conquering (Rev. 6:1-2). Daniel 11, which abruptly shifts from Antiochus Epiphanes (vv. 21-35) to Antichrist (vv. 36ff), provides some additional insight. In Daniel 11, what Antichrist does not regard—the gods of his fathers—is contrasted with what he regards—warfare and military spending and the homage of the conquered (vv. 37-39). Following these "general policies and practices,"[195] some of Antichrist's military engagements are cited (vv. 40-44), which likely take place prior to the midpoint of the Tribulation. Antichrist's disregard for any god and his magnifying of himself (v. 37), dedication to war (v. 38), and reward of his followers (v. 39) will be evident in the first half of the seventieth week and amplified during the Great Tribulation.

Having linked Daniel's coming prince with John's beast of Revelation and having established the two periods of Antichrist's rule, we are ready to delve into new information about Antichrist provided exclusively by the Book of Revelation. This new information is critical to discovering the true identity of the strange-looking beast that John saw in the lake of fire.

Brand-New Revelation

John enhanced our understanding of Antichrist when he wrote: "I saw one of his heads as if it had been slain, and his fatal wound was healed. And the whole earth was amazed and followed after the beast" (Rev. 13:3, NASB). A few verses later, John confirms that the beast himself suffered the fatal wound (13:12, 14). Thomas writes,

> Revelation 13:12, 14 with v. 3 require the equivalence of the head to the beast and vice versa. The healing of the head is

> the healing of the beast, and the healing of the beast is the healing of the head....
>
> It is best to identify this restoration to life with an end-time satanically controlled king who will come to the world as a false Christ.[196]

One reason to understand the fatal wound as applying to Antichrist personally is that his dramatic resurrection surely takes place at the midpoint of the Tribulation as the healed beast is given authority for forty-two months, at the end of which Christ returns. The idea that the little horn's iron and clay empire, which will exercise significant power at the start of Daniel's seventieth week, is to be destroyed and suddenly reestablished to rule the world is beyond difficult to envision.

Another reason in favor of the physical death of Antichrist is found in Revelation 5:6, "where the Lamb carried the scars of death."[197] Ryrie writes,

> One of the heads of the Beast was (literally) "as having been slain to death." This is... the same word that was used in 5:6 of the Lamb, where it is translated "as if slain." Since Christ died actually, it appears that Antichrist will also actually die.[198]

Seiss states,

> John tells us that he beheld one of the Beast's heads "as having been slain to death." The expression is so strong, definite, and intensified, that nothing less can be grammatically made of it than that real death meant to be affirmed. It is further described as a sword-wound, "the stroke of his death," or a stroke which carries death to him who experiences it. A man who has undergone physical death is therefore in contemplation.... Similar phraseology is used in this Book

with regard to Christ, but all agree that it there means return to life by resurrection after a real bodily killing. How, then, can it mean less here? In the subsequent portions of the history this Beast is repeatedly spoken of as "he whose stroke of death was healed;" "the beast which had the stroke of the sword, and *lived*," or became alive again, — "the beast that was, and is not, and *yet is*,"... These expressions inevitably carry with them the notion of a violent and real death, and as real a return again to presence and activity on the earth. Indeed, it seems to be this revivescence and remanifestation of one known to have been dead that causes the universal wondering after this Beast.[199]

Newell states, "One who has been slain with the death-stroke of a sword is 'healed'; a killed body stands up!"[200]

The beast of Revelation is clearly a man at the start of the seven-year period known as Daniel's seventieth week. Moreover, in Daniel 7 and 9, Antichrist's career continues through the Great Tribulation. Thus, the death of the beast in Revelation catches us off guard. How does Antichrist live to rule the second half of Daniel's seventieth week?

Can the Devil Duplicate the Resurrection of Christ?

McGee answers,

Satan does not have power to raise the dead; that power has not been given to him at all.... Therefore, I take it that the restoration is a false, a fake resurrection....

Nobody can duplicate the resurrection of Christ; they might imitate it, but they cannot duplicate it. Yet Antichrist is going to imitate it in a way that will fool the world—it is the big lie.[201]

RESCUE FROM DEATH

While it is surely beyond the power of Satan to duplicate Christ's resurrection, the strong evidence that the beast actually dies drives some futurists to teach that the beast will be brought back from the realm of the dead "by permitted Satanic agency."[202] Resurrection, however, is the great evidence of Christ's deity. Jesus Christ was "declared to be the Son of God with power, according to the Spirit of holiness, by the resurrection from the dead" (Rom. 1:4). The idea that God would grant Satan power to raise the dead should not be a consideration.

If Antichrist actually dies and Satan cannot raise him from the dead, what is the solution to this dilemma? Some futurists maintain that the beast's resurrection is a counterfeit, without suggesting how this is accomplished. Some call it resuscitation. Morris suggests it is a matter of "suspended animation" and "some kind of occult supernatural phenomenon."[203] One of the most novel solutions comes from Gregory H. Harris, who argues that the beast and false prophet are human beings who die, undergo the supernatural transformation by which the unsaved receive bodies fit for eternal damnation, and then operate in these supernatural bodies during the Great Tribulation.[204]

Futuristic traditionalists offer various explanations but no satisfactory answer. Typically, the reality of Antichrist's death is denied in some way. Harris avoids this problem without ascribing undue power to Satan, but the idea that Antichrist and the false prophet receive bodies fit for eternal misery in hell, in accordance with traditionalism, and subsequently spend three and a half years ruling the world is highly unlikely. Solving the mystery of the beast's return to life will require another of John's exclusive revelations.

The Abyss Factor

A future iron and clay empire is foretold in Daniel 2, but Daniel 2 does not provide the slightest hint that there will be an eleventh ruler, the little horn. To have an accurate understanding of prophecy, we must watch for and assimilate new revelation. So far in Revelation, we have seen that Antichrist has suffered a fatal wound. Another prophetic truth exclusive to Revelation is that Antichrist will ascend out of the abyss, or bottomless pit.

We are first informed that the beast will ascend out of the abyss in Revelation 11:7: "Now when they [God's two witnesses] finish their testimony [of 1260 days], *the beast that ascends out of the bottomless pit* will make war against them, overcome them, and kill them." In Revelation 17, an angel explains the mystery of the beast which has seven heads and ten horns to John, saying, "The beast that you saw was, and is not, and *will ascend out of the bottomless pit* and go to perdition. And those who dwell on the earth will marvel, whose names are not written in the Book of Life from the foundation of the world, when they see the beast that was, and is not, and yet is" (Rev. 17:8). Thomas writes,

> The designation of the beast as the one who "was and is not, and is about to ascend out of the abyss"... ties him to the beast with the death-wound who was healed in 13:3, 12, 14. Both there and here the earth-dwellers express amazement (Johnson). The words "is not" refer to the beast's death, and his ascent from the abyss means he will come to life again (cf. 13:14)....
>
> This is most probably a point at the very middle of the seventieth week, between the beast's human and superhuman careers (Walvoord).[205]

The abyss is clearly highly significant to our understanding of the beast. So what do we know about the abyss from which the beast ascends? It literally means "unfathomably deep"[206] and is a place of confinement for demonic spirits prior to them being cast into the lake of fire. In Luke, demons beg Jesus to not send them into the abyss (Luke 8:31), where certain fallen angels were already being held (2 Pet. 2:4).[207] Satan will be confined in the abyss during the millennial reign of Christ (Rev. 20:1-3). Revelation 9 also provides insight:

> Then the fifth angel blew his trumpet, and I saw a star that had fallen from the sky to the earth, and he was given the key to the shaft of the abyss. He opened the shaft of the abyss and smoke rose out of it like smoke from a giant furnace. The sun and the air were darkened with smoke from the shaft. Then out of the smoke came locusts onto the earth, and they were given power like that of the scorpions of the earth. They were told not to damage the grass of the earth, or any green plant or tree, but only those people who did not have the seal of God on their forehead. The locusts were not given permission to kill them, but only to torture them for five months, and their torture was like that of a scorpion when it stings a person. In those days people will seek death, but will not be able to find it; they will long to die, but death will flee from them.
>
> Now the locusts looked like horses equipped for battle. On their heads were something like crowns similar to gold, and their faces looked like men's faces.

They had hair like women's hair, and their teeth were like lions' teeth. They had breastplates like iron breastplates, and the sound of their wings was like the noise of many horse-drawn chariots charging into battle. They have tails and stingers like scorpions, and their ability to injure people for five months is in their tails. They have as king over them the angel of the abyss, whose name in Hebrew is *Abaddon*, and in Greek, *Apollyon* [Destroyer].

The first woe has passed, but two woes are still coming after these things! (Rev. 9:1-12, NET)

An incredibly massive amount of smoke comes out of the abyss. Locusts do not live in such an environment. Moreover, the description of the creatures in Revelation 9 does not remotely match that of the insects we call locusts. The details of the text lead to the conclusion that the tormentors in Revelation 9 are demonic beings. Thomas writes,

> Heavy evidence favors the identification of these locusts as demons or fallen angels... They have an angel as their leader (9:11). They come from the abyss where evil spirits are imprisoned (Beckwith, Lenski). Their attack against men rather than consuming of green vegetation points to their demonic nature (Beasley-Murray). They have a form such as no human being has ever seen (Bullinger, Seiss, Walvoord).[208]

In Revelation, Satan is released from the abyss to deceive the nations at the end of the millennium (20:7-8) and demonic beings are released from this same pit to torment those "who do not have the seal of God" during the Tribulation (9:1-12). Are we not also to understand that a demonic spirit ascends out of the abyss to assume the identity of the beast?

Putting the Slain Prince and the Abyss Together

When the evil prince to come suffers a deathblow, his soul goes to Hades as is customary for the unsaved. The slain prince "lives again" when a demonic spirit ascends out of the abyss to possess and animate the prince's dead body.[209]

This is the one view that accounts for all of the key issues. It satisfies the strong wording that the beast is slain. It protects rather than threatens the great evidence of Christ's deity by assuring us that the resurrection of Antichrist is a counterfeit resurrection. It does not grant power to Satan to bring a man back from the dead. It takes the beast's ascension out of the bottomless pit at face value. It is also consistent with the fact that the unsaved world will marvel.

It is possible that Antichrist's recovery from a deathblow will be witnessed on live TV, but think of the effect that fingerprints and DNA might provide if a demonic spirit were to possess the prince's slain body. Imagine the impact of watching Antichrist pass eye-scan security measures. With scientific verification that death has been conquered, no wonder the unsaved world will marvel and follow Antichrist.[210]

The Number of the Beast

In Revelation, Antichrist is pictured as a composite beast with seven heads and ten horns to establish connection with Daniel's little horn, the prince to come who makes a seven-year covenant with Israel. Covenants are signed by human beings, and the number of the beast is that of a man:

> And he [the false prophet] causes all, the small and the great... to be given a mark on their right hand or on their forehead, and he provides that no one will be able to buy or to sell, except the one who has the mark, either the name of the beast or the number of his name. Here is wisdom. Let him who has understanding calculate the number of the beast, for the number is that of a man; and his number is six hundred and sixty-six. (Rev. 13:16-18, NASB)

Antichrist controls commerce. To legally do business, one must receive Antichrist's name or identifying number on the forehead or right hand. These external markings do not necessarily address the interior reality of Antichrist. They do, however, help assure us that Antichrist's human form and prince identity remain intact during the Great Tribulation.

This is important because we come to the Book of Revelation with the understanding that the signing of the treaty with Israel, its breaking at the midpoint, and the subsequent persecution of the saints for three and a half years are all attributed to the prince to come. Because the fallen angel who ascends out of the bottomless pit will maintain the identity of the treacherous prince by possessing his body during the second half of the seventieth week, requisite continuity will not be lacking.

Outwardly and to the world, Antichrist was killed and rose from the dead. People will believe this because of what their eyes

RESCUE FROM DEATH

see and their science verifies, but the world will be deceived; if Antichrist's dead body is resurrected, it will be because a demonic spirit from the bottomless pit possesses it.

Spirit Beings in Human Form

Angels are "ministering spirits" (Heb. 1:14). "They are both finite and spacial."[211] Though angels do not have bodies of flesh that can be seen or handled (Luke 24:39), they are capable of operating in human form (Heb. 13:2). In Genesis, three *men* visited Abraham in Mamre (18:1-2). Abraham's hospitality included providing water to wash the men's *feet* (18:4) and food, which the men *ate* under the shade of a tree (18:8). Afterward, "the *men* rose from there and looked toward Sodom, and Abraham went with them to send them on the way" (18:16). Upon learning of Sodom's impending judgment from one of his guests, Abraham stood before the Lord and talked with Him while the two "*men* turned away from there and went toward Sodom" (18:22) where some of Abraham's relatives lived. This story continues in Genesis 19, where we learn that the two men are actually two *angels* (v. 1).

Abraham's nephew Lot greeted the angels and offered them water for their *feet* (v. 2) and insisted that they lodge under his roof (v. 3). Then Lot prepared a meal that the two *ate* (v. 3). Before long, the men of Sodom surrounded Lot's house (v. 4), wanting Lot to bring out "the *men* who came to you tonight" (v. 5). Lot stepped out of his house, shutting the door behind him, in an attempt to protect his guests, but the crowd threatened Lot and were close to breaking his door down when, from within the house, "the *men* reached out their *hands* and pulled Lot into the house with them, and shut the door" (v. 10). Then Lot's two guests ended the confrontation by striking the men outside the doorway with blindness (v. 11).

These two angels were in the physical form of men, were recognized as men by all who met them, and performed everyday human tasks. Most significant to our study is the fact that *scripture repeatedly refers to these angels as men.* The same is true in the New Testament. Following Christ's resurrection, the women entering the tomb "saw a young *man* clothed in a long white robe" (Mark 16:5). This "man" was an angel (Matt. 28:5-8).[212]

Given the precedent of angels appearing in the form of men and the teaching of scripture that the beast ascends out of the abyss, should we be surprised if an evil angel operates in the form of an evil man during the Tribulation? And in light of the fact that scripture refers to angelic beings in human form as men, should we be surprised if the mark of a fallen angel operating in human form is said to be the mark of a man?

THE SATANIC TRINITY

Satan is an imitator who seeks to take the place of God. The devil's ambition to be like the Most High is widely recognized by students of the Bible. In Revelation, we see Satan form a tri-unity with the beast and false prophet:

> And I saw a beast rising up out of the sea... The dragon gave him his power, his throne, and great authority. (Rev. 13:1-2)

Then I saw *another* [Gr. *allo* "one like in kind"²¹³] beast [aka the false prophet] coming up out of the earth, and he had two horns like a lamb and *spoke like a dragon*. And he *exercises all the authority of the first beast* in his presence, and causes the earth and those who dwell in it to worship the first beast, whose deadly wound was healed. (Rev. 13:11-12)

Satan receives worship as the invisible member of this tri-unity (Rev. 13:4); the beast receives worship as one who was slain and yet lives (Rev. 13:3); the false prophet performs great signs to cause the world to worship the beast (Rev. 13:11-13). William H. Marty writes,

> Satan's goal from the beginning has been to overthrow God and to rule the world. At the end of the age, he will turn to two beasts, forming an unholy trinity that is a clever and sinister imitation of God the Father, God the Son, and God the Holy Spirit. Satan assumes the place of God, the Antichrist the place of Christ, and the False Prophet the place of the Holy Spirit.²¹⁴

Futuristic traditionalists customarily teach that Satan will form his counterfeit tri-unity with two human beings. The matchless, utterly unique, divine Holy Trinity, however, is a tri-unity of coequal Persons. Angels and humans are not equals (2 Pet. 2:11). Because Satan is a fallen cherub, should we not expect that he would form his imitation trinity with other fallen angels?

And I saw three unclean spirits like frogs coming out of the mouth of the dragon, out of the mouth of the beast, and out of the mouth of the false prophet. For they are *spirits of demons*, performing signs, which go out to the kings of the earth and of the whole world, to gather them to the battle of that great day of God Almighty. (Rev. 16:13-14)

Out of the mouth of the dragon, beast, and false prophet come unclean spirits that are explicitly declared to be spirits of *demons*. Is this not a picture of a demonic trio?

The Book of Revelation looks beyond the human realm. Prior to Adam's sin in Eden, a cosmic conflict between God and Satan was underway. This conflict began when Satan became corrupted through pride (Ezek. 28:17; 1 Tim. 3:6). Glimpses of Satan's rebellion are provided throughout scripture, but the rebellion is fully out in the open in the Book of Revelation. Satan and his angels fight with Michael and the holy angels in heaven (Rev. 12:7). The holy angels prevail, and Satan and his angels are cast out of heaven, down to earth (Rev. 12:8-10). Enraged, Satan vents his wrath against God on Israel (Rev. 12:13) and prepares for yet more warfare with his Creator (Rev. 16:13-14).

Satan presently rules this world in conjunction with his angels. We should not expect this to change during the Great Tribulation. Scriptural testimony indicates that during the Great Tribulation, a counterfeit trinity will emerge, composed of Satan and two fallen angels who operate in human form (Rev. 11:7, 13:3-5, 11-12, 18, 16:13-14, 17:8).

THE SATANIC TRINITY IN THE LAKE OF FIRE

Our investigation discovered that Antichrist and the false prophet are in reality fallen angels. Halfway through the Tribulation, a demonic spirit ascends out of the abyss to possess Antichrist's slain body. The false prophet is another like Antichrist. In Revelation 20:10, then, we have a picture of the devil and his angels in the fire prepared for them, where they suffer day and night while unsaved humanity faces final judgment before God's Great White Throne (Rev. 20:11-12).[215]

When futuristic traditionalists come to Revelation 20:10, however, they see Satan and two human beings in the lake of fire and argue that the beast and false prophet's presence there for a thousand years indicates that unsaved men are not annihilated. This traditionalist argument does not account for the demonic identity of the beast and false prophet or the enormity of their sin.

The scope of Antichrist's and the false prophet's sin is utterly beyond that of human beings, even the most notorious. In a time of unprecedented trouble, the beast and false prophet will be responsible for unprecedented sin. Having been granted authority over every tribe, tongue, and nation, Antichrist and the false prophet will assault the entire world—small and great, rich and poor, free and slave—with a devastating combination of deceit and coercion designed to force humanity to reject the Creator. Antichrist, utilizing lying wonders and unrighteous deception, will claim to be God and will demand the world's worship. The false prophet will use the very real threat of death to pressure *billions* to worship the beast and take his mark.

To overlook the sin of Antichrist and the false prophet is to fail to interpret Revelation 20:10 in light of its context. This is a common problem. Notice how Alcorn argues against annihilationism,

> Another view states that unbelievers are destroyed not at death, but sometime later. They suffer some punishment appropriate to their offenses... some shorter and some longer, then are snuffed out of existence.
>
> But as we've seen, two human beings, the antichrist and the false prophet, will [still be in]... the lake of fire after a thousand years of suffering. If it is wrong for punishment [torment] to last forever, wouldn't it seem wrong to last over a thousand years?[216]

If we were talking about two ordinary sinners, yes, more than a thousand years of torment would seem too much, but Revelation 20:10 does not present us with two nondescript individuals. Why, then, do traditionalists?

Alcorn states that "God records all human works so that all punishment will be commensurate to the evil committed," ensuring that the unsaved "will bear only the sins they have committed."[217] Thus, should not traditionalists expect that the vastly greater sin of Antichrist and the false prophet will result in a vastly greater amount of suffering for this dreadful duo than what the impenitent of Adam's race will experience?

Viewing Antichrist and the false prophet as representative of humanity is a key component of the argument made by futuristic traditionalists; however, the biblical picture does not cooperate, not even *if* the beast and false prophet are demon-possessed men as most futuristic traditionalists hold.

Even if Antichrist's ascension from the abyss simply indicated demon possession, the powerful dominant fallen angel would not be along for the ride; he would be the driver. Whether the fallen angel possesses a dead body or a living human person, the words and actions of the beast from the midpoint of the Tribulation forward are the words and actions of a demonic being. As Seiss admits, Antichrist is "in some sense an incarnation of the Devil."[218] Thomas writes, "After his death he will come to life again. When he does, he will come back in a demonic rather than a purely human form to establish his world domination (Beckwith)."[219]

If the beast is representative, he is representative of those inhabiting the abyss from which he ascended: the fallen angels. "Out of the mouth of the dragon, out of the mouth of the beast, and out of the mouth of the false prophet" come "spirits of demons" (Rev. 16:13-14). If we see a satanic trinity in Revelation 16, should we not see the devil and his angels in Revelation 20:10?

REVELATION 20:10-15—A MISNOMER

Some traditionalists do not consider the identity of the beast and false prophet to be a critical issue. Laying aside the identity of the beast and the false prophet, Peterson argues,

> Revelation 20:10 tells us that the devil will be thrown into the lake of fire. Five verses later we read that human beings will be cast into the same lake of fire. Wouldn't normal hermeneutics dictate the understanding that human beings will be heading for eternal torment too?...
> The lake of fire signifies eternal torment in verse 10. John does not tell his readers that the meaning of the lake of

fire is different in verse 15. So annihilationists have no right to change the meaning.[220]

Peterson presents us with an assumption. If John does not tell his readers that the meaning of the lake of fire has changed, neither does he tell them that the result of being cast into the lake of fire is the same for Adam's race as it is for the devil and his angels. Peterson reads Revelation 20:10-15 as if the words "as the devil is tormented in the lake of fire, so unsaved human beings will be tormented in the lake of fire" *were in the text,* but no such words are there.

Normal hermeneutics dictate that the author's flow of thought and organization of content should be respected. It is not our place to reorganize scripture, yet this is essentially what traditionalists have done with Revelation 20.

Scripture can change subjects quickly, and it does so in the key latter chapters of Revelation. Revelation 20:7-10 and Revelation 20:11-15 are two distinct visions with two distinct subjects: Satan and his angels, and the unsaved of Adam's race, respectively.

The proximity of the visions hardly relieves the interpreter of the responsibility to assess each passage on its own merits. The lake of fire is common to both visions, but Satan and Adam are very different creations of God. Furthermore, with regard to sin, God has clearly dealt differently with humans than He has with Satan. As noted in Chapter 4, Jesus died for fallen human beings, but He did not die for fallen angelic beings. It is not for us to assume that a human being's experience in the lake of fire is identical to that of the devil. Our job is to carefully observe what the text actually does and does not teach.

RESCUE FROM DEATH

The Visions of John: Revelation 19:11–21:2

In the latter portion of Revelation, John has one vision after another.

In Revelation 19:11, we read, "*Then I saw* heaven opened, and behold, a white horse. And He who sat on him was called Faithful and True, and in righteousness He judges and makes war." In 19:11-16, Jesus is the subject of John's vision.

In Revelation 19:17, we read, "*Then I saw* an angel standing in the sun; and he cried with a loud voice, saying to all the birds that fly in the midst of heaven, 'Come and gather together for the supper of the great God.'" In 19:17-21, the defeat of the beast and his armies is declared.

In Revelation 20:1, we read, "*Then I saw* an angel coming down from heaven, having the key to the bottomless pit and a great chain in his hand." In 20:1-3, we learn that Satan is bound for a thousand years.

In Revelation 20:4, we read, "*And I saw* thrones, and they sat on them, and judgment was committed to them." In 20:4-6, the focus is the saints' thousand-year reign with Christ.

In Revelation 20:7, we read, "*Now when* the thousand years have expired, Satan will be released from his prison." In 20:7-10, we have the last evil act of Satan on earth and his subsequent casting into the lake of fire.

In Revelation 20:11-12, we read, "*Then I saw* a great white throne and Him who sat on it, from whose face the earth and the heaven fled away. And there was found no place for them. And I saw the dead, small and great, standing before God, and books were opened." In 20:11-15, the final judgment of those who died without faith in Christ is recorded.

In Revelation 21:1, we read, "*And I saw* a new heaven and a new earth."

In Revelation 21:2, we read, "*Then I*, John, *saw* the holy city, New Jerusalem, coming down out of heaven from God, prepared as a bride adorned for her husband."

A Fundamental Error of Traditionalism

Revelation 20:7-10 is one vision, one context, one passage of scripture. Revelation 20:11-15 is another vision, another context, another passage.

In Revelation 20:7-10, Satan's casting into the lake of fire and the torment of the satanic trinity are declared. After the Revelation 20:7-10 vision, John receives a new vision:

> *Then I saw a great white throne and Him who sat on it,* from whose face the earth and the heaven fled away. And there was found no place for them. And I saw the dead, small and great, standing before God, and books were opened. And another book was opened, which is the Book of Life. And the dead were judged according to their works, by the things which were written in the books. The sea gave up the dead who were in it, and Death and Hades delivered up the dead who were in them. And they were judged, each one according to his works. Then Death and Hades were cast into the lake of fire. This is the second death. And anyone not found

written in the Book of Life was cast into the lake of fire. (Rev. 20:11-15)

The judgment of unbelievers *begins* in Revelation 20:11: "*Then I saw* a great white throne." The importance of this simple fact should not be minimized. Revelation 20:10 is *not* the first verse of what God has to say about the judgment of humanity; nevertheless, traditionalists link Revelation 20:10 with Revelation 20:11-15 as if this were the case. Recall Peterson's words "Arguably the second most important passage on the doctrine of hell (after Mt 25:41, 46) is Revelation 20:10-15."[221]

Citing Revelation 20:10-15 as the second most important *passage* of scripture about hell fails to respect the distinction between the visions of Revelation 20:7-10 and Revelation 20:11-15. This is a fundamental error of traditionalism.

Torment is not the penalty for sin established in Eden (Gen. 2:17; Rom. 1:32), and torment does not appear in John's vision of unsaved humanity in Revelation 20:11-15. To support their theology, traditionalists assign torment foretold for Satan in one vision to humankind in another vision. This is not responsible hermeneutics.

DISTINCT SCOPE OF SIN, DISTINCT EXTENT OF SUFFERING

Directly created by God as a fully formed powerful cherub, Satan was the first to rebel against God. Constantly sinning against God by continually working to corrupt human beings, Satan's sinful actions span the globe and human history. His offenses are astronomical. It is altogether appropriate that Satan, like the beast and false prophet, should suffer in the lake of fire for a very great period of time. Humanity's situation is quite different.

Subject to death by virtue of membership in a fallen race (Gen. 5:3; Rom. 5:12), every grandchild of Adam and Eve is born utterly helpless and precious beyond words. The love that fills parents' and grandparents' hearts at the birth of a child is something angels have never experienced. Nurtured and cared for, in time, the child grows to an age of accountability. Some die shortly thereafter, meaning that some people die with few entries in the books of heaven by which the unsaved are judged. Does it seem reasonable that the unsaved person who commits *almost* no punishable offenses against God should spend the same amount of time in the lake of fire as Satan?

Traditionalists hold that Satan's Revelation 20:10 experience in the lake of fire illustrates the eternal destiny of the unsaved teachers who taught us to read and write and the unsaved doctors who performed life-saving surgery on our loved ones and the unsaved men who gave their lives on the beaches of Normandy. Conditionalists believe that God expects us to find the fate of unsaved humanity in scriptures such as Genesis 2:17; Psalm 37:20; Ezekiel 18:4; Matthew 3:12, 7:13, 10:28, 13:40, 21:44; John 3:16; Romans 1:32, 6:23; Philippians 3:18-19; and 2 Peter 2:6.

The death of the sinner in the lake of fire will be as prolonged and painful as the record of his life merits, but as the scale of the unsaved sinner's sin is immensely less than that of Satan, surely the extent of his suffering will be immensely less as well.

RESCUE FROM DEATH

REVELATION 20:11-15 IN A NUTSHELL

The unsaved will be resurrected to stand before God's Great White Throne for judgment. Wrongs in this world will be brought to light as the deeds and secrets of unsaved humanity recorded in the books of heaven are made public (Rev. 20:11-12). No member of Adam's race will be lost to eternal death without a review of his or her life that will affirm that the penalty for sin is merited. The effort put into this judgment reflects the importance of people to God and the need for closure. Every unsaved sinner will be accounted for, even those lost at sea (20:13).

"Then Death and Hades were cast into the lake of fire. This is the second death" (20:14). Death will be no more (Rev. 21:4), and Hades, an intermediate state, will also be no more. This is arresting because annihilation appears to be set before the reader immediately prior to the words "And anyone not found written in the Book of Life was cast into the lake of fire" (20:15).

We witness the execution of the Genesis 2:17 penalty for sin as the unsaved are cast into the lake of fire, which is the second death. It is unnecessary for the Book of Revelation to elaborate, the penalty for sin having already been unequivocally declared. The fire of which Jesus and His forerunner both warned *burns up* chaff and tares—the unsaved of Adam's race.

NEW HEAVEN, NEW EARTH

"And I saw a new heaven and a new earth, for the first heaven and the first earth had passed away. Also there was no more sea" (Rev. 21:1). Some think that "new" simply means refreshed from the damages of sin, but scripture seems to indicate an end to the first universe, followed by the creation of a new one. Newell states,

> Three great passages, Isaiah 65:17; 66:22; II Peter 3:10-13 and the present Revelation passage, deal with this stupendous subject, the new creation. The definite and repeated statements that the old earth and heaven "flee away," "pass away with a great noise," and are "burned up"; together with the statement that "there was found no place for them," compel the conclusion that those who argue that these words indicate only a "cleansing by fire" and not actual eternal dissolution and disappearance, shrink from the *searching realities* of this subject.... We know that *create* in Genesis 1:1 cannot mean anything but the calling into existence of that which did not before have being *(Hebrews 11:3)*. And certainly Revelation 21:1 is just as new a beginning!...
>
> This Revelation 21:1 plainly discriminates the two creations, in that one must pass away before the other appears.
>
> The matter thus lay also in the mind of our blessed Lord who said: "Heaven and earth shall pass away, but my word shall not pass away." To one of the simplicity of a child, all these Scriptures convey nothing else than the complete disappearance of a former creation and the appearing by the Word of God of a material creation absolutely new.[222]

Walvoord writes,

> It would be most natural that the present earth and heaven, the scene of the struggle with Satan and sin, should be displaced by an entirely new order suited for eternity. The whole structure of the universe is operating on the principle of a clock that is running down. Though many billions of years would be required to accomplish this, the natural world would eventually come to a state of total inactivity if the physical laws of the universe as now understood should remain unchanged. What could be simpler than for God to

create a new heaven and a new earth by divine fiat in keeping with His purposes for eternity to come?[223]

An entirely new universe is coming. To witness God creating a new earth and heavens is one of the innumerable blessings waiting for those who love God. In keeping with God's nature, the new earth and heavens will be a place where righteousness dwells. Newell writes,

> The first creation was the sphere and scene of what God calls "the first things." Sin, beginning in heaven and with the highest of the creatures, challenging the will of the Creator as the creature's highest good, came in to mar, ruin, and wreck the first creation. Now comes at last, based upon Christ and His work, a wholly new creation which will never pass away, and in which the apostle Peter announces that "righteousness will be *at home*" (II Peter 3:13, Greek).[224]

We have seen that impenitent human beings have no place in God's glorious new creation. What about the devil and demons? Will demonic beings be part of God's righteous new universe?

IS THERE A PLACE FOR SATAN AND HIS ANGELS IN THE NEW HEAVENS?

"Then God saw *everything* that He had made, and indeed it was *very good*" (Gen. 1:31). All was good in God's original creation until the cherub (now known as Satan) sinned:

> You were anointed as a guardian cherub, for so I ordained you. You were on the holy mount of God; you walked among the fiery stones. You were blameless in your ways

from the day you were created till wickedness was found in you. (Ezek. 28:14-15, NIV)

Satan contributed to Adam's fall (Gen. 3:1-7) and works to prevent sinners from coming to faith in Christ (2 Cor. 4:3-4). Fittingly, Revelation 20 closes with two visions best appreciated as if playing on a split prophecy screen. On one side of the screen, Satan and his angels are being tormented without relief; on the other side, those who died without Christ face final judgment.

Every unsaved individual will be judged in accordance with his or her words (Matt. 12:36-37), deeds (Rom. 2:4-6), secrets (Rom. 2:16), and privilege (Luke 12:47-48). How long it will take to complete the Great White Throne judgment is not revealed, but it could be a very great amount of time. The church, comprised of finite human beings, will be involved in this judgment (1 Cor. 6:2), and potentially billions of unsaved lives will come before God's throne. As thoroughly deserved, Satan and his angels will suffer throughout the judgment of each and every unbeliever.

Satan's suffering will be continual while the unsaved from throughout the ages of human history stand before the Great White Throne, but it will not necessarily last eternally. "Forever and ever," as previously discovered, requires contextual investigation to determine whether or not eternity is in view. It makes good sense that Satan would suffer during the judgment of those whom he deceived. Satan in the eternal state, however, is problematic. The unrighteous nature of Satan and his angels argues against their inclusion in the new heavens. As God's original creation was entirely good, should we not expect that the new heavens and earth will be entirely good?

Interestingly, fallen angels acknowledge that God has both torment (Matt. 8:29) and destruction (ἀπολέσαι, Mark 1:24; Luke 4:34) in store for them. Recall that with regard to humanity, ἀπολέσαι consistently means to kill in the Gospels. Will God ultimately kill Satan and the fallen angels? Ezekiel 28:11-19 seems to indicate that He will.

The human ruler of Tyre is the subject of Ezekiel 28:1-10. The next section (vv. 11-19), however, contains language that points to Satan, the spirit ruler of this world. For example, this "king of Tyre" (v. 12) was "in Eden, the garden of God" (v. 13), is said to be "the anointed cherub" who walked "in the midst of fiery stones" (v. 14), and remained "perfect" from the day he was "created" till iniquity was found in him (v. 15). Chafer writes,

> In this one context [Ezek. 28:11-19] God records the origin, estate, character, and sin of the greatest of angels. The importance of this revelation as it bears upon the doctrine of the angels... cannot be overestimated. God did not create Satan as such; He created an angel who was perfect in all his ways, and that angel sinned by opposing the will of God. By this act he became Satan the resister, and all else that all his titles imply. The ancient question raised by the skeptics of the past with respect to who made the devil has been answered in this passage just considered. There it is seen that God created a holy angel possessing the power of choice between good and evil, and he chose to do the evil.[225]

It is appropriate that a lament for the ruler of Tyre provides insight into Satan. As the prince of this world, Satan exercised influence over the ruler of Tyre. Ezekiel's reference to Satan is significant to our study because the passage concludes, "You have come to a horrible end and will be no more" (28:19, NIV). Guillebaud states,

> The King of Tyre is denounced and threatened but the prophet recognizes behind him a power mightier than he. Of this dread being, who was once "the anointed cherub that covereth" and was in Eden the garden of God, it is said "thou art become a terror, and thou shalt never be any more" (verse 19)... the same prophecy that had been applied to the city of Tyre in Ezekiel 27:36. We have seen that Paul's statement in *1 Corinthians 15:28* that God shall be all in all seems impossible to reconcile with the eternal existence of the devil, even in hell. Now in addition we have this definite statement in Ezekiel that the devil shall "never be any more," which seems to mean that his existence shall come to an end.[226]

God did not allow sin and pain to enter the first creation that it might continue forever but to do away with it forever. Peter teaches that "the earth and the works that are in it will be burned up" (2 Pet. 3:10). John tells us that all that is in the world, including lust and pride, will pass away (1 John 2:16-17). Satan is full of pride (Ezek. 28:17), is behind the evil works of the world today (Eph. 2:2), and will be cast down to earth during the Tribulation (Rev. 12:9, 13). Are not Satan and his angels too integral to the world and its works to be outside the scope of Peter and John's words?

In Revelation 20:11-15, mention is made of the present earth and heaven's end: "there was found no place for them" (v. 11). This cannot fully take place by verse 11, however, as we find the sea giving up the dead in it when we come to verse 13. Hades, which is also part of the present creation, is not cast into the lake of fire until verse 14. Next, we read that the unsaved are cast into the lake of fire, and, thereafter, John sees a new heaven and earth, the first earth and heaven having passed away (Rev. 21:1). Does the burning of the tares ignite the fiery end of the present universe?

Peter wrote that the present heavens and earth are reserved for fire: "kept for the day of judgment and destruction of ungodly men" (2 Pet. 3:7, NASB). Could it be that the lake of fire either merges with or develops into the fire whereby the heavens will be dissolved and the elements melt (2 Pet. 3:12)? In any case, only that which is unshakable will enter the new earth and heavens.

The writer of Hebrews links God as *consuming* fire (Heb. 12:29) with the day when God will "shake not only the earth, but also heaven" (Heb. 12:26), resulting in the "removal of those things that are being shaken… that the things which cannot be shaken may remain" (Heb. 12:27). What cannot be shaken is the kingdom of God (Heb. 12:28), which includes: heavenly Jerusalem, the holy angels, the church of the firstborn who are registered in heaven, the spirits of just men made perfect, the new covenant, and the shed blood of Christ (Heb. 12:22-24).

Neither the devil nor demons have any part in the one and only unshakable kingdom. Since it is God's kingdom alone that will remain, and since Satan and his angels have no part in it, does it not follow that demonic beings will be annihilated?

Though it may be an unfamiliar thought, upon reflection, should the exclusion of demonic beings from the eternal universe in which righteousness dwells and God is all in all surprise us? What sense would it make for the greatest evil of the present universe to be brought into the coming new righteous one? God is infinite in power, but why eternally give attention and energy to Satan? Do we really expect a holy God to endlessly sustain sinfulness that He absolutely abhors?

As becoming a servant *forever* to a fellow Israelite (Deut. 15:12-17) lasts for a generation, and the territory given to Israel *forever* (Gen. 13:15) remains her promised land while this earth endures, and the smoke rising from Babylon *forever and ever* (Rev. 19:3) ascends until the city can no longer be found, it certainly would be well within the norm if the *forever and ever* torment of the devil, beast, and false prophet terminates with the passing away of the present universe.

MAINTAINING PERSPECTIVE

We should never lose sight of the fact that Satan's fate and the fate of human beings are not connected. As previously noted, Satan and humanity are distinct creations that God has dealt distinctly with regarding sin. Understandably, just as the Bible has much more to say about human beings than demonic beings, so the judgment of the impenitent of Adam's race is far more extensively documented in scripture. It should also be noted that one can be a conditionalist and believe that Satan will suffer ECT. Conditionalism properly encompasses only humanity, as it is only Adam's race which is offered immortality on the condition of faith in the Lord Jesus Christ.

Most importantly, no matter what the experience of Satan and his angels in the lake of fire may be, it would be a tragic mishandling of the Word for a difficult phrase in the difficult prophetic Book of Revelation to overturn the explicit teachings of John the Baptist, Jesus, and the apostles regarding the fate of impenitent human beings.

GOD DWELLS WITH HIS PEOPLE

On a new earth in a new universe, God will dwell with His people (Rev. 21:1, 3). God's throne and the holy city, New Jerusalem, will descend out of heaven to the new earth (Rev. 21:2-22:3). The transition from the Messianic reign of Christ in the first creation to the Father's throne established on the new earth is touched on by McClain:

> As we pass from chapter 20 into chapter 21 of the Apocalypse, therefore, we stand at the junction point between two worlds and between two kingdoms. It is the end of the "first" or "natural" order of things, and the beginning of the final order of things. Here also the Mediatorial Kingdom of our Lord ends, not by abolition, but by its mergence into the Universal Kingdom of God. Thus it is perpetuated forever, no longer as a separate entity, but in indissoluble union with the original Kingdom of God from which it sprang. What will happen is succinctly described in St. Paul's classic passage on the subject: "Then cometh the end, when he shall have delivered up the kingdom to God, even the Father; when he shall have put down all rule and all authority and power.... And when all things shall be subdued unto him, then shall the Son also himself be subject unto him that put all things under him, that God may be all in all" (I Cor. 15:24, 28).... There are no longer two thrones: one His Messianic throne and the other the Father's throne, as our Lord indicated in Revelation 3:21. In the final Kingdom there is but one throne, and it is "the throne of God and of the Lamb" (22:3).[227]

What will it be like when the throne of God and the Lamb is on the new earth? The opening verses of Revelation 21 are revealing:

> And I heard a loud voice from the throne saying: "Look! The residence of God is among human beings. He will live among them, and they will be his people, and God himself will be with them. He will wipe away every tear from their eyes, and death will not exist any more—or mourning, or crying, or pain, for the former things have ceased to exist." (Rev. 21:3-4, NET)

Think of it—an eternity without pain or sorrow or death. Yet believers have something even more priceless to look forward to: God, who is love, will dwell with us. Newell writes,

> Do we not see this great Bible He has given us going right forward against all obstacles, over all mountains, through all valleys, yea, to Gethsemane and Calvary—to come to this sweet, eternal consummation, *that God may be with men, their God?*[228]

Our study has not dodged the obstacles and challenges that must be faced in order to have a universe where no resistance to the love of God exists. The present chapter has tackled especially difficult issues. It is therefore fitting that we close with reflections on the ultimate end. In *Close to His Majesty*, David Needham speaks of the love of God that believers can know today and that will fill our hearts throughout eternity:

> Some of us have developed such unbalanced concepts of God. The awesome supreme Judge of the universe... Yes, He

is all of that. But first... He is love. He is the God who longs to fill our lives and our days with the wealth of His presence. A God who cherishes our companionship....

I can't think of anything that expresses the love and tenderness we feel toward our young children more than this act of wiping away tears. At this very moment I can look back over the years and see my little daughter running to me with tears streaming down her face. Squeezing her close, I would gently wipe away those tears with my hand. And wipe and wipe until at last the tears were gone.

God will not delegate any "tear wiping" committee when we arrive in heaven. No! "He Himself... shall wipe away every tear."...

God wants us to understand the eternal intimacy He shares with His Son *because this is precisely the kind of love the Father and Son have for you and me.*

That same evening before Gethsemane Jesus said: "As the Father has loved me, *so* I have loved you. Now remain in my love." (John 15:9 NIV)

Later, as He prayed to His Father, He requested "that the world may know that Thou didst send Me, and didst love them, *even as* Thou didst love Me." (17:23)

"Even as!" It would seem as though the intimacy of love that exists between Father and Son—so sacred, so pure—should be theirs privately forever. We should be seen as intruders. But no! We are actually invited inside this love. Their love. Each of us is loved by God *that* way.[229]

7
WHAT MUST I DO TO BE SAVED?

Traumatic experiences have a way of shaking us up and making us consider life and death. After an earthquake rocked a prison in Philippi, unfastening the prisoners' bonds and opening all the doors, the jailor asked Paul and Silas, "Sirs, what must I do to be saved?" (Acts 16:30).

GOOD WORKS ARE NOT THE ANSWER

The world seems to think that good works are the path to heaven. Many reason, "I've done more good than bad, so I should be fine." There are at least two flaws in this thinking. First, God doesn't grade on the curve, so any amount of sin is enough to bring condemnation (James 2:10). Second, all of us have sinned (Rom. 3:9, 23).

In spite of the fact that man is powerless to save himself, the false gospel of salvation by works has always thrived in Christendom. Even in the evangelical world, some confuse the demanding cost of discipleship with the free gift of salvation. Seeking forgiveness of sins and eternal life on the basis of commitment to the cause of Christ may sound noble, but it is actually an insult to God.

Martin Luther was keenly aware of this. Reflecting on the price Christ paid at the cross, Luther wrote,

> Again, these words, "the Son of God loved me, and gave Himself for me", are mighty thunderings and lightnings from heaven against the righteousness of the law and all the works thereof....
>
> If thou couldst rightly consider this incomparable price, thou shouldst hold as accursed all... ceremonies, vows, works, and merits... there is nothing which is able to pacify Him but this inestimable price, even the death and the blood of the Son of God, one drop whereof is more precious than the whole world....
>
> To teach that righteousness may be acquired by any other means than by Christ alone, is a horrible blasphemy, and yet it commonly reigneth.[230]

Newell explains,

The reason God hates your trust in your "good works" is, that you offer them to Him instead of resting on the all-glorious work of His Son for you at the cross.

Reflect:

1. What it cost God to give Christ.

2. What it cost Christ to put away sin,—your sin, at the cross.

3. What honor God has given Him "because of the suffering of death."

4. What plans for the future God has arranged through Christ's having made peace by the blood of His cross, to reconcile "things upon the earth and things in the heavens, unto Himself."...

It is ominously bold presumption, when God is calling all to behold His Lamb, to be found asking God to behold your goodness, your works![231]

But what about the rich young ruler? Didn't Jesus tell him to sell all he had and give everything away to the poor? Needham responds,

> Here was a man who wanted eternal life. He wanted what God alone could give. Yet he was unable to open his hands and heart to receive that gift because they were already filled with images of his own riches. His dreams, his hopes, and his values were tied up in his possessions and Jesus knew it. In a sense, Jesus was saying to him, "You say you want Me... yet you don't have any room for Me. You can't receive God's gift—your arms are already too full of your own things. Drop them and receive! Let them go. Open yourself to Me!"
>
> It's still that way. Nothing's changed. What must I do with a God who says "I love you"? Give Him something? Bargain with Him? No, just one thing... unconditionally receive His self-giving—Himself.
>
> Just receive.[232]

SALVATION BY GRACE THROUGH FAITH

Heaven is not a place full of self-righteous pride. It is a place full of praise for God. Justification by grace through faith eliminates self-centered boasting because it limits the believer's role in salvation to acceptance of Christ. "Where is boasting then? It is excluded. By what law? Of works? No, but by the law of faith" (Rom. 3:27). To realize you are worthy only of condemnation, unable to atone for your shortcomings, and totally dependent on Another to save you is humbling. When a person is rescued from death on the basis of Christ's work, he has nothing to boast about except the Savior and His death on the cross (Gal. 6:14; Rev. 5:12).

Faith is the means whereby a sinner may receive "Christ with all His benefits for oneself."[233] Mitchell writes,

> We are justified *by God* (Romans 3). This is the source of our justification. We are justified *by grace*, as Romans 3:24 says, "Being justified freely by his grace." That's the principle of it. We are justified *by faith*, as Romans 5:1 says, "Therefore being justified by faith, we have peace with God." This is the method of receiving justification. And then we are justified *by His blood*, and this is the ground of justification. Romans 5:9 says, "Much more then, being now justified by his blood, we shall be saved from wrath through him."[234]

Samuel Fisk states,

> To be saved, man must do something in the sense of exercising faith, believing the gospel, actively receiving the Saviour... his exercise of that faith is nothing meritorious... Faith, as will be seen, is the mere channel, not the ground of man's salvation. The ground or basis of salvation from sin, of course, is the divine provision in the finished work of Christ; the means or instrument of making effective that heavenly boon is an unworthy person casting himself on God's mercy and accepting it all for himself. This he must do, and he alone can do.[235]

Faith is a basic aspect of life, but all do not have *saving* faith in God. Willard M. Aldrich, who served as president of Multnomah for thirty-five years, writes,

> The Bible not only teaches that men are saved by faith but that men are lost by faith. Faith brings salvation when it lays hold upon God as Creator and Redeemer. This is saving faith. On the other hand, faith may bring disappointment and slavery to sin and death because it is placed upon an

unworthy and incapable object. And this may prove to be condemning faith.

The Apostle Paul tells us that if Jesus Christ had not been raised from the dead... our faith [in Him] would be in vain.... But thank God, He was delivered to death because of our offenses and was raised again because through His death He won forgiveness and justification for those who trust Him (Romans 4:25; 1 Corinthians 15:3-4, 14, 17)....

Failure to believe on the Lord Jesus Christ does not arise out of a lack of capacity for faith but rather because there is a rival faith which precludes confidence in the Saviour....

Many, like the Pharisees, trust in themselves that they are righteous (Luke 18:9). Jesus spoke a parable to the self-righteous Pharisees about the prayers of a self-abasing tax collector. And the despised tax man who prayed, "God be merciful to me a sinner," went down to his house justified rather than the proud Pharisee.

If your faith is resting upon your own righteousness and upon your religious rites and ceremonies, it may well be *condemning* rather than *saving* faith.

Others are like the prosperous farmer whose folly is the subject of another of the parables. He had such bumper crops that he tore down his barns to build larger ones. He made the mistake of believing, however, that prosperity meant security for his soul. And his *false faith* cost him his soul. For God said, "Thou fool, this night thy soul shall be required of thee" (Luke 12:20).

The Bible tells of many others who were lost or destroyed by their faith. They trusted in military might, wealth, lying words and lying vanities, graven images or in their own beauty, righteousness and ways (Psalm 20:7; 44:6; Proverbs 11:28; Jeremiah 7:4, 8; Psalm 31:6; Isaiah 59:4; 42:17; Ezekiel 16:15; 33:13; Hosea 10:13).

History repeats itself, but the mistakes of history can be avoided if we will learn from them.

In the beginning of the race, man fell by faith. He fell from faith in God through faith in Satan and in himself.

Satan first questioned the restriction God had placed upon Adam's freedom to enjoy all things. Then he denied that disobedience would bring death. And finally, he promised that to eat of the fruit of the tree of the knowledge of good and evil would make Adam and Eve as God, wise enough to make moral judgments independent of God. And, because Adam and Eve believed Satan, sin and death entered the race....

Whether you are saved by faith or lost by faith depends upon whom or what you trust....

You are living by faith. Is it faith in the Lord Jesus Christ?[236]

Jesus said, "And this is the will of Him who sent Me, that everyone who sees the Son and believes in Him may have everlasting life; and I will raise him up at the last day" (John 6:40). "It is written in the prophets, 'And they shall all be taught by God.' Therefore everyone who has heard and learned from the Father comes to Me" (John 6:45). Commenting on John 6, Mitchell states,

> Every time a person hears the Gospel, God is teaching men: "This is My Son. This is the One who can save. This is the One who can give life." Everyone has the right to come to Jesus, but many refuse to do so....
>
> Jesus said, "Whoever comes to Me, I will not cast out. Whoever comes to Me, I will give eternal life. Whoever comes to Me, I will give satisfying life. Whoever comes to Me, I will give resurrection life."[237]

Over and over again, Jesus extends a personal invitation to us: "If anyone thirsts, let him come to Me and drink" (John 7:37); "Behold, I stand at the door and knock. If anyone hears My voice and opens the door, I will come in to him and dine with him, and he with Me" (Rev. 3:20); "he who receives Me receives Him who sent Me" (Matt. 10:40).

True Christianity is fundamentally a matter of personal relationship with God. The one who receives Christ becomes a member of God's family: "As many as received Him, to them He gave the right to become children of God, even to those who believe in His name" (John 1:12). The one who receives Jesus also receives eternal life: "And this is the testimony: God has given us eternal life, and this life is in his Son. The one who has the Son has this eternal life; the one who does not have the Son of God does not have this eternal life" (1 John 5:11-12, NET).

He knew all about you when He chose to die for you (John 1:1-3, 14, 29, 3:14-16). Call upon Him: Jesus, Son of God…

RECEIVING CHRIST

There are no magical words. In fact, faith is really a matter of the heart. If you truly want Jesus to be your Savior and are not sure how to begin, know that faith can be expressed in a prayer. As an example, "Jesus, Son of God, thank you for dying for my sins on the cross and for Your resurrection from the dead. I am not worthy of You, but come into my heart. I want to be part of Your family. I trust solely in Your shed blood for the forgiveness of my sins and future home with You. Thank you, God, for loving me so much."

LIFE IN CHRIST

If you receive the Savior, you will gain new capacity to know God and new desire for the things of God (1 Cor. 2:9-12; 1 Pet. 2:2; 2 Pet. 1:2-4). God will never leave you, nor forsake you (Heb. 13:5), and nothing will be able to separate you from His love (Rom. 8:31-39). As you experience His love and grace and come to know Him more and more, it will have a profound impact on you. Good works done out of gratitude to God will enrich your life and bring rewards in the future.

Make reading the Bible a regular part of your life. Read it to see your Savior and to hear from Him. Be sure to pay close attention to the context. There are lessons to be learned from each passage of scripture, but not everything will *directly* apply to you. Take your cares and concerns to Jesus. Be honest with Him. He is there for you (1 Pet. 5:7; Heb. 4:14-16). Learn to rely on His strength; yours isn't sufficient.

Find fellowship with others who believe in the Savior. You need your brothers and sisters in Christ, and they need you. Be sure to be baptized in the name of the Father and of the Son and of the Holy Spirit. This special act is an important part of the Great Commission (Matt. 28:18-20).

As long as we live on this present earth in these mortal bodies of ours, there will be challenges and difficulties and failures. Ultimately, believers will be completely free from sin and all the damage that comes from it. We will have new imperishable bodies that are like Jesus' own glorious body (Phil. 3:21), and we will be thoroughly like Him in character "for we shall see Him as He is" (1 John 3:2).

8

REFLECTIONS AND PRACTICAL ISSUES

With the exegesis of the major passages completed, we take up some personal reflections and practical issues.

INADEQUATE WARNING, INADEQUATE DOCTRINE

Eternal conscious torment represents danger far above all other dangers. Given the importance of providing warning (Ezek. 33:1-9), if ECT were true, it would surely be unambiguously declared throughout God's Word, yet we found no hint of eternal torment in Genesis. Indeed, the entire Old Testament is devoid of the concept.

Of the some 23,000 verses in the Old Testament, there are only *two* from which traditionalists even attempt to make a case. One is Isaiah 66:24. We thoroughly examined this verse in Chapter 3. We found that it spoke of literal corpses on Israeli soil following the Battle of Armageddon—a gruesome picture of death unrelated to torment. The other is Daniel 12:2, a verse that assures us that there will be a resurrection of the unsaved without elaborating on punishment. It appears that the righteous will have fixed contempt for the shameful evil of the ungodly who rise to condemnation, but little else can be concluded with certainty.

Neither torment nor any equivalent term is found in Matthew 25:46. Likewise, in Matthew 25:41 and Revelation 20:15, nothing is said about ECT when the unsaved are cast into the lake of fire. Torment is involved in the story of the rich man and Lazarus, but the context is the temporal intermediate state—*not* hell. In Revelation, the context of 14:11 is the Great Tribulation, and a satanic trinity is in view in 20:10. "Wailing and gnashing of teeth" is never said to be eternal.

If great danger exists, subtlety doesn't cut it. Some doctrines are pieced together from various passages of scripture; the enormity of the danger represented by eternal torment, however, demands straightforward declaration: crystal-clear warning in scripture. It just isn't there.

THE PRODIGAL SON'S FATHER— TRADITIONALIST OR CONDITIONALIST?

Jesus told the story of a man who had two sons. The younger son requested and received an inheritance from his father and left for a far country where he squandered all of his resources with wild living. Flat broke as a severe famine hit, the prodigal son found himself friendless and starving. In the midst of his suffering, however, he came to his senses and headed back home. What happens next is one of the most moving pictures in all of scripture:

And he arose and came to his father. But when he was still a great way off, his father saw him and had compassion, and ran and fell on his neck and kissed him. (Luke 15:20)

Jesus' portrait of the Father is all the more moving in light of a comment that the late Multnomah professor James Braga made in class one day: "As far as I know, this is the only time in scripture when God was ever said to be in a hurry."

But what if the prodigal son had not returned home? How might the story have ended?

Let's consider two alternative endings.

In the first alternative ending, the prodigal son does not repent and dies by starvation in that far country. The father mourns his son's life coming to an end. At the same time, the father knows that to return home or not was his son's choice to make. This ending is in keeping with the conditionalist view that the ultimate fate of the unsaved is to suffer an irreversible death that is painful in accordance with one's sin.

A traditionalist ending would have the father say to his older son: "Your brother is suffering greatly in a far country and near to death due to his waywardness and impenitence; however, a painful death by starvation would not be near enough justice. He deserves to be sustained forever in a perpetual state of starvation. His suffering will never end because there is no end to my wrath toward the impenitent."

Does the "traditionalist" father even remotely resemble the father of the prodigal son?

RESCUE FROM DEATH

TRADITIONALISM'S INCOMPATIBILITY WITH THE ESSENCE OF CHRISTIANITY

God is not some impersonal force. He is the infinite personal Creator of the universe. Adam and Eve were created in God's image. This does not mean that they were created all-powerful or all-knowing or everywhere present or as immortal beings. "Man," notes Francis Schaeffer, "being made in the image of God, was made to have a personal relationship with Him."[238] And not just any personal relationship; God seeks a love relationship. A true love relationship requires two truly willing partners. Alcorn writes,

> C. S. Lewis said, "Why, then, did God give them free will? Because free will, though it makes evil possible, is also the only thing that makes possible any love or goodness or joy worth having. A world of automata—of creatures that worked like machines—would hardly be worth creating."
>
> Can real love exist without freedom? Suppose that through threats, drugs, or hypnotism I could coerce my wife to love me. First, it would be a contradiction in terms. Her "loving" words and actions would be an illusion, meaning nothing if they originated in me, not in her. I don't want to force her to love me; I want her to love me simply because she does, because she wants to. I may inspire or "win" her love through my devotion to her, but I cannot dictate it, nor would I if I could. Forced love is no love at all. Love requires the freedom not to love.[239]

True love cannot be coerced, yet isn't ECT the ultimate threat? What greater coercion could there possibly be?

Alcorn recognizes that God "doesn't want people who merely desire to escape Hell. He wants people who value and treasure him above all else, who long to be with him."[240] Why, then, would God establish a hell so horrific that escaping it would be paramount for anyone who took the peril seriously? Moreover, while the manipulative potential of ECT is evident, it is difficult to see how the terrifying threat of endless unbearable pain serves God's desire for a truly genuine love relationship.

If forced love is no love at all, is not ECT incompatible with the essence of Christianity?

THE TRADITIONALIST'S UNRESOLVED CONFLICT

The Father's giving of the Son who left the glory of heaven for the cross is the greatest of all love stories. The thought of fathers and mothers and sons and daughters being tormented eternally, in contrast, is horrific. As John Stott famously said of ECT,

> Well, emotionally, I find the concept intolerable and do not understand how people can live with it without either cauterising their feelings or cracking under the strain.[241]

Not surprisingly, most traditionalists are conflicted. In *Erasing Hell*, Francis Chan sides with ECT, which prompts a confession that surely resonates with many:

> What causes my heart to ache right now as I'm writing this is that my life shows little evidence that I actually believe this. Every time my thoughts wander to the future of unbelievers, I quickly brush them aside so they don't ruin my day.... We can talk about the fate of some hypothetical person, but as I look up and see their smiles, I have to ask myself if I really believe what I have written in this book....

As I have said all along, I don't *feel like* believing in hell. And yet I do. Maybe someday I will stand in complete agreement with Him, but for now I attribute the discrepancy to an underdeveloped sense of justice on my part. God is perfect.[242]

So how do traditionalists cope? Ignoring the subject as much as possible is one coping mechanism. Another is to put ECT in the category of things beyond our understanding. Chan writes, "He hasn't asked us to figure out why He does the things He does. We can't. We are not capable. Our thinking is inferior to His."[243] This leads to Chan's suggestion that we "put our energy toward submitting rather than overanalyzing"[244] and "cling to Abraham's words in Genesis 18:25: 'Shall not the Judge of all the earth do what is just?'"[245]

But does this approach really work? Is final judgment not to be understood in this life? Henry Constable writes,

> Future punishment is a matter fully placed before us. No question occupies a more distinct position than it does in divine revelation. We are clearly told its cause and its nature: we are told to ponder on and study it.... In the question of future punishment we have the highest case on which any tribunal shall have ever sat; and we may be sure that the Judge of all the Earth will do right, not merely in His own eyes, but in those of all His intelligent creation; of the angels who stand round His throne; of the redeemed who rejoice in their acceptance; of the very damned who listen to their sentence.
>
> But we are often told that, while no doubt God's conduct towards sinners will one day appear to the redeemed and even to the lost to have been just, yet that we must be content *to wait* until it shall so appear. This life is to pass away, the hour of resurrection must come, the throne of

judgment must be set, the guilt of the lost be displayed, the everlasting sentence be passed, *and then*, the redeemed and the lost alike will see that God's ways were just. Not so, we reply. God appeals to us now to judge.... When the judgment is set, and the sentence passed, *it is too late*.[246]

Jesus came to reveal the Father to a broken world. He went to where people lived, broke bread with them, heard their concerns, answered their questions, healed the sick, brought sight to the blind, demonstrated the magnificence of God's grace at Calvary, and brought hope of immortality by rising from the dead. Josh McDowell would call it evidence that demands a verdict. McDowell writes,

> My heart and head were created to work and believe together in harmony. Christ commanded us to "... love the Lord your God with all your heart, and with all your soul, and with all your *mind*" (Matthew 22:37).
> When Jesus Christ and the apostles called upon a person to exercise faith, it was not a "blind faith" but rather an "intelligent faith."...
> I took the evidence that I could gather and put it on the scales. The scales tipped the way of Christ being the Son of God and resurrected from the dead. It was so overwhelmingly leaning to Christ that when I became a Christian, it was a "step into the light" rather than a "leap into the darkness."[247]

The penalty for sin that Jesus rescues believers from is not only part and parcel of the Gospel but is an expression of divine justice and a revelation of God's character. How could it not be essential evidence that demands a verdict? Constable continues,

> But they who tell us to *wait in faith* wholly miscalculate the real position of the question before us. *They suppose faith in*

God is to sustain the mind against the appearance of injustice in God's dealings with men. They reverse the mode of God's own proceeding. They suppose faith first to exist, and this faith is to withstand and subdue all that may appear unjust. The exact opposite to this is the way in which God deals with man. *He has come to an unbelieving and alienated world and put his character before them to win their fear, their repentance, and their love.... It was to a world of unbelievers* that God was proposed as a God of justice, as well as pity and of love. To this world, which had no faith, God was proposed for acceptance.... God's character and conduct are to win faith; not to be sustained by faith against appearances. The missionary tells the unbeliever what kind of God the God of the Christian is, to convert the unbeliever to the faith.[248]

If believers who grew up in traditionalist churches struggle with ECT, how much more problematic is ECT when it comes to evangelism? Blind faith in the justice of ECT collides with the realities of evangelism. It is the *goodness* of God that leads to repentance (Rom. 2:4). God "did not leave Himself without witness, in that He *did good*" (Acts 14:17). "We love Him because He first *loved* us" (1 John 4:19). These truths are so powerful that most traditionalists abandon ECT when asking the unsaved to believe in Christ.

Bill Bright's Gospel tract, *Have You Heard of the Four Spiritual Laws?*, with over 100 million copies in circulation worldwide, begins with the love of God and says nothing about ECT.[249] The Navigators' tract, *The Bridge to Life,* says nothing about ECT. It proclaims salvation from "death and certain judgment" through faith in Christ.[250] Billy Graham's online "Peace with God" Gospel presentation emphasizes the love of God and is devoid of ECT.[251]

The Gideons International began the Bible Project in 1908. Serving more than 190 countries, in more than 90 languages, the Gideons have distributed more than 2 *billion* Bibles and New Testaments.[252] I received a pocket New Testament with Psalms and Proverbs from the Gideons in the sixth grade at Star Lake Elementary, a public school. In the back is given the plan of salvation. There are four statements with corresponding scripture verses typed out: God Loves You (John 3:16; Romans 5:8), All Are Sinners (Romans 3:23, 3:10), God's Remedy for Sin (Romans 6:23; John 1:12; 1 Corinthians 15:3-4), and All May Be Saved Now (Revelation 3:20; Romans 10:13). There is not a hint of ECT in the Gideons' presentation of the Gospel.[253]

Erasing Hell ends with an invitation to respond to God in love and trust. Interestingly, Chan's *"Finally... Are You Sure?"* conclusion adopts conditionalist language when calling people to trust Christ. Chan writes, "And so we all have a choice before us. Choose life or choose death."[254]

Traditionalists understand the second death to represent ECT. Moreover, Chan strongly urges that it is time to stop being embarrassed and stop trying to "cover" for God.[255] So why doesn't Chan state that the choice is between eternal life and eternal suffering?

Some traditionalists do preach eternal torment in presenting the Gospel, but the great verses of the Bible commonly used in evangelism do not readily accommodate ECT. Moreover, it is awkward to speak metaphorically of death as endless misery while sharing the story of Christ's literal crucifixion, literal burial, literal empty tomb, and literal bodily resurrection. Primarily, though, to verbalize God's love for people and the eternal torment of sons and daughters and mothers and fathers *in the same breath* is simply too incoherent.

Conditionalists need not hesitate to affirm their understanding of final judgment when sharing the Gospel. The essence of conditionalism is evident in verses such as Romans 6:23 and John 3:16. Traditionalists typically remain conflicted, holding to ECT in doctrinal statements while avoiding its mention when doing evangelism.

A WORD OF ENCOURAGEMENT TO RELUCTANT TRADITIONALISTS

If you are one who hasn't had the heart to preach the endless suffering that is in the doctrinal statement of your church or ministry, don't beat yourself up. You've been on the right track, practically speaking. Fudge observes,

> We do find early Christian apostles, evangelists, and other disciples telling listeners across the Roman Empire about Jesus. God raised Jesus from the dead, they say. Through Jesus, anyone—Jews, Romans, people from all nations—can enjoy forgiveness of sins, receive God's Spirit, become children of God. But the message that rings most distinctly, as Acts reports the gospel's movement across the Greco-Roman world, is the offer of *life in Christ.*
>
> What about *gehenna*, the "hell" of final punishment? It is never mentioned in Acts. Maybe it's listed under "Lake of Fire"? Not so. Perhaps graphic warnings of eternal torment? Not even once. Warning of torment but not so graphic? Sorry. Still completely missing. One begins to suspect that the apostles motivated people with something better than fear.[256]

Steve Gregg writes,

> It was not fear of his father's wrath, nor threats of his punishment, that converted the prodigal in the far country. It was the memory of the goodness of his father toward his servants (Luke 15:17).[257]

God does not threaten the world with endless suffering. The Bible's graphic warnings of hell assure us that eternal *loss of life* is to be *taken seriously*. The lake of fire is *where* the eternal death of the unsaved takes place. Fire, or the power it represents, is the *means* of accomplishing the bottom-line reality that Paul faithfully declared: "The wages of sin is death."

Those who preach rescue from death and an everlasting love relationship with the Creator through faith in the death and resurrection of the Lord Jesus are in good company, that of the apostles.

WHAT'S AT STAKE—A PERSONAL TESTIMONY

I grew up in a home where neither God nor religion was ever mentioned or discussed. Church was never on the radar. Christmas was for presents. Easter was about chocolate bunnies and dyeing eggs to hide for my younger brothers. My only exposure to scripture came in the seventh grade. The Bible given to me by the Gideons was quickly hidden in my room without a word to anyone. The next year, I got it out and, for a time, read some of the Psalms, but it would not be until after I graduated from high school that Christ would reach me.

RESCUE FROM DEATH

In the summer of 1969, a friend invited me to go on a youth retreat in the San Juan Islands. Camping out on beautiful Orcas Island, I encountered a group of people who loved Jesus. The joyful spirit of these believers and the testimonies of what Christ meant to them were impossible to ignore. By the end of the retreat, I wanted to know about Christ and sought out one of the leaders.

As we waited for the ferry and rode it to the mainland, Richard shared from God's Word: "In the beginning was the Word, and the Word was with God, and the Word was God. And the Word became flesh and dwelt among us" (John 1:1, 14). I listened intently to each verse, nodded, and wanted to hear more. "All have sinned and fall short of the glory of God" (Rom. 3:23); "Christ died for our sins according to the Scriptures, and that He was buried, and that He rose again the third day" (1 Cor. 15:3-4). No verse mentioned hell, and no trace of ECT was involved.

In the ferry terminal on the mainland, I was still trying to take it all in as the time came for everyone to pile into cars for the trip home. Richard wanted to pray. It was the first time anyone had ever prayed for me in my presence, and I think there might have been a tear in the corner of my eye as I headed for the cars. Waiting for the caravan to get on the road, I looked out over the water, the sun bright above the horizon, and the realization came over me that I was loved by God. I said to Him, "When I get home, I'm going to ask You into my life."

Like snowflakes and fingerprints, probably no two salvation stories are alike. I share mine in the hope that traditionalists might take a "where the rubber meets the road" look at their teaching.

Suppose Richard had used the parable of the rich man and Lazarus in Luke 16 to explain the wages of sin. Imagine if I had been asked to visualize the rich man suffering in flames and hearing him say, "This... is it. Too late. No release. No hope. For eternity."[258]

I can't say for sure what I would have thought or how I would have reacted, because I wasn't presented with a traditionalist message. I'll leave it to you, the reader, to mull over how the prospect of my family and most of my friends being tormented forever might have affected me in the most important moment of my young life.

I'm eternally grateful that I left the San Juan Islands with the overwhelming sense that God loved me. Does your presentation of the Gospel facilitate or hinder a deep-down sense within that God is good and loves the world?

THE MAKING OF A TRADITIONALIST

When I first began my investigation of the key texts, around 2001, I thought the conditionalist viewpoint was something that I had no experience with.[259] Recently, upon reflection, it dawned on me that early in my Christian life, I had actually been a conditionalist. So many years had passed by that it seemed like I had always held to ECT, but that was not the case.

The first scriptures I ever read, the Psalms, are pregnant with the perishing of the ungodly. The idea that the unsaved continue on forever is utterly foreign to God's songbook. In the Gospel, Jesus is crucified and His body buried in a tomb. I took John 3:16 and Romans 6:23 at face value when Richard shared the Gospel with me because I had no reason not to. If someone had asked if I were a conditionalist or a traditionalist, I wouldn't have known what they were talking about, but my initial understanding was conditionalist.

How did I become a traditionalist? I drifted into it. Traditionalism isn't so much formally taught as it is caught. In the evangelical world where I fellowshipped, many issues were studied and debated: the sovereignty of God and free will of man, eternal security, Lordship salvation, Calvinism, Arminianism, tongues, prophecy, and biblical church leadership, for example. Hell, however, we never studied or debated. There was a common understanding that "eternal separation from God" constituted hell. This popular version of traditionalism is communicated through expressions such as "everyone must exist somewhere forever." Repeated exposure to this way of thinking resulted in my believing that God had created man as an eternal being, which, coupled with the power of choice, logically led to eternal conscious separation from God for the impenitent.[260] I wrote my traditionalist understanding down long ago in some teaching notes:

> God created Adam and Eve with the power of *choice*. People would not be human without the power of choice.
>
> When a person chooses to reject his Creator, he also rejects all that belongs to the Creator and all that reflects His glory—the beauty of the earth, the singing of the birds, the blue of the sky, the warmth of the sun. The reason that hell is such a terrible place is because the only aspect of God that is evident in hell is His wrath against sin.
>
> God created man not only with the power of choice but as an *eternal being*. Thus, to argue against the existence of an eternal hell is to argue against man being created as an eternal being.
>
> In short, the consequences of sin are great because the capacities that God created people with are great. Being eternal, everyone must exist somewhere, and those who reject

the only remedy for their sin cannot abide in the favor and fellowship of their glorious Creator, life apart from Whom is hell.

Notice that my traditionalist explanation of hell did not cite a single verse of scripture. In the case of hell, I had accepted a predetermined conclusion. This was uncharacteristic of how I normally operated. I believe that all doctrine should be established by thorough exegesis of scripture, but rather than recognizing ECT as an issue to be tested (1 Thess. 5:21), for decades, I did little more than look for a way to justify the eternal-separation view that I had been schooled in. In the sphere of my fellowship, ECT was considered a closed subject, and I had succumbed to the status quo.

WHAT WERE WE THINKING?

My former traditionalist position suggested that ECT was a product of the immortality of the soul and choice. I failed to account for a crucial question, however: Why would an all-wise and maximally good God bring two factors into being that inevitably result in endless suffering for some? Had I pondered this question, I might have realized sooner that living forever was conditional (Gen. 3:22; John 6:51; 2 Tim. 1:10).

Traditionalist literature contains many "what were we thinking" moments. One common argument virtually admits that the unsaved do not merit endless torment. Alcorn writes,

> D. A. Carson argues that rebellion may continue eternally in Hell, and if so, then Hell is eternal precisely because the sinful rebellion is eternal. Hell would then be a place where

"sinners go on sinning and receiving the recompense of their sin, refusing, always refusing, to bend the knee." Hell would be ever-ongoing punishment for ever-ongoing sins.[261]

This is an inexplicable suggestion for a traditionalist. If it takes the sins of this life *plus* sins committed throughout eternity to merit ECT, then the sins of this life do not merit ECT.

Moreover, this traditionalist argument prompts the question: Why would God eternally sustain what His holiness abhors?

The reality is that it has never been the intention of God that people should continue in a sinful state forever. In Genesis 3, we saw cherubim and a flaming sword prevent sinners from reaching the fruit on the tree of life. Contrary to the traditionalist claim that the flames of hell do not consume sinners, chaff utterly burns up (*katakaio*) in unquenchable fire (Matt. 3:12). Likewise, weeds are consumed (*katakaio*) by God's judgment fire (Matt 13:40). Sodom and Gomorrah, which serve as examples to the ungodly of God's judgment fire, are no more. Dyer writes,

> In my many travels to Israel I have taken over four thousand slides and pictures, but I have yet to get a picture of Sodom or Gomorrah. When God destroyed these cities in the time of Abraham, he "rained down burning sulphur on Sodom and Gomorrah" (Genesis 19:24).... From the moment God overthrew them, these cities ceased to exist and were never again inhabited as cities.[262]

It is not that God has failed to plainly declare the penalty for sin; it is that His efforts are for naught if one reads words such as perish, die, kill, death, consume, destruction, and burn up utterly *and thinks* "exist somewhere forever" or "endless misery."

Another issue is the mental aspect of an eternity in hell. Drawing upon the rich man and Lazarus as if the context were hell rather than the intermediate state, Hades/Sheol, Alcorn writes,

> Jesus taught that an unbridgeable chasm separates the wicked in Hell from the righteous in paradise. The wicked suffer terribly, remain conscious, retain their desires and memories, long for relief, cannot find comfort, cannot leave their torment, and have no hope (see Luke 16:19-31).[263]

The rich man was in torment, yet he conversed with Abraham and expressed concern for his brothers. That is, he seemed to be functioning normally. *How would this be possible throughout eternity in hell?* If a person is put in a position of continual pain and agony, what happens when hope of deliverance fades? Sooner or later, he will break down. Logically, the eternal torment of human beings would essentially turn hell into an enormous hospital with two sections: the intensive care unit and the psychiatric ward. How can an eternity of torment awful beyond words not cause the psychological disintegration of the sinner? For the traditionalist understanding of hell to be true, would not God have to continuously grant superhuman mental health to the impenitent?

Traditionalism is truly burdened with problems.

ABOUT CHURCH TRADITION

"The Church has taught for the past 2,000 years that hell is eternal conscious torment," states Phil Fernandes.[264] Many traditionalists make this claim. How true is it? How much legitimate weight does church history provide ECT?

RESCUE FROM DEATH

During the first 500 years there was no consensus on hell. There were three major views: conditionalism, universalism, and ECT. Gregg writes,

> All three views of hell were prevalent, existing side-by-side from the second century onward, and were regarded as acceptable for Christians to believe, at least for the first four or five centuries of the church.[265]

Glenn Peoples states,

> Historically, many of the proponents of the doctrine of the eternal torments of the lost—in fact those who were responsible for cementing the place of that view within Christian theology—did indeed argue from the immortality of every human soul to the doctrine of eternal torment in hell. Clement of Alexandria made the argument in approximately AD 195: "All souls are immortal, even those of the wicked, for whom it were better that they were not deathless. For, punished with the endless vengeance of quenchless fire, and not dying, it is impossible for them to have a period put to their misery." But it was Augustine of Hippo, more than any other theologian of the first half millennium of Christian history, who galvanized the doctrine of the immortality of all human souls, as well as the role that this belief was to play in the doctrine of hell....
>
> There were, however, other voices among the church fathers who did not share the stance of Clement of Alexandria and Augustine. Among writers like Ignatius of Antioch, the author of the *Epistle of Barnabas*, Irenaeus of Lyons, Arnobius of Cicca, and even Athanasius the Great, modern conditionalists find a view much more like their own than like that of many Christians. In the view of these fathers—representing the earliest post-apostolic perspective, Christ came so that he could save people from the impending consequences of sin, and thereby "breathe immortality into

His church" so that those within would not "perish," [*Ign. Eph.* 17; *ANF* 1:56] saying that if God did not save us and chose instead "to reward us according to our works, we should cease to be." [*Ign. Magn.* 10; *ANF* 1:63] They taught that instead of living forever, the one who rejects God's kingdom in favor of other things "shall be destroyed with his works." [*Barn.* 21; *ANF* 1:149] They taught Christians that we are like God's other creations in the sense that they "endure as long as God wills that they should have an existence and continuance," and that "it is the Father of all who imparts continuance for ever and ever on those who are saved." The one who rejects the gift of life, however, "deprives himself of continuance for ever and ever," and he "shall justly not receive from Him length of days for ever and ever." [*Against Heresies* 2.34.3; *ANF* 1:412] This is a punishment which is eternal, but not because the lost themselves will live forever. Instead the punishment is eternal insofar as what the lost will miss out on is eternal. "That punishment falls upon them because they are destitute of all that is good. Now, good things are eternal and without end with God, and therefore the loss of these is also eternal and never-ending." [*Against Heresies* 5.27.2; *ANF* 1:556] Among these fathers we read that a being "cannot be immortal which does suffer pain," and that those who are finally lost, regardless of whether their souls survive the death of their bodies in this world, will finally die "man's real death, this which leaves nothing behind," and "being annihilated, pass away vainly in everlasting destruction." [*Against the Heathen* 2:14; *ANF* 6:439-40][266]

Augustine's position was adopted by the Roman Catholic Church. Traditionalists claim the Roman Catholic years between the church fathers and the Reformation as if they add weight to their view, yet are traditionalists also willing to own the role that ECT played in the inquisitions?

The traditional view of hell also prevailed during the Reformation. The story is not a pretty one, however. During the days of the Reformation, conditionalism was favored by "many of the radical reformers known as Anabaptists."[267] Anabaptists, however, were scorned by Luther, Calvin, and Catholics. *Eerdmans' Handbook to the History of Christianity* states,

> The Anabaptists made the most radical attempt of the Reformation era to renew the church. They did not consist of a single, coherent organization, but a loose grouping of movements. All rejected infant baptism and practiced the baptism of adults upon confession of faith. They never accepted the label "Anabaptist" (meaning "rebaptizer")—a term of reproach which was coined by their opponents. They objected to the implication that the ceremonial sprinkling which they had received as infants had in fact been a valid baptism....
>
> Anabaptist beliefs about the church were very distinctive. They were not interested in simply reforming the church; they were committed to *restoring* it to the vigor and faithfulness of its earliest centuries. In the Scriptures they read of a church which was not a wealthy and powerful institution—but a brotherhood, a family of faith. It existed, not because it was recognized by some outside ecclesiastical or political organization, but because God was at work among his people....
>
> In their congregations, all members were to be believers, baptized voluntarily as adults upon confession of faith. Decision-making was to be by the entire membership. In deciding matters of doctrine, the authority of Scripture was to be interpreted, not by a dogmatic tradition or by an ecclesiastical leader, but by the consensus of the local gathering—in which all could speak, and listen critically....
>
> A fourth major Anabaptist conviction was the insistence upon the separation of church and state. Christians, they

claimed, were a "free, unforced, uncompelled people." Faith is a free gift of God, and the authorities exceed their competence when they "champion the Word of God with a fist." The Anabaptists also believed that the church was distinct from society, even if society claimed to be Christian. Christ's true followers were a pilgrim people; and his church was an association of perpetual aliens.

To the established leaders of Protestant and Catholic Europe, these beliefs (and the personalities and movements which gave rise to them) were alarming indeed....

By 1527 [the Reformers] had determined to use all necessary means to root out Anabaptism. They were joined in this determination by the Catholic authorities. To Protestants and Catholics alike, the Anabaptists seemed not only to be dangerous heretics; they also seemed to threaten the religious and social stability of Christian Europe. In the carnage of the next quarter of a century thousands of Anabaptists were put to death (by fire in the Catholic territories, by drowning and the sword under Protestant regimes). Thousands more saved their skins by recanting.[268]

Rather than learning from each other, sadly, blood was shed and a unique opportunity for theological discourse and advancement was missed. Fudge writes,

> As Augustine had fixed the tradition for later Catholicism, so Calvin sealed it with the Protestant stamp of approval 1100 years later. The understanding of Tertullian and Augustine, of Chrysostom and Anselm and Aquinas, of Calvin and Bullinger, would receive official status in many Protestant creeds. Opposition from "outsiders" such as many Anabaptists (and later Adventist groups), or from heretical groups such as the Socinians (and later Jehovah's Witnesses), would only harden the established churches in the received interpretation and would effectively prevent any full-scale

exegetical study of the subject in the same open-minded manner other important subjects might receive.[269]

The modern era has seen a slow but steady shift from ECT to conditionalism. During the twentieth century, opposition to ECT was especially strong in England. Harold Guillebaud, Basil Atkinson, John Wenham, and John Stott are among those who set forth cases for conditionalism. A sense of the exegetically robust international rejection of ECT is captured in *Rethinking Hell: Readings in Evangelical Conditionalism*. In this excellent collection of writings, conditionalism is affirmed by the aforementioned British scholars and a host of others, including Earle Ellis, Philip Hughes, and Edward Fudge. John G. Stackhouse Jr. writes,

> There are chapters upon chapters of high-quality argument: exegesis of Scriptures, logical deductions, inferences to best explanations, metaphors and thought experiments, and more. I've never seen such a book, in fact, that piled up such a rich array of reasons to hold to a particular theological idea.[270]

Are the outstanding evangelical leaders who taught conditionalism and those who embraced their teaching not part of the church?

Are the Seventh Day Adventists, over 17 million strong, who hold to the deity, virgin birth, sinless life, miracles, substitutionary atonement, and bodily resurrection of the Lord Jesus Christ not part of the church?

In 1989, over 600 evangelical leaders convened at Trinity Evangelical Divinity School to discuss "Evangelical Essentials."

Packer presented a paper that sought to put annihilationism outside of evangelicalism. The attempt failed. Packer writes,

> It turns out that the conference was split down the middle over the annihilation question. The *Christianity Today* report said: "Strong disagreements did surface over the position of annihilationism... the conference was almost evenly divided as to how to deal with the issue in the affirmations statement, and no renunciation of the position was included in the draft document."[271]

In 2000, the Evangelical Alliance Commission on Unity and Truth among Evangelicals (ACUTE), under the auspices of the Evangelical Alliance, "the largest and oldest body representing the UK's two million evangelical Christians,"[272] released a report entitled *The Nature of Hell*. The report "concluded that annihilationism and conditional immortality represented a 'significant minority evangelical view,' and that this view fell within the parameters set by the 1970 Basis of Faith."[273] The ACUTE report also declared,

> Furthermore, we believe that the traditionalist-conditionalist debate on hell should be regarded as a secondary rather than a primary issue for evangelical theology. Although hell is a profoundly serious matter, we view the holding of either one of these two views of it over against the other to be neither essential in respect of Christian doctrine, nor finally definitive of what it means to be an evangelical Christian.[274]

In short, as Packer overestimated anticipated support for ECT, even so traditionalists overreach when they claim ECT to be "the view of the church for 2000 years."

THE CATCH-22 THAT SUSTAINS ECT

A Christian worldview once was dominant in the United States. The late nineteenth and early twentieth century, however, saw an assault on the scriptures that eventually produced our modern secular society. David O. Beale cites three driving factors of liberalism:

> There were three main weapons in the arsenal of liberalism that opened the way for the rapid expansion of liberalism in America after the Civil War: Darwinian evolution, comparative religion, and higher criticism. Evolution attacked the biblical account of creation, as well as bringing into question the depravity of man and the significance of the work of Christ. Comparative religion attacked the uniqueness of Christianity as the way of salvation and the need for divine revelation. Biblical criticism attacked the integrity and historicity of Scripture. Hence, the focus of the assault was the authority and reliability of the Bible.[275]

Fudge wrote in 1982:

> Truly, the "fundamentals" of Christianity were at stake, and emotions rightfully ran high. There are older preachers today who still remember the trauma of this fight they beheld or survived forty and fifty years ago.
>
> Anything remotely associated with the "modernists" was understandably tainted for orthodox folk. "Modernists" denied that anyone would burn forever in conscious torment; *ergo*, anyone who even looked askance at the traditionalist hell came under immediate suspicion as a latent or closet "modernist."[276]

It was in the midst of the turmoil and controversy brought about by the rise of liberalism that the doctrinal statements of most American evangelical Bible colleges and seminaries were formulated. When the ink dried on these critical documents, ECT was placed on an equal footing with the virgin birth and deity of Christ. Because most evangelical schools require faculty members to sign doctrinal statements, the inclusion of ECT meant that just as one cannot deny the deity of Christ and teach at Moody Bible Institute, for example, neither can one move from ECT to a conditional immortality understanding of hell without suffering loss of employment.

> To maintain continuity and consistency with the heritage entrusted to its care, Moody expects faculty and administration to agree with, personally adhere to and support Moody's doctrinal distinctives as noted above and defined in the following Institutional Positions Related to the Moody Bible Institute Doctrinal Statement (1928)....
> The retribution of the wicked and unbelieving and the rewards of the righteous are everlasting, and as the reward is conscious, so is the retribution....
> This statement excludes any position which asserts a... complete cessation of consciousness... or annihilation of the damned[277]

One of the most outstanding expositors of God's Word ever to serve at Moody Bible Institute was William R. Newell. I built on Newell's work to make the key point: *Jesus died a redemptive death at Calvary that we might not die a redemptionless death in the lake of fire.* Moody is a premillennial school, and *Rescue from Death* is written from a premillennial viewpoint, yet the faculty of Moody Bible Institute are not free to examine the argument for conditionalism made in *Rescue from Death* without potential loss of employment hanging over head. Indeed, unless one is truly prepared to lose his or her dream job, it is difficult to see how the faculties of conservative evangelical schools can consider conditionalism with the heart of a Berean, no matter who were to make the presentation.

In 2012, I sent copies of the original *Rescue from Death* (subtitled *John 3:16 Salvation*) across the country. Interestingly, those with jobs on the line didn't acknowledge receiving *Rescue*.[278] In contrast, evangelicals without jobs on the line responded with thankfulness and positive feedback. Most had switched from ECT to conditionalism.

One professor, loved and respected by many after over forty years of teaching Bible and Theology at a well-known evangelical school, shared that he hadn't taken time to seriously grapple with final punishment until after he had retired. He had chosen to focus on other issues because further investigation into hell might result in him not being able to sign the doctrinal statement. The blunt reality, as he called it, of having to sign the doctrinal statement not only inhibited his willingness to rethink hell while employed but in retirement also made him hesitant to ask colleagues yet under contract to join him in taking a closer look at the subject, even though he now had serious reservations about the scriptural basis for ECT.

What a predicament. A proper examination of hell requires the freedom to believe whatever scripture affirms, but conservative evangelical schools will terminate the employment of teachers who take verses such as Matthew 10:28 at face value. Might this help explain why ECT has been the dominant view in conservative evangelical circles in our own day?

IS A LEVEL PLAYING FIELD TOO MUCH TO HOPE FOR?

The realization that cessation of life is heaven's ultimate solution for the impenitent set me free to think about ECT in a way that wasn't previously possible. I was free to shudder and to be repulsed without fear of offending my Savior. Now I wonder how I could have ever attributed ECT to God. Forgive me, Lord, for having thought the unthinkable about You.

Understandably, I've wanted to see evangelical institutions reject ECT and embrace conditionalism in doctrinal statements. Upon reflection, however, I think unity, research, and a Berean spirit would be better served if Bible colleges and seminaries adopted language specific enough to affirm the resurrection of the unsaved to face final judgment and general enough to allow for either ECT or conditionalism. This could be accomplished by sticking to biblical language, such as resurrection to condemnation (John 5:29).[279]

As terrible an error as I believe ECT to be, the fact remains that many were indoctrinated in ECT at a young age by believers who had themselves been likewise trained. We should keep this in mind, especially if conditionalism becomes the dominant view. I don't want to see traditionalists fired or denied employment. We can well afford to be charitable to our traditionalist brethren, trusting that the truth about hell will be evident where the opportunity to freely discuss the biblical texts is allowed.

Will we see a level playing field before the Lord returns? It has been more than a quarter of a century since John Stott wrote,

> I do plead for frank dialogue among Evangelicals on the basis of Scripture. I also believe that the ultimate annihilation of the wicked should at least be accepted as a legitimate, biblically founded alternative to their eternal conscious torment.[280]

Do you want to be counted among those who refused such a reasonable request? If you don't, why not speak up? Why not echo John Stott's plea to level the playing field? Every voice matters. Will yours be heard?

MY JOHN 3:16 PRAYER

I have always loved John 3:16 because it is such a beautiful expression of the Gospel. Though deeply committed to taking John 3:16 at face value, I had a blind spot. For decades, instead of being instructed by the word *perish*, I read John 3:16 as if the words "suffer endlessly" were in the text. Today, I read every word of John 3:16 with the heart of a child. I rejoice in a Savior who loves everyone, died for the world, and rescues from death all who believe in Him.

My prayer is that the true love and true justice of John 3:16 will reach a world desperately in need of the Savior. May every heart be filled with an overwhelming sense of the goodness of God.

SMALL GROUP DISCUSSION QUESTIONS

CHAPTER 1

1) What is the worst pain you have ever experienced? How long did it last? Can you imagine anyone suffering forever?

2) According to Romans 1, what was the original understanding of God's righteous penalty for sin?

3) If God had not acted in grace when Adam and Eve sinned, would the human race exist?

4) Compare and contrast: What do the traditional view of hell and conditional immortality have in common? How do these two views differ?

5) If a person rejects the Creator, does he deserve to live in the Creator's universe?

6) If eternal suffering is the penalty for sin, was the Garden of Eden a paradise or an immensely fearful danger zone?

7) The idea that the human soul is immortal was foundational to Tertullian and Augustine's belief in ECT. Did Tertullian and Augustine build on a faulty premise? (Genesis 3:22, John 6:51, 2 Timothy 1:10)

8) In light of Ezekiel 33:1-9, how important is it to provide warning of impending danger?

9) Given the gravity of the danger, if ECT were true, would it not be plainly declared throughout the Bible? What are we to conclude, then, if this is not the case?

10) The earliest scripture typically cited by traditionalists in support of their position is Isaiah 66:24. Therefore, if traditionalism is true, for more than half of human history, God kept silent about the penalty of ECT that loomed over one generation after the next. Does such silence seem reasonable?

11) Does it seem reasonable that God would eternally sustain what His holiness abhors? In Genesis 3:22-24, does God act to prevent sinners from continuing forever in a sinful condition?

CHAPTER 2

1) *Gehenna* (hell) is found in Mathew 5:22, 29, 30, 10:28, 18:9, 23:15, 33, Mark 9:43, 45, 47, Luke 12:5, and James 3:6. Hades is found in Matthew 11:23, 16:18, Luke 10:15, 16:23, Acts 2:27, 31, 1 Corinthians 15:55, and Revelation 1:18, 6:8, 20:13-14. Does the translation of the Bible that you read properly distinguish between hell and Hades?

2) Has the story of the rich man and Lazarus (Luke 16) influenced your view of hell? If so, should it have? Why or why not?

3) Wailing and gnashing of teeth is found seven times in the Gospels—Matthew 8:12, 13:42, 50, 22:13, 24:51, 25:30, and Luke 13:28. Do any of these passages state that wailing and gnashing of teeth lasts eternally?

4) When John the Baptist speaks of God's unquenchable fire in Matthew 3:7-12, is he talking about final judgment? (Compare what John the Baptist said about Christ gathering His wheat into His barn with Jesus' own teaching in Matthew 13:24-30, 37-43.)

5) What happens to chaff and weeds when thrown into a blazing fire?

6) The chaff (Matt. 3:12) and tares (Matt. 13:30, 40) provide the clearest and most specific explanation of what happens to the unsaved in the final judgment fire. Agree or disagree?

7) When a word has a range of meaning, which is the preferred understanding: The meaning that best fits one's theology or best fits the context of the passage under consideration?

8) Did W. E. Vine or John Stott do a better job of defining *apollumi*?

9) With regard to humanity, the exact same word for "destroy" in Matthew 10:28 (ἀπολέσαι) is also found in Matthew 2:13, Luke 6:9, 9:56, 19:47, and James 4:12. Based on a review of these verses, how would you define ἀπολέσαι?

10) Paraphrase Matthew 10:28 without using the word *destroy*.

11) Do you think that Jesus' warning of what God is *able* to do to both soul and body in hell is merely theoretical or what is in store for the impenitent?

12) If the unsaved burn up like weeds in a furnace of fire, would such a death appropriately be called annihilation?

CHAPTER 3

1) Are you more familiar with the New Testament or the Old Testament? What are your favorite Old Testament books?

2) Read Mark 9:43-48. Is the function of worm and fire obvious, or would background information on undying worm and unquenchable fire be helpful?

3) How familiar do you think Jesus' original audience was with the Book of Isaiah? Do you think Jesus expected His original audience to understand undying worm and unquenchable fire in light of Isaiah 66?

4) Symbols are found in prophecy. For example, in Revelation 19:15, we read of the King of kings—"out of His mouth goes a sharp sword, that with it He should strike the nations." What do you understand the sword to represent? Does the symbolic nature of the sword prevent us from understanding that Revelation 19:11-21 speaks of a literal battle in which the armies of the world are slain by Christ at His Second Coming?

5) Political developments of his day influenced Augustine to abandon premillennialism. At the time of the Reformation, Israel had been scattered about the earth for some 1400 years and no restoration of the nation was in sight. If Augustine and the mainstream Reformers were here today, do you think

they might reconsider their denial of a future millennial reign of Christ?

6) The details of Isaiah 66:23 indicate that the setting of Isaiah 66:24 is the millennial Messianic reign of Christ that takes place prior to the creation of the new heavens and new earth. Agree or disagree?

7) If there is to be a millennial reign of Christ on this earth following the battle of Armageddon, how important would it be to cleanse the battlefield, the land of Israel? How difficult of a job might that be?

8) Complete the following statement: Unquenchable fire in the writings of Jeremiah (17:27) and Ezekiel (20:45-48) is fire that...

9) The worshippers in Isaiah 66:23 go forth in Isaiah 66:24 to see dead bodies being consumed by worms and fire. Agree or disagree?

10) In Mark 9:43-48, did Jesus illuminate the danger of *Gehenna* by citing a portrait of torment or a gruesome picture of literal physical death?

11) Is the traditionalist understanding of Mark 9:43-48 consistent or inconsistent with the reality of what happens to chaff and weeds cast into a furnace of fire?

CHAPTER 4

1) Why is Matthew's Gospel so important to the study of hell?

2) Biblically, is conscious suffering the only form of punishment? (Exod. 21:12, 14, 15, 16, 17, 23, 29)

3) When a government executes a criminal, we call it capital punishment. How does capital punishment *punish* a criminal?

4) If every day that believers are blessed with throughout eternity is a day denied to the unsaved (by virtue of annihilation), would the punishment of the unsaved be just as eternal as the life that believers enjoy?

5) Whether thought of in terms of conscious separation from a good God or ECT, the traditional view of hell is fundamentally terrifying beyond comprehension. True or False?

6) Jesus spoke of some who would be beaten with few stripes (Luke 12:47-48). Are few stripes and eternal suffering compatible concepts?

7) As death on earth commonly involves pain to one degree or another, it is reasonable that final irreversible death in the lake of fire would involve suffering based on the hardness

and impenitence of the unbeliever's heart (Rom. 1:32-2:12). Agree or disagree?

8) Does Matthew 25:46 provide enough detail to establish the penalty for sin?

9) In Matthew's Gospel, a number of passages address the final judgment of unbelievers. Do you think God expects us to notice these texts and keep them in mind when interpreting the judgment of the goats in Matthew 25:41-46?

10) According to Matthew 3:12, 7:13, 10:28, 13:40-42, and 21:44-45, what is the destiny of the unsaved?

11) Is there biblical precedent for a one-time act of eternal consequence being deemed eternal? (Heb. 6:2, 7:27, 9:12)

12) What verse or verses would you say are scripture's own commentary on eternal punishment?

CHAPTER 5

1) Christ is both divine and human. Do His two natures blend in some way, or do they remain distinct?

2) Some teach that Christ experienced infinite suffering in His divine nature at Calvary. Are you familiar with this teaching? Has it influenced you to believe in ECT?

3) According to scriptures such as Galatians 4:4-5, Hebrews 2:9, Colossians 1:21-22, and 1 Peter 2:24: In which nature did Jesus pay for the sins of the world?

4) What gives the blood of the Lamb its immeasurable value?

5) Scripture places great emphasis on Christ's blood. Indeed, "apart from blood-shedding forgiveness doth not come" (Heb. 9:22, YLT). Shouldn't the blood of Christ inform our understanding of His saving death?

6) The blood of the Lamb shed for our sins at Calvary speaks of a life sacrificially *laid down*. Jesus *died* for our sins (as verified by the *burial* of His crucified body) and rose from the *dead* (speaking of His *lifeless body* lying in the tomb). Do any of these truths suggest that we should understand *death* in terms of endless misery or ongoing killing that never ends?

7) Conditional immortality affirms final judgment to encompass suffering, appropriate to one's sin, followed by death. Traditionalism, in contrast, affirms suffering followed only by more suffering. Which view is consistent with the experience of Christ at the cross?

8) Death is the penalty for sin. Jesus died at Calvary so believers would not perish. The believer in Christ is counted as having died with Christ at the cross. What price should we expect that the impenitent will pay in the lake of fire?

9) Conditionalism holds that under God's death penalty, a life ceases or comes to an end. When the blood of the sacrificial goat was sprinkled upon and before the mercy seat (Lev. 16:15), what did it signify?

10) When Christ rose, did He resume His earthly flesh and blood life? Or, did that life end at the cross? (Eph. 1:20-23; Phil. 3:21; 1 Cor. 15:45-49)

11) Why is the chance to share in Christ's crucifixion, in the sight of God, such an incredible gift of grace?

12) Why is the distinction between Christ's redemptive death and the unbeliever's redemptionless death so important?

CHAPTER 6

1) Christians have developed distinct ways of understanding the Book of Revelation. What perspective is taken in *Rescue from Death?*

2) Explain the parallel between God's land redemption program for Israel and the message of the Book of Revelation?

3) Is there a strong connection between Revelation 14:9-11 and the trumpet and bowl judgments of the Great Tribulation?

4) Some teachers say "forever and ever" always means eternal. Others disagree. Does the smoke rising "forever and ever" from Babylon during the Tribulation (Rev. 19:3), smoke that surely won't cloud the skies throughout the millennial reign of Christ (Rev. 20:4-6), nor pollute the new earth (Rev. 21:1), help us resolve this issue?

5) If the trumpets and bowls include torment by fire and brimstone that takes place in the presence of holy angels and the Lamb, and if temporal smoke from the city of Babylon is said to ascend "forever and ever," could it be that smoke will rise "forever and ever" from fire and brimstone that torments beast-worshippers during the Great Tribulation? Could the "no rest day or night" of Revelation 14:11 also be accounted for by relentless trumpet and bowl judgments?

6) Is there biblical evidence to suggest a transition in the career of Antichrist from human being to demonic being?

7) Given the precedent of angels appearing in the form of men and the teaching of scripture that the beast ascends out of the abyss, should we be surprised if an evil angel operates in the form of an evil man during the Tribulation? And in light of the fact that scripture refers to angelic beings in human form as men, should we be surprised if the mark of a fallen angel operating in human form is said to be the mark of a man?

8) In Revelation 20:10, is it Satan and two human beings or a satanic trinity that is seen suffering in the lake of fire?

9) What fundamental error do traditionalists make when citing Revelation 20:10-15 as a passage of scripture in support of their position?

10) Does Revelation 20:11-15 say anything about ECT?

11) Are Satan and his angels compatible with God's intentions for the new heavens?

12) What do you look forward to the most about the new heavens and new earth?

CHAPTER 7

1) Does virtually everyone trust in something or someone?

2) If a person thinks that he can earn his way to heaven by good works, what is he blind to?

3) How many have sinned? How many are guilty before God? (Rom. 3:9-19)

4) How many did Jesus die for? (1 John 2:2) How many does He want to rescue from death? (2 Pet. 3:9)

5) Jesus not only died for our sins, He also was bodily resurrected from the dead. Why is the resurrection an essential part of the Gospel (1 Cor. 15:1-4)?

6) God's salvation is not for sale; it is freely given to sinners who believe in Jesus (Rom. 3:24-26). Why does God's plan for justifying sinners call for faith rather than works? (Rom. 3:27-4:8)

7) Read the story of Naaman in 2 Kings 5:1-14. What almost prevented Naaman from being healed? How does Naaman's story illustrate the challenge of salvation by faith?

8) Read John 1:12, 4:7-14, 7:37-38, 20:30-31 as well as 1 John 4:9-10, 5:12 and finish the thought: Jesus calls sinners to…

9) When does faith become saving faith?

10) Read the prayer at the end of Chapter 7. If you have not yet put your trust in Christ for salvation, would you like to pray this prayer?

11) If you have a salvation testimony, would you like to share it with the group?

CHAPTER 8

1) If the prodigal son had not returned home, do you think that his father would have condemned him to endless suffering?

2) If God seeks to bring sinners into a true love relationship with Himself, is the threat of endless suffering compatible or incompatible with the heart of Christianity?

3) Why is it especially difficult for most Christians to talk about ECT when it comes to evangelism?

4) According to the Book of Acts, did the apostles preach ECT?

5) Did Paul's Gospel say anything about endless suffering? (Rom. 1:1-5; 1 Cor. 15:1-4)

6) If our message of salvation does not contain ECT, should our doctrinal statements?

7) Inasmuch as ECT became a dominant view in conjunction with the rise of Roman Catholicism, could the Rethinking Hell movement be seen as a continuation of the Reformation?

8) If you grew up holding to the traditional view of hell, what factors were most responsible for this?

9) Should evangelical churches, ministries, and schools fully welcome conditionalists? What can be done to make this a reality?

10) If the Bible does not actually teach ECT, God has been misrepresented in a most terrible way and His love tragically obscured. Agree or disagree?

11) If evangelicals were to embrace conditional immortality, could it energize evangelistic outreach and bring revival? Consider: (1) In our literate secular world, ECT is cited as a primary reason for the rejection of Christianity; (2) Christians not only lack a satisfactory answer for why a loving God would allow fathers and mothers and daughters and sons to eternally suffer unbearable pain, many find ECT deeply disturbing; (3) While ECT is incomprehensible, the cessation of life is a profound concern that the world longs for an answer to.

12) Given the stakes involved, shouldn't the study of hell be a top priority for today's church? Does it not merit a thorough Berean examination by believers everywhere? Will you encourage those in your sphere of fellowship to take a closer look at what the Bible actually says about the righteous judgment of God?

ENDNOTES

1. *The Englishman's Hebrew and Chaldee Concordance of the Old Testament* (Grand Rapids: Zondervan Publishing House, 1970), pp675-680.
2. The Hebrew text "does not refer to two aspects of death ('dying spiritually, you will then die physically')" (*NET Bible*, Genesis 2:17 study note).
3. Bodie Hodge, "Why Didn't Adam and Eve Die the Instant They Ate the Fruit?" *Answers Magazine*, March 9, 2010, https://answersingenesis.org/bible-characters/adam-and-eve/why-didnt-adam-and-eve-die-the-instant-they-ate-the-fruit/.
4. http://www.talkgenesis.org/why-didnt-adam-die-the-day-he-ate/ (November 2, 2015).
5. The verb occurs consecutively in distinct tenses.
6. John H. Sailhamer, "Genesis," *The Expositor's Bible Commentary*, Vol. 2, Frank E. Gaebelein, General Editor (Grand Rapids: Zondervan Publishing House, 1990), p48.
7. Lawrence O. Richards, *Expository Dictionary of Bible Words* (Grand Rapids: Regency Reference Library, 1985), pp407-408.
8. Of *thnesko*, W. E. Vine states, "To die (in the perf. tense, to be dead), in the N.T. is always used of physical death, except in I Timothy 5:6, where it is metaphorically used of the loss of spiritual

life" (*An Expository Dictionary of New Testament Words*, Vol I [Old Tappan: Fleming H. Revell Co, 1966], p308).

Of *anairesis*, Vine states, "Another word for death... as of the taking of a life, or putting to death; it is found in Acts 8:1, of the murder of Stephen" (Ibid., p276).

Of *teleute*, Vine states, "An end, limit... hence, the end of life, death, is used of the death of Herod, Matt. 2:15" (Ibid., p276).

Thanatos is translated as *death*, e. g., "Now brother will deliver up brother to *death*" (Matt. 10:21); "I persecuted this Way to the *death*" (Acts 22:4); "And there were many priests, because they were prevented by *death* from continuing" (Heb. 7:23).

Apothnesko is primarily rendered as *die* or *died*, e. g., "When he heard that Jesus had come out of Judea into Galilee, he went to Him and implored Him to come down and heal his son, for he was at the point of *death*.... The nobleman said to Him, 'Sir, come down before my child *dies*!'" (John 4:47-49); "For scarcely for a righteous man will one *die*; yet perhaps for a good man someone would even dare to *die*. But God demonstrates His own love toward us, in that while we were still sinners, Christ *died* for us" (Rom. 5:7-8).

It is unfortunate that many believers have been conditioned by traditionalism to think of death in terms of separation. While it is true that the human soul departs from the body in the first death, the fact remains that Luke and Jesus and the nobleman and Paul plainly speak of death in its ordinary sense—the absence or cessation of life. Indeed, this is the primary meaning of dead/death/die throughout the Bible.

[9] Ignatius, *The Epistle of Ignatius to the Magnesians*, Chapter 10, http://www.newadvent.org/fathers/0105.htm.

Contrary to common traditionalist rhetoric, there was no consensus on hell in the early centuries of church history. The reality is that the dominance of the eternal-torment view formed in conjunction with the development of Roman Catholicism. See Chapter 8 ("About Church Tradition").

[10] Henry Clarence Thiessen, *Introductory Lectures in Systematic Theology* (Grand Rapids: Eerdmans Publishing Co, 1949), p271.

[11] Ibid.

[12] Robert P. Lightner, *Sin, the Savior, and Salvation* (Grand Rapids: Kregel Publications, 1991), pp28-29.

[13] Robert A. Peterson and Edward William Fudge, *Two Views of Hell: A Biblical and Theological Dialogue* (Downers Grove: InterVarsity Press, 2000), p147.

Peterson is a leading proponent of traditionalism. Fudge has labored for decades, arguing for conditionalism. He wrote *The Fire That Consumes* (Verdict Publications) in 1982.

[14] Ibid., 118.

[15] Millard J. Erickson, *Christian Theology* (Grand Rapids: Baker Book House, 1985), p1239.

[16] Christopher W. Morgan, "Annihilationism," *Hell under Fire*, Christopher W. Morgan and Robert A. Peterson, General Editors (Grand Rapids: Zondervan, 2004), p210.

[17] Robert A. Peterson, *Two Views of Hell*, p121.

[18] Edward William Fudge, *Two Views of Hell*, pp191-192.

[19] Millard J. Erickson, *Christian Theology*, p613.

[20] John W. Wenham, "The Case for Conditional Immortality," *Rethinking Hell: Readings in Evangelical Conditionalism*, ed. by Christopher M. Date, Gregory G. Stump, and Joshua W. Anderson (Eugene: Cascade Books, 2014), p83.

21. Norman Shepherd, "Immortality," *The Zondervan Pictorial Encyclopedia of the Bible*, Vol. 3, Merrill C. Tenney, Gen. Editor (Grand Rapids: Regency Reference Library, 1975), p263.
22. Robert A. Peterson, *Two Views of Hell*, pp88-89.
23. Ibid., p119.
24. Ibid.
25. Tertullian, *On the Resurrection of the Flesh*, Chapter 35, http://www.newadvent.org/fathers/0316.htm.
26. Tertullian, *A Treatise on the Soul*, Chapter 22, http://www.newadvent.org/fathers/0310.htm.
27. Tertullian, *On the Resurrection of the Flesh*, Chapter 3, http://www.newadvent.org/fathers/0316.htm: "For some things are known even by nature: the immortality of the soul, for instance, is held by many; the knowledge of our God is possessed by all. I may use, therefore, the opinion of a Plato, when he declares, 'Every soul is immortal.'"
28. Ibid., Chapter 34.
29. Edward William Fudge, *Two Views of Hell*, p187.
30. Augustine of Hippo, *The City of God*, Book 13, Chapter 24, http://newadvent.org/fathers/1201.htm.
31. Ibid., Book 13, Chapter 2.
32. Ibid., Book 21, Chapter 3, Italics mine.
33. Philip E. Hughes, "Is the Soul Immortal?," *Rethinking Hell: Readings in Evangelical Conditionalism*, p192.
34. *Westminster Confession of Faith*, Chapter IV: Of Creation.
35. Clark H. Pinnock, "The Destruction of the Finally Impenitent," *Rethinking Hell: Readings in Evangelical Conditionalism*, pp66-67.
36. This truth is normative. The goats in Matthew 25 face final judgment at Christ's return to earth and from that judgment are

cast into the lake of fire. The goats are a very small percentage of Adam's race and foreshadow the main judgment before the Great White Throne that takes place after the millennium. See Chapter 4 for greater detail.

37 M. R. Vincent, *Word Studies in the New Testament*, Vol. 1 (Mac Dill AFB: MacDonald Publishing Co., n. d.), p31.

38 Paul Enns, *The Moody Handbook of Theology* (Chicago: Moody Press, 1989), p375.

Traditionalists and conditionalists affirm that the lake of fire is a terrifying place where God's justice is executed. The only real difference between the two views is whether hell is ultimately a place of unending suffering or perishing.

39 Kenneth S. Wuest, *Wuest's Word Studies from the Greek New Testament*, Vol. Three (Grand Rapids: Wm. B. Eerdmans Publishing Co., 1966), p45.

40 M. R. Vincent, *Word Studies in the New Testament*, Vol. 1, p58.

41 Robert W. Yarbrough, "Jesus on Hell," *Hell under Fire*, p74.

42 Jesus' words were directed at the Pharisees who scoffed at His teaching that one cannot serve both God and money (Luke 16:13-14). Lovers of money (Luke 16:14), the Pharisees saw themselves as Abraham's heirs (Matt. 3:9; John 8:33, 39) but did not walk in Abraham's ways (John 8:39-41). Rather than live by faith in God's Word as Abraham had (Gen. 15:1-6), the Pharisees demanded miraculous works of Christ (John 6:30). Interpreted in light of its context, the parable of the rich man and Lazarus is seen as a powerful rebuke to the Pharisaic view that wealth is an indication of God's favor. John W. Cooper of Calvin Theological Seminary writes, "This is a parable whose point is not to teach about death or the intermediate state, but to warn its hearers about the dangers

of riches" (*Body, Soul & Life Everlasting*, Wm. B. Eerdmans Publishing Co., Grand Rapids, 2000, p126).

Jesus also emphasizes that salvation actually belongs to those who believe God's Word. This is seen in the parable's conclusion:

> Then he [the rich man] said, "I beg you therefore, father, that you would send him [Lazarus] to my father's house, for I have five brothers, that he may testify to them, lest they also come to this place of torment." Abraham said to him, "They have Moses and the prophets; let them hear them." And he said, "No, father Abraham; but if one goes to them from the dead, they will repent." But he said to him, "If they do not hear Moses and the prophets, neither will they be persuaded though one rise from the dead." (Luke 16:27-31)

John A. Martin states, "Jesus was obviously suggesting that the rich man symbolized the Pharisees. They wanted signs—signs so clear that they would compel people to believe. But since they refused to believe the Scriptures, they would not believe any sign no matter how great. Just a short time later Jesus did raise a man from the dead, another man named Lazarus (John 11:38-44). The result was that the religious leaders began to plot more earnestly to kill both Jesus and Lazarus" ("Luke," *The Bible Knowledge Commentary* [Victor Books, 1983], p247).

Alfred Edersheim warns that when interpreting the parable of the rich man and Lazarus: "Its Parabolic details must not be exploited, nor doctrines of any kind derived from them, either as to the character of the other world, the question of the duration of future punishments, or the possible moral improvement of those in *Gehinnom*. All such things are foreign to the Parable" (*The Life* and Times of Jesus the Messiah, Book IV [Grand Rapids: Wm. B. Eerdmans Publishing Co., 1971], p277).

43   Geerhardus Vos, "Hades," *The International Standard Bible Encyclopaedia*, Vol II (Grand Rapids: Wm. B. Eerdmans Publishing Co., 1939), p1315.

44   John F. Walvoord, *The Revelation of Jesus Christ* (Chicago: Moody Press, 1966), p307.

45   Robert W. Yarbrough, "Jesus on Hell," *Hell under Fire*, pp73-74.

46   Traditionalists would seem to agree. Matthew 23:15 is not cited in *Two Views of Hell*, and James 3:6 is not cited in *Hell under Fire*.

47   Alan W. Gomes, "Annihilation of Hell," *Christian Research Journal*, Summer 1991, p11.

48   Basil Atkinson, *Life and Immortality*, Chapter 4, "Unquenchable Fire," https://lifebeyonddeath.wordpress.com/2013/11/25/life-and-immortality-by-basil-atkinson/.

Atkinson (1895-1971) had a key role in the formation of Inter-Varsity Fellowship of Evangelical Unions.

49   John F. Walvoord, *Matthew Thy Kingdom Come* (Chicago: Moody Press, 1974), p32.

50   Harry Allan Ironside, *Matthew* (Neptune: Loizeaux Brothers, 1948), pp28-29.

51   Basil Atkinson, *Life and Immortality*, Chapter 4, "Unquenchable Fire."

52   Alan W. Gomes, "Evangelicals and the Annihilation of Hell," *Christian Research Journal*, Spring 1991, p19.

53   Harold E. Guillebaud, *The Righteous Judge*, Chapter 4, "Separation from God: Penal Suffering," http://lifebeyonddeath.wordpress.com/2013/11/12/the-righteous-judge-by-harold-e-guillebaud/.

Guillebaud (1888-1941) was an Anglican missionary and translator of the New Testament.

54 Alan W. Gomes, "Annihilation of Hell," p11.

55 D. A. Carson, "Matthew," *The Expositor's Bible Commentary*, Vol 8 (Grand Rapids: Zondervan Publishing House, 1984), p242.

56 Robert W. Yarbrough, "Jesus on Hell," *Hell under Fire*, p81.

The Greek letter Upsilon can be transliterated either with "u" or "y"; hence, both *apollumi* and *apollymi* are acceptable. Accent marks not retained.

57 W. E. Vine, *An Expository Dictionary of New Testament Words*, Vol. I (Old Tappan: Fleming H. Revell Co, 1966), p302.

This definition appears under the heading DESTROY, DESTROYER, DESTRUCTION, DESTRUCTIVE. As it is the definition traditionalists cite in support of their view, we will examine it closely. Vine also provides definitions of *apollumi* under the headings of LOSE, (Suffer) LOSS, LOST, and PERISH.

58 John Stott, *Essentials: A liberal-evangelical dialogue*, by David L. Edwards with John Stott (London: Hodder & Stoughton, 1988), p315.

59 A. Oepke, "*apollymi*," *Theological Dictionary of the New Testament*, Gerhard Kittle and Gerhard Friedrich, Editors, abridged in one volume by Geoffrey W. Bromiley (Grand Rapids: William B. Eerdmans Publishing Co., 1985), p67.

60 W. E. Vine, *An Expository Dictionary of New Testament Words*, Vol. III, pp18-19.

61 Ibid., p18.

62 Edwin A. Blum, "John," *The Bible Knowledge Commentary*, NT, ed. by John F. Walvoord and Roy B. Zuck (Victor Books, 1983), p310. Bold emphasis not retained.

63   Douglas J. Moo, "Paul on Hell," *Hell under Fire*, p105.

64   Categories A thru E are organized in order of importance. We want to know what Jesus meant when He said that God can ἀπολέσαι both soul and body in hell, so other instances where Jesus uses ἀπολέσαι are of primary importance. Since our target verse is in Matthew, we look at how ἀπολέσαι is used in Matthew before considering the other Gospels and the balance of the New Testament.

        In Categories A thru D, every occurrence of ἀπολέσαι in the New Testament is cited, except for two where unclean spirits ask Jesus if He has come to destroy them (Mark 1:24; Luke 4:34). A Category F could be created for these verses but the further from Category A, the less relevant the input and a line must be drawn somewhere. Moreover, Categories A thru E keep the focus on *apollumi* in relation to human beings, the truth we seek.

        Fallen angels are a distinct entity that God has dealt distinctly with regarding sin (e.g., Christ did not die for angels, Heb. 2:14-16); nevertheless, in Chapter 6, we will find strong evidence that Satan and his angels will not only experience torment in the lake of fire but ultimately utter destruction, even as feared by unclean spirits in Mark 1:24 and Luke 4:34.

65   Christopher W. Morgan, "Biblical Theology: Three Pictures of Hell," *Hell under Fire*, p137.

        Morgan's strong assertion follows the wording of the NKJV in Mark 9:43 which calls hell "the fire that shall never be quenched." Yet, as noted in Chapter 2, the Greek simply reads: "τὸ πῦρ τὸ ἄσβεστον" (SBLGNT)—"the fire—the unquenchable" (YLT).

66   Robert A. Peterson, *Two Views of Hell*, p93.

67   Paul Lee Tan, *The Interpretation of Prophecy* (Winona Lake: BMH BOOKS, 1974), pp30-31, 142-143.

68 Charles C. Ryrie, *Dispensationalism Today* (Chicago: Moody Press, 1965), pp88-89.

69 J. K. Grider, "Allegory," *The Zondervan Pictorial Encyclopedia of the Bible*, Vol. 1, Merrill C. Tenney, Gen. Editor (Grand Rapids: Regency Reference Library, 1975), pp105-106.

70 Bernard Ramm, *Protestant Biblical Interpretation* (Grand Rapids: Baker Book House, 1970), pp28, 24.

71 Ibid., pp54, 58.

72 Renald E. Showers, *There Really Is a Difference! A Comparison of Covenant and Dispensational Theology* (Bellmawr: The Friends of Israel Gospel Ministry, 1990), pp24-25.

Highly recommended; provides a solid foundation for studying the end-times.

73 Paul Enns, *The Moody Handbook of Theology*, p389. Leaders cited by Enns; dates approximate.

74 Renald E. Showers, *There Really Is a Difference!*, pp115-126.

Showers' documentation is excellent.

75 Millard J. Erickson, *Christian Theology*, p1212.

76 Paul Enns, *The Moody Handbook of Theology*, p380.

77 Renald E. Showers, *There Really Is a Difference!*, pp127-135.

78 Alva J. McClain, *The Greatness of the Kingdom* (Winona Lake: BMH BOOKS, 1974), pp137-138.

This book is a must read.

79 Ibid., p244.

80 Robert A. Peterson, *Two Views of Hell*, pp130-131.

81 Ibid., p131.

82 Ibid., pp92-93, 132-133.

83 John F. Walvoord, *The Prophecy Knowledge Handbook* (Scripture Press Publications, 1990), p119.

[84] Charles L. Feinberg, *The Minor Prophets* (Chicago: Moody Press, 1990), p312.
[85] John A. Martin, "Isaiah," *The Bible Knowledge Commentary*, OT, ed. by John F. Walvoord and Roy B. Zuck (Victor Books, 1985), p1121. Bold emphasis not retained.
[86] Charles L. Feinberg, *The Minor Prophets*, p343.
[87] Alva J. McClain, *The Greatness of the Kingdom*, pp251-252.
[88] J. Dwight Pentecost, *Things To Come* (Grand Rapids: Zondervan Publishing House, 1958), pp111, 444, 481, 512.
[89] Alva J. McClain, *The Greatness of the Kingdom*, pp189-194.
[90] Robert L. Thomas, *Revelation 8-22: An Exegetical Commentary* (Chicago: Moody Press, 1995), pp393-394.
[91] William R. Newell, *Revelation: Chapter-by-Chapter* (Grand Rapids: Kregel Classics, 1994), p313. (Originally published in 1935 by Grace Publications.)
[92] Ralph H. Alexander, *Ezekiel* an Everyman's Bible Commentary (Chicago: Moody Press, 1976), pp69-70.
[93] The NIV states that unquenchable fire will *consume* Jerusalem's fortresses (Jer. 27:17).
[94] Robert A. Peterson, *Two Views of Hell*, p133.
[95] John A. Martin, "Isaiah," *The Bible Knowledge Commentary*, OT, p1121.
[96] Ibid., pp1120-1121.
[97] One can only imagine the struggle that McClain might have experienced when writing *The Greatness of the Kingdom*. McClain's keen awareness of, and fierce opposition to, the allegorical method would have made it very difficult for him to have interpreted the slain soldiers in Isaiah 66:24 as living human beings suffering torment. For the record, McClain's masterpiece, which extensively

discusses the return of Christ and the Messianic millennial earth, does not contain a single reference to Isaiah 66:24.

[98] Paul teaches that the end of "the enemies of the cross of Christ" will be *destruction* (Phil. 3:18-19) and declares *death* to be the righteous judgment of God—the wage that unbelievers merit (Rom. 1:32, 6:23). He holds that unbelievers *perish* (Rom. 2:12). Paul *never* speaks of eternal torment. This fact is like a huge flashing caution sign through which traditionalists speed.

There has been an attempt to understand destruction in terms of eternal torment by coupling Revelation 17:8, 11, where it is said that the beast goes to destruction, with the beast's torment in the lake of fire. Peterson sees this as a strong traditionalist response to the conditionalist position that perishing and being destroyed should be taken at face value ("Undying Worm, Unquenchable Fire," *Christianity Today*, Oct. 23, 2000). For Peterson to cite the beast of Revelation 17 as strong support for the traditionalist understanding of destruction is telling because Revelation 17 is a complex prophecy and the least clear of all the destruction passages. Moreover, futurists affirm the beast not only as a personal entity but as a kingdom that Christ will obliterate in conjunction with His Second Coming, raising the possibility of destruction being the annihilation of the beast's empire on earth, something integral to the Revelation 17 landscape (vv. 11-14). Additionally, the beast ascends out of the abyss (Rev. 17:8) which houses demonic beings (Luke 8:31; 2 Pet. 2:4; Rev. 20:3). So it is not at all clear that Peterson's argument is even related to the fate of impenitent human beings. Further, while the beast suffers in the lake of fire, several scriptures suggest that this is not the end of the beast's story (see Chapter 6).

99 John G. Mitchell, *Outline of Luke* (Portland: Multnomah Press, 1974), p4. Underline emphasis not retained.
100 John G. Mitchell, *Matthew* (Portland: Multnomah Press, 1974), p5. Underline emphasis not retained.
101 Robert A. Peterson, *Two Views of Hell*, p108.
102 Charles B. Williams, *The New Testament* (Chicago: Moody Press, 1950), p59.
103 The authorship of the Book of Daniel as a sixth century BC work by God's prophet is well supported. For significant historical and linguistic evidence see, *The International Standard Bible Encyclopaedia*, Volume II (Grand Rapids: Eerdmans Publishing Co., 1939); *A Commentary on Daniel* by Leon Wood (Grand Rapids: Regency Reference Library, 1973); *Daniel* by John C. Whitcomb in the *Everyman's Bible Commentary* series (Chicago: Moody Press, 1985); *Daniel* by Gleason L. Archer Jr. in *The Expositor's Bible Commentary*, Volume 7 (Grand Rapids: Regency Reference Library, 1985).
104 E. A. Judge, "Alexander," *The Zondervan Pictorial Encyclopedia of the Bible*, Volume One, pp97-98.
105 John C. Whitcomb, *Daniel* (Chicago: Moody Press, 1985), pp47-48.
106 Renald E. Showers, *The Most High God* (Bellmawr: The Friends of Israel Gospel Ministry, 1982), pp21-23.
107 Robert A. Peterson, *Two Views of Hell*, p145.
108 Ibid., p110.
109 J. I. Packer, "Universalism: Will Everyone Ultimately Be Saved?," *Hell under Fire*, p183.
110 Alan W. Gomes, "Evangelicals and the Annihilation of Hell," p17.
111 Ibid.
112 Ibid., pp17-18.

113 Ibid., p18.
114 John G. Mitchell, *Outline of Hebrews* (Multnomah School of the Bible, n. d.), p21.
115 J. Dwight Pentecost, *Prophecy for Today* (Grand Rapids: Zondervan, 1961), pp178-179.
116 Paul Enns, *The Moody Handbook of Theology*, p379.
117 Alan W. Gomes, "Evangelicals and the Annihilation of Hell," p18. Accent marks not retained.
118 Randy Alcorn, *If God Is Good* (Colorado Springs: Multnomah Books, 2010), p312.
119 Ibid., 314.
120 Mark Galli, *God Wins* (Carol Stream: Tyndale House Publishers, 2011), pp127-128.
121 E. Earle Ellis, "New Testament Teaching on Hell," *Rethinking Hell: Readings in Evangelical Conditionalism*, p132. (This is a widespread understanding among evangelical conditionalists.)
122 Ibid.
123 Two passages are sufficient to establish such devastation: Revelation 6:8 and 9:15-18. Much more detail on the Tribulation is provided in Chapter 6, The Revelation Passages. For additional study, I recommend *Maranatha: Our Lord, Come!* by Renald Showers (published by the Friends of Israel Gospel Ministry). This book provides extensive substantiation for designating the entire seventieth week of Daniel 9 as the Tribulation, something widely held by futurists. It also provides an excellent analysis of the rapture of the church as both imminent and prior to the seven-year Tribulation.
124 John F. Walvoord, *Matthew Thy Kingdom Come*, pp200-201.
125 Ibid., p202.

126. Harry Allan Ironside, *Matthew*, p339.
127. J. Vernon McGee, *Matthew*, Volume II (Pasadena: Thru The Bible Books, 1973), p148.
128. J. Dwight Pentecost, *Things To Come*, pp425-426.
129. Ibid., p422.
130. Harry Allan Ironside, *Matthew*, pp337, 340-341. Italics mine.
131. Bernard Ramm, *Protestant Biblical Interpretation*, pp104-105.
132. I spent more than three years at Multnomah, 1971-1974. I went there because of Dr. Mitchell. When it comes to understanding the Bible, no one has had a bigger impact on me. The time I spent with him in the last summer of his life is among my most treasured memories.
133. Dick Bohrer, *Lion of God* (Multnomah Bible College, 1994), pp87-88.
134. Robert A. Peterson, *Two Views of Hell*, p110.
135. William R. Newell, *Romans Verse by Verse* (Iowa Falls: World Bible Publishers, 1987), p62.
136. Christopher D. Marshall, "Divine and Human Punishment in the New Testament," *Rethinking Hell: Readings in Evangelical Conditionalism*, p223.
137. W. E. Vine, *An Expository Dictionary of New Testament Words*, Vol. I, p159.

    F. Wilbur Gingrich and Frederick W. Danker's *A Greek-English Lexicon of the New Testament* states that *katakaio* means to "*burn down, burn up, consume* by fire" (2nd ed., University of Chicago Press, 1979, p411).
138. Alfred Marshall, *The Interlinear Greek-English New Testament* (Grand Rapids: Zondervan Publishing House, 1958), p57.

139 Henry M. Morris, *The Revelation Record* (Wheaton: Tyndale House Publishers, 1983), pp430-431.

140 Robert A. Peterson, *Two Views of Hell*, p150.

141 Ibid., pp150-151.

142 Henry M. Morris, *The Bible Has the Answer* (Grand Rapids: Baker Book House, 1971), p43.

143 All four Gospels recognize both the deity and the humanity of Christ. Still, each Gospel has its own emphasis.

144 Lewis Sperry Chafer, *Systematic Theology*, Vol. 1 (Dallas: Dallas Seminary Press, 1947), p314.

145 Paul Enns, *The Moody Handbook of Theology*, p227. Italics mine.

146 Henry C. Thiessen, *Introductory Lectures in Systematic Theology*, pp305-306.

147 Norman L. Geisler and Bill Roach, *The Shack: Helpful or Heretical?*, from http://www.normangeisler.net/theshack.html (2011).

148 Lewis Sperry Chafer, *Systematic Theology*, Vol. 3 (Dallas: Dallas Seminary Press, 1948), p68.

149 Robert A. Peterson, *Two Views of Hell*, p175.

150 Ibid.

151 William R. Newell's definition of propitiation from his tract "Paul's Gospel."

152 William R. Newell, *Romans Verse by Verse*, p173.

153 Ponder it: The Judge of all the earth neither requires nor is satisfied by infinite suffering; "apart from blood-shedding forgiveness doth not come" (Heb. 9:22, YLT).

154 Clark H. Pinnock, *Set Forth Your Case* (New Jersey: The Craig Press, 1968), pp42-43, 66-67.

155 John G. Mitchell, *Right With God* (Portland: Multnomah Press, 1990), p105.

156 Allen P. Ross, "Genesis," *The Bible Knowledge Commentary*, OT, p33. Bold emphasis not retained.
157 William R. Newell, *Hebrews Verse by Verse* (Grand Rapids: Baker Book House, 1987), pp316-317.
158 Arthur D. Jackson, *New Testament Mysteries* (Bemidji: Focus Publishing, 1996), pp115-116.

Commenting on the fact that there will be no sea in the new earth, Henry Morris writes,

> The present sea is needed, as was the original antediluvian sea, as a basic reservoir for the maintenance of the hydrologic cycle and the water-based ecology and physiology of the animal and human inhabitants of the earth. In the new earth... presumably all the men and women who live there will have glorified bodies with no more need of water. Their resurrected bodies will be composed, like that of the Lord Jesus, of flesh and bone (Luke 24:39; Philippians 3:21) but apparently with no need of blood (1 Corinthians 15:50) to serve as a cleanser and restorer of the body's flesh as at present. This, in turn, eliminates the major need for water on the earth (blood is about 90 percent water, and present-day human flesh about 65 percent water). (*The Revelation Record*, p437)

159 John G. Mitchell, *Right With God*, pp118-120, 122.
160 William R. Newell, *Romans Verse by Verse*, pp207-208.
161 Alva McClain, *Romans: The Gospel of God's Grace* (Winona Lake: BMH Books, 1973), p144.
162 H. A. Ironside, *Lectures on the Epistle to the Romans* (Neptune: Loizeaux Brothers, 1928), pp77-78.

163 William R. Newell, *Romans Verse by Verse*, pp207, 222.

164 John G. Mitchell, *Right With God*, pp126-127.

165 Gregory K. Beale, "The Revelation on Hell," *Hell under Fire*, p134.

166 I say that New Jerusalem is the *primary* focus of Revelation 21 in part because there is an evangelistic pause in Revelation 21:6-8: Today is the day God freely offers the water of life to him that thirsts (v. 6); two ends are in the balance: life with God as your Father in the new earth or second death in the lake of fire (vv. 7-8). Evangelistic concern is also found in the epilogue. This is especially clear in 22:17: "And the Spirit and the bride say, 'Come!' And let him who hears say, 'Come!' And let him who thirsts come. And whoever desires, let him take the water of life freely." Regarding Revelation 22:11, J. Hampton Keathley III states,

> Verse 11, which at first seems fatalistic, is closely related to verse 10, the unsealed character of this book and the imminent return of the Lord. Actually it is evangelistic. It is an appeal to men to respond to this book, for if one does not, there is no other message which can change him. Concerning this verse Walvoord writes: "If the warnings of the book are not sufficient, there is no more that God has to say. The wicked must continue in their wicked way and be judged by the Lord when He comes. The same rule, however, applies to the righteous. Their reaction to the prophecy, of course, will be different, but the exhortation in their case is to continue in righteousness and holiness. It is an either/or proposition with no neutrality possible." (*Studies in Revelation*, https://bible.org/seriespage/29-epilogue-rev-226-21#P4376_1108164)

167 Charles C. Ryrie, *Revelation* (Chicago: Moody Publishers, 1996), p53.

168 Other chronologies have been suggested; however, differences should not affect our study, because virtually all futuristic views have the same understanding of the nature of the trumpets and bowls.

169 Charles C. Ryrie, *Revelation*, p54.

170 Henry M. Morris, *The Revelation Record*, p96.

171 Renald E. Showers, *Maranatha: Our Lord, Come!* (Bellmawr: The Friends of Israel Gospel Ministry, Inc., 1995), p84.

172 Ibid., pp85, 89, 92, 94-96.

173 H. A. Ironside, *Notes on the Prophecy and Lamentations of Jeremiah* (Neptune: Loizeaux Brothers, 1906), pp169-170.

174 Though Christ's Second Advent continuously gets closer, we have, and will continue to have, questions that puzzle us. Though we know in part, we can wholly trust God's Word.

175 Robert A. Peterson, *Two Views of Hell*, pp159-160.

176 In Revelation 14, we read of an everlasting Gospel: "Fear God and give glory to Him... and worship Him who made heaven and earth, the sea and springs of water." We should not be surprised by this. As John G. Mitchell wrote, "Creation was man's first Bible. Even if he knew nothing of the writing of books, he could find God through creation" (*Right With God*, p45).

The heavens are a message from God broadcast throughout the world (Ps. 19:1-4). When the preincarnate Christ put the stars in place, when He caused the ocean waves to pound upon the shore, and when His breath caused Adam's heart to beat, a continuous revelation of the one true God was established (John 1:1-3, 14; Rom. 1:20). Because creation is a work of the Son and witness to His divine nature, it is possible to see the eternal Son through creation and to respond in worship. The Father will apply the shed blood of Christ to a true worshipper, even though his understanding may be very limited, because he has seen and believed in the Son (John 6:40).

Many say that one must have knowledge of the 1 Corinthians 15 Gospel to be saved. Willard Aldrich points out, however, that the implementation of the 1 Corinthians 15 Gospel has a schedule. God determined that the proclamation of Christ's death and resurrection would *begin* in Jerusalem (Luke 24:47) and branch out from there by means of human ambassadors (Matt. 28:18-20; 2 Cor. 5:20). In short, the obligation to know and believe 1 Corinthians 15:1-4 takes effect as its message moves throughout the world in accordance with the words of Christ: "You shall be witnesses to Me in Jerusalem, and in all Judea and Samaria, and to the end of the earth" (Acts 1:8). If the 1 Corinthians 15 Gospel never reaches an individual, he is yet responsible for, and able to exercise faith in God through, the revelation that God *has given* to him, whether Old Testament scripture or creation. (Insight from a 1972 classroom discussion with Willard Aldrich at Multnomah.)

Aldrich writes, "My position is a dispensational one, and it includes the idea that the stewardships of truth may be running concurrently. God's forgiveness is always based upon the sacrifice of Christ (none other name), but its application is not limited to those who understand its theology" (personal letter, April 12, 1997).

It is not the extent of one's knowledge of the Son but rather one's response to Him that is critical (Isa. 66:1-2; Rom. 1:21; Heb. 11:6; Rev. 14:7). We do not take the 1 Corinthians 15 Gospel to the world because God's hands are otherwise tied. We go, first and foremost, out of love for and obedience to God. We go to implore people to turn to God. Moreover, we go to declare not only the greatest revelation of God (Phil. 2:6-11) but the whole counsel of God (Matt. 28:20; Acts 20:27).

[177] Charles C. Ryrie, *Revelation*, p103.
[178] Harry Allan Ironside, *Lectures on the Book of Revelation* (Neptune: Loizeaux Brothers, 1973), pp258-259.
[179] Robert L. Thomas, *Revelation 8-22: An Exegetical Commentary*, p204.
[180] Robert A. Peterson, *Two Views of Hell*, p160.
[181] Renald E. Showers, *Maranatha: Our Lord, Come!*, pp24-25.
[182] Mark Robinson, "The Beginning of Sorrows," *Israel My Glory*, April/May 1994, p10.
[183] Robert A. Peterson, *Two Views of Hell*, p161.
[184] W. E. Vine, *An Expository Dictionary of New Testament Words*, Vol. II, p47.
[185] Gregory K. Beale, "The Revelation on Hell," *Hell under Fire*, pp128-129.
[186] Fritz Rienecker, *A Linguistic Key to the Greek New Testament*, Cleon Rogers, Editor (Grand Rapids: Zondervan, 1976), p844.
[187] James Strong, "Greek Dictionary of the New Testament," *The New Strong's Exhaustive Concordance of the Bible* (Nashville: Thomas Nelson, 1990), pp8-9. Entries 104, 165.

Though an idiomatic expression is not to be taken literally, the similarity between the origin of *age* and the common characteristic of the "forever and ever" passages may be more than coincidental.

[188] Charles H. Dyer, *World News and Bible Prophecy* (Wheaton: Tyndale House Publishers, 1993), p145.

189 Many commentators have recognized this. The first beast, for example, is like a lion and has eagle's wings. The lion and the eagle are both designations for Babylon in the OT prophets. Moreover, the details of Daniel 7:4 well fit the experience of Nebuchadnezzar in Daniel 4.

190 Joseph A. Seiss, *The Apocalypse* (Grand Rapids: Kregel Publications, 1987), pp391-393. Originally published in 1900.

191 Harold W. Hoehner, *Chronological Aspects of the Life of Christ* (Grand Rapids: Zondervan, 1977), pp119-139.

192 Leon Wood, *A Commentary on Daniel* (Grand Rapids: Regency Reference Library, 1973), p258.

193 Charles C. Ryrie, *Revelation*, pp99-100.

194 Renald E. Showers, *Maranatha: Our Lord, Come!*, pp65-66.

195 Leon Wood, *A Commentary on Daniel*, p308.

196 Robert L. Thomas, *Revelation 8-22: An Exegetical Commentary*, p158.

197 Ibid., p157.

198 Charles C. Ryrie, *Revelation*, p96.

199 Joseph A. Seiss, *The Apocalypse*, pp325-326.

200 William R. Newell, *Revelation: Chapter-by-Chapter*, p186.

201 J. Vernon McGee, *Thru the Bible*, Vol. V (Nashville: Thomas Nelson Publishers, 1983), pp999-1000.

202 William R. Newell, *Revelation: Chapter-by-Chapter*, p188.

203 Henry M. Morris, *The Revelation Record*, p238.

204 Gregory H. Harris, "Can Satan Raise the Dead? Toward a Biblical View of the Beast's Wound," *The Master's Seminary Journal*, Spring 2007, pp23-41.

   This article confronts problems facing futurists with regard to the beast's death stroke and offers a solution that solves some key issues. It is a bit of a two-edged sword for futuristic traditionalists, however. Harris' view affirms the genuine death of the beast and his return to life without attributing undue power to Satan, but it also demonstrates how far futuristic traditionalists must reach to account for the beast's death wound.

[205] Robert L. Thomas, *Revelation 8-22: An Exegetical Commentary*, pp292-293.

[206] Fritz Rienecker, *A Linguistic Key to the Greek New Testament*, p832.

[207] "Peter uses the verb *tartaroo* ('to hold captive in Tartarus') to tell where the sinning angels were sent" (Edwin A. Blum, *The Expositor's Bible Commentary*, Volume 12, Zondervan, 1981, p278).

[208] Robert L. Thomas, *Revelation 8-22: An Exegetical Commentary*, p30.

[209] Less probable, though still a possibility, is that a fallen angel might take on a human form similar to that of the slain prince. In either case, a satanic being ascends out of the abyss to assume the identity of the treacherous end-time prince.

[210] This paragraph includes details not recorded in scripture but rather derived from reasonable assumptions based on early twenty-first century reality.

[211] Lewis Sperry Chafer, *Systematic Theology*, Vol. II (Dallas: Dallas Seminary Press, 1947), p12.

[212] A. T. Robertson, *A Harmony of the Gospels* (Harper & Row, 1922), pp240-241.

[213] John F. Walvoord, *The Revelation of Jesus Christ*, p205.

[214] William H. Marty, "The Nations in Transition: The Shape of the Final Superpower," *Storm Clouds on the Horizon*, Charles H. Dyer, General Editor (Chicago: Moody Press, 2001), p58.

215 We have seen that the duration of "forever and ever" is contextually determined; its meaning with regard to Satan and his angels will be discussed in a later section. See: "Is There a Place for Satan and His Angels in the New Heavens?"

216 Randy Alcorn, *If God Is Good*, p313.

The only support Alcorn offers for the beast and false prophet as human beings is Rev. 19:20, which simply states that they are captured alive. The beast's death wound and ascension from the abyss are not addressed.

217 Ibid., 317.

218 Joseph A. Seiss, *The Apocalypse*, p326.

219 Robert L. Thomas, *Revelation 8-22: An Exegetical Commentary*, p294.

220 Robert A. Peterson, *Two Views of Hell*, pp111-112.

221 Ibid., 110.

222 William R. Newell, *Revelation: Chapter-by-Chapter*, pp335-337.

223 John F. Walvoord, *The Revelation of Jesus Christ*, p306.

224 William R. Newell, *Revelation: Chapter-by-Chapter*, p338.

225 Lewis Sperry Chafer, *Systematic Theology*, Vol II, pp 43-44.

Chafer states that it is obvious that the end of the passage points out the final judgment of God upon Satan (p43), yet he declines to comment on what Ezekiel actually wrote concerning Satan's fate. Later, he simply cites Revelation 20:10 without elaboration (p61).

226 Harold E. Guillebaud, *The Righteous Judge*, Chapter 5, "The Four Excepted Passages," http://lifebeyonddeath.wordpress.com/2013/11/12/the-righteous-judge-by-harold-e-guillebaud/ (edited to conform to American spelling).

227 Alva J. McClain, *The Greatness of the Kingdom*, p513.

[228] William R. Newell, *Revelation: Chapter-by-Chapter*, p347. All capital letter emphasis not retained.
[229] David C. Needham, *Close to His Majesty* (Portland: Multnomah Press, 1987), pp89, 118, 124-125.
[230] Martin Luther, *Commentary on Galatians*, English translation by Erasmus Middleton (Grand Rapids: Kregel Publications, 1979), pp94-95, 97.
[231] William R. Newell, *Romans Verse by Verse*, p143.
[232] David C. Needham, *Close To His Majesty*, p86.
[233] William R. Newell, *Romans Verse by Verse*, p107.
[234] John G. Mitchell, *Right With God*, p105.
[235] Samuel Fisk, *Divine Sovereignty and Human Freedom* (Neptune: Loizeaux Brothers, 1973), p26.
[236] Willard M. Aldrich, *The battle for your faith* (Portland: Multnomah Press, 1975), pp20-22.
[237] John G. Mitchell, *An Everlasting Love* (Portland: Multnomah Press, 1982), pp135-136.
[238] Francis A. Schaeffer, *Escape from Reason* (Downers Grove: Inter-Varsity Press, 1968), p26.
[239] Randy Alcorn, *If God Is Good*, p255.
[240] Ibid., p320.
[241] John Stott, *Essentials: A liberal-evangelical dialogue*, p314.
[242] Francis Chan and Preston Sprinkle, *Erasing Hell* (Colorado Springs: David C. Cook, 2011), pp107-108, 141.
Erasing Hell was written with one voice: Chan's.
[243] Ibid., p133.
[244] Ibid., p134.
[245] Ibid., p163.

246. Henry Constable, *The Duration and Nature of Future Punishment*, Chapter 8, "The Divine Justice," 1868.
247. Josh McDowell, *Evidence That Demands a Verdict* (San Bernardino: Here's Life Publishers, 1988), pp3-4, 10.
248. Henry Constable, *The Duration and Nature of Future Punishment*, Chapter 8, "The Divine Justice."
249. http://www.crustore.org/downloads/4laws.pdf.
250. *Bridge to Life*, Navigators Gospel Track (Colorado Springs: Navpress, 1969), p5.
251. http://peacewithgod.net/god-so-loved-the-world/?.
252. http://www.gideons.org/AboutUs/OurHistory.aspx.
253. http://www.gideons.org/BecomeAChristian/BecomeAChristian.aspx.
254. Francis Chan and Preston Sprinkle, *Erasing Hell*, p149.
255. Ibid., pp132-133, 138.

    Chan and Sprinkle began work on *Erasing Hell* thoroughly indoctrinated in ECT. While their review of hell left them siding with (and attempting to defend) ECT, they weren't completely certain and they urged further study (p86). Preston's continuing studies now have him strongly leaning toward annihilationism.
256. Edward William Fudge, *Hell: A Final Word* (Abilene: Leafwood Publishers, 2012), p120.
257. Steve Gregg, *All You Want to Know about Hell* (Nashville: Thomas Nelson, 2013), p66.
258. Randy Alcorn, *Eternity* (Kingstone Comics, 2013), p112.
259. My initial Berean look at the key scriptures was brief but compelling. The texts I looked at in Matthew led me to believe that hell was a place of perishing rather than eternal torment. I found death rather than ECT in Paul's letters and "forever and

ever" in Revelation didn't automatically equal eternal. It wasn't until July of 2009, however, that I committed myself to the extensive investigation that I knew the subject deserved and the evangelical world would demand of anyone opposing ECT.

260 *Eternal conscious separation from God* is perhaps the most prevalent traditionalist understanding today. This version of traditionalism does not explicitly mention torment. If one took the time to consider what eternal existence apart from the goodness of God would do to someone, you'd arrive at endless suffering, to be sure, but that inescapable conclusion is rarely contemplated for long. It is easier to simply think in terms of separation from a good God.

261 Randy Alcorn, *If God Is Good*, p318.

It is also baffling that one who is passionate about the value of life in the womb and the importance of maintaining an eternal perspective ascribes little value to human life when it comes to final judgment, calling eternal loss of life "mere nonexistence" (p314). More shocking yet is Alcorn's argument that the magnificence of Christ's redemptive work is tied to the ECT of impenitent human beings (pp312-315), in which he strongly implies that if Christ shed His blood on the cross to rescue us from a final permanent death, then "perhaps the grace he showed us on the cross isn't big enough to warrant eternal praise" (p315).

Dying to save us from utter capital punishment wouldn't warrant our eternal praise? Perhaps the lesson here is that the harder one tries to justify the traditional view of hell, the further afield they get.

262 Charles H. Dyer, *The Rise of Babylon* (Wheaton: Tyndale House Publishers, 1991), pp175-176.

263 Randy Alcorn, *If God Is Good*, p310.

264 Phil Fernandes, *Is Hell Forever?*, Debate with Chris Date (Create Space Independent Publishing Platform, September 5, 2013), p22. Bold emphasis not retained.

265 Steve Gregg, *All You Want to Know about Hell*, p130.

266 Glenn Peoples, "Introduction to Evangelical Conditionalism," *Rethinking Hell: Readings in Evangelical Conditionalism*, pp13-15. (References in brackets from Peoples' footnotes. *ANF* is for *Ante-Nicene Fathers*, edited by Philip Schaff et al., Hendrickson, 1996.)

267 Edward William Fudge, *Two Views of Hell*, p193.

268 John H. Yoder and Alan Kreider, "The Anabaptists," *Eerdmans' Handbook to the History of Christianity* (Grand Rapids: Wm. B. Eerdmans Publishing Co., 1977), pp399, 401-402. Edited to conform to American spelling and punctuation.

269 Edward William Fudge, *The Fire That Consumes* (iUniverse.com. Inc., 2001), p383.

270 John G. Stackhouse Jr., "Foreword," *Rethinking Hell: Readings in Evangelical Conditionalism*, pxii.

    This collection of conditionalist writings was put together by the Rethinking Hell project. Check out rethinkinghell.com for additional helpful resources.

271 J. I. Packer, "Evangelical Annihilationism in Review," *Reformation & Revival*, Volume 6, Number 2, Spring 1997, http://www.graceonlinelibrary.org/eschatology/eternal-punishment/evangelical-annihilationism-in-review-by-j-i-packer/.

272 The Evangelical Alliance, "About Us," http://www.eauk.org/connect/about-us/.

273 The Evangelical Alliance, "Introduction," *The Nature of Hell: Conclusions and Recommendations*, http://www.eauk.org/church/resources/theological-articles/the-nature-of-hell.cfm.

274 The Evangelical Alliance, "The Nature of Hell: Conclusions and Recommendations," *The Nature of Hell: A Report by the Evangelical Alliance Commission on Unity and Truth among Evangelicals (ACUTE)* (Carlisle: Paternoster Press, 2000), http://eauk.org/church/resources/theological-articles/upload/The-Nature-of-Hell-2.pdf, conclusion #19.

275 David O. Beale, *In Pursuit of Purity: American Fundamentalism Since 1850* (Greenville: Unusual Publications, 1986), p80.

276 Edward William Fudge, *The Fire That Consumes*, p405.

277 http://www.moodyglobal.org/beliefs/.
    I look forward to the day when this quote is outdated.

278 In fairness, it should be noted that the 2012 Outskirts Press edition of *Rescue from Death* was not nearly as thorough.

279 Churches would also do well to utilize biblical language; moreover, churches ought to consider crafting membership statements of faith that are limited to what is truly essential to being a Christian.

280 John Stott, *Essentials: A liberal-evangelical dialogue*, p320.

www.ingramcontent.com/pod-product-compliance
Lightning Source LLC
Chambersburg PA
CBHW020300010526
44108CB00037B/224